Hands-On Microservices with JavaScript

Build scalable web applications with JavaScript, Node.js, and Docker

Tural Suleymani

Hands-On Microservices with JavaScript

Group Product Manager: Kaustubh Manglurkar

Publishing Product Manager: Bhavya Rao

Book Project Manager: Sonam Pandey

Senior Editor: Ayushi Bulani

Technical Editor: K Bimala Singha

Copy Editor: Safis Editing

Indexer: Manju Arasan

Production Designer: Prashant Ghare

First published: December 2024

Production reference: 1221124

Published by Packt Publishing Ltd.
Grosvenor House
11 St Paul's Square
Birmingham
B3 1RB, UK

ISBN 978-1-78862-540-1

www.packtpub.com

To Elvira, my steadfast companion, whose unwavering love and support has been the bedrock of my life and work. To Turgut and Farah, my beloved children, whose existence fills my world with immeasurable joy and purpose.

Every challenge I've faced has been a crucible, forging the strength and resilience necessary for this journey. I am eternally grateful for the trials that have shaped me, and for the love that has carried me through.

– Tural Suleymani

Contributors

About the author

Tural Suleymani is a seasoned software development expert with over a decade of industry experience. Renowned as Azerbaijan's first Microsoft MVP in .NET and a three-time C# Corner MVP, he has established himself as a leading authority in his field. With a passion for sharing knowledge, Tural has dedicated ten years to mentoring developers through comprehensive programming languages and technology tools instruction. A self-taught pioneer, he empowers a global audience through his *TuralSuleymaniTech* YouTube channel, where he delivers in-depth tutorials and insights on C#, Apache Kafka, SQL, JavaScript, Domain-Driven Design, software architecture, microservices, and more. His deep technical knowledge and practical insights have empowered countless developers through his work as a mentor, educator, and public speaker. He also holds prestigious certifications including MCP, MCSA, and MSCD from Microsoft. Tural is also a Udemy instructor, further expanding his educational reach. Currently, Tural holds the position of Chief Software Architect at VOE Consulting, where he continues to innovate and lead in the software development industry.

About the reviewer(s)

Rasul Huseynov is a senior software developer and consultant with over seven years of experience in delivering high-quality software solutions. He graduated with high honors in computer engineering and brings deep expertise in **Object-Oriented Analysis and Design** (**OOAD**), Extreme Programming, and Distributed Systems. Holding certifications such as MCP, MCSA, and MCSD, Rasul has a solid foundation in Microsoft technologies and has successfully delivered numerous web projects. His experience extends to ensuring that software solutions are robust, maintainable, and efficient while adhering to industry best practices.

Adewole Caleb is a skilled backend engineer with a solid foundation in JavaScript, Golang, and TypeScript. Over his five years of professional experience, he has built a reputation for his curiosity, problem-solving abilities, and dedication to continuous learning. Having recently graduated, Caleb is now exploring a career transition into distributed and system engineering. Beyond his professional work, Caleb is deeply passionate about music. He finds joy in playing the guitar, singing, and participating in other activities that allow him to express his creativity. Caleb volunteers as a boot camp tutor, where he shares his knowledge and experience to inspire budding developers.

Joel Edmond Nguemeta is a full-stack developer and mentor with expertise in web application development and system design. He has worked as a mentor and evaluator at OpenClassrooms, providing personalized support to numerous students and contributing to their professional growth. As a mobile developer at Tamangwa Shipping, he designed several custom systems tailored to the company's specific needs. Joel also has solid experience in creating and implementing microservices architectures, ensuring scalability and performance. He regularly shares his knowledge and technical advice on his YouTube channel, which is dedicated to the developer community.

Jean Clayton Seraphin is an accomplished full-stack developer with over five years of experience in the industry. He has honed his skills in building robust APIs using Python and Django, as well as crafting engaging frontend applications with ReactJS. Beyond his expertise in web development, Jean Clayton Seraphin boasts an advanced understanding of servers and cloud services, particularly in the realm of AWS. He is well-versed in Linux administration and proficient in utilizing infrastructure-as-code tools such as Docker, CircleCI, and Nginx to streamline deployment and ensure the scalability and reliability of his projects.

Table of Contents

Part 2: Building and Managing Microservices

6

Synchronous Microservices   133

7

Asynchronous Microservices   169

8

Real-Time Data Streaming Using Microservices   195

Part 3: Securing, Testing, and Deploying Microservices

9

Securing Microservices   221

10

Monitoring Microservices   251

11

Microservices Architecture   269

12

Testing Microservices   311

Preface

Hello there! Welcome to *Hands-On Microservices with JavaScript*, a journey through the fascinating intersection of one of the most popular programming languages and the ever-evolving world of microservices architecture. JavaScript, with its versatility and ubiquity, combined with the modular, scalable power of microservices, forms the perfect duo for modern software development. This book is designed to bridge these two worlds, offering a comprehensive guide to building, managing, and scaling microservices with JavaScript.

The rise of microservices has revolutionized the way we think about software architecture. Gone are the days when monolithic applications dominated the landscape, offering simplicity but at the cost of scalability and flexibility. Microservices, with their promise of independent, self-contained units, have brought about a new era of development: agile, resilient, and highly scalable. However, with great power comes great responsibility, and the challenges of adopting a microservices architecture should not be underestimated.

In this book, we'll take you step by step through the process of understanding and implementing microservices using JavaScript. Each chapter is crafted to not only introduce you to the theoretical concepts but also to provide hands-on guidance that you can apply in real-world scenarios.

We will start with an introduction to microservices, exploring their core principles, benefits, and challenges. From there, we will delve into the internals of microservices, focusing on communication techniques and patterns that are essential for building robust systems. We'll also cover the foundational knowledge you need in JavaScript and Node.js before diving into more advanced topics, such as real-time data streaming, securing your microservices, and deploying them to production.

This book is not just about writing code; it's also about understanding the architectural patterns and best practices that will allow you to build scalable, maintainable, and efficient microservices. Whether you're an experienced developer looking to expand your skill set or a newcomer eager to explore the world of microservices, this book is designed to be your guide.

Thank you for embarking on this journey with me. I hope this book will not only enhance your technical skills but also inspire you to push the boundaries of what you can achieve with microservices and JavaScript.

Let's dive in!

Who this book is for

This book is designed for software developers, architects, and IT professionals who are eager to dive into the world of microservices using JavaScript. Whether you're new to microservices or looking to enhance your existing knowledge, this book provides practical insights and hands-on experience to help you build, manage, and scale microservices in a real-world context.

You are likely to benefit from this book if you belong to one of the following groups:

JavaScript developers: If you're a JavaScript developer interested in expanding your skill set into the microservices architecture, this book will guide you through the process. You'll learn how to apply your existing JavaScript knowledge to build scalable and resilient microservices, gaining insights into best practices, common challenges, and effective solutions.

Software architects: For architects looking to design and implement microservices architectures, this book offers a comprehensive exploration of patterns, tools, and strategies. You'll learn how to make informed decisions on structuring and deploying microservices, ensuring that your systems are both flexible and robust.

DevOps and IT professionals: If you're involved in the deployment, monitoring, and maintenance of microservices, this book will equip you with the knowledge to manage these systems effectively. You'll gain a deep understanding of CI/CD pipelines, containerization, orchestration, and monitoring techniques that are critical for running microservices in production environments.

This book will provide you with the practical knowledge and tools you need to successfully navigate the complexities of microservices architecture with JavaScript, positioning you for success in today's fast-paced development landscape.

What this book covers

Chapter 1, Introduction to Microservices, provides an introduction to microservices architecture, exploring its core principles and defining microservices as small, independent units focused on specific functionalities. This chapter also contrasts microservices with traditional monolithic architecture, highlighting the pros and cons of each approach and setting the stage for the rest of the book.

Chapter 2, Diving into Microservices Internals, delves deeper into the internal workings of microservices. It covers microservice communication techniques, including REST, GraphQL, and **Remote Procedure Call** (**RPC**), and explains both synchronous and asynchronous communication methodologies. The chapter also explores popular communication patterns such as API gateways and message queues, providing a theoretical foundation that is essential for practical implementation.

Chapter 3, What Do You Need Before Getting Started?, focuses on the essential concepts of JavaScript and Node.js that you need to understand before building microservices. This chapter covers JavaScript engine internals, asynchronous programming, the Node.js runtime environment, and the crucial role of threading and runtime management in building effective microservices.

Chapter 4, Stack Development Technologies, introduces the essential tools and technologies required to develop and manage microservices with JavaScript. This includes a deep dive into Node.js and various frameworks, choosing the right IDE, and the installation and use of Docker and Git. The chapter also covers Postman, a key tool for testing APIs and interacting with microservices during development.

Chapter 5, Basic CRUD Microservices, takes a practical approach by guiding you through the development of your first microservice using Express.js. This chapter covers the tools required, the internal architecture of microservices, and the step-by-step process of creating and testing a basic **CRUD (Create, Read/ Retrieve, Update, Delete)** microservice, preparing you for more complex implementations.

Chapter 6, Synchronous Microservices, explores the creation and orchestration of synchronous communication between microservices. This chapter focuses on building a second microservice using NestJS and establishing communication between services.

Chapter 7, Asynchronous Microservices, delves into the world of asynchronous communication, a crucial aspect of building scalable systems. The chapter covers the implementation of Apache Kafka for asynchronous messaging, setting up the infrastructure for Kafka with NestJS, and building an asynchronous transaction service. It also breaks down Kafka's core concepts and explains how to incorporate asynchronous communication into your microservices architecture.

Chapter 8, Real-Time Data Streaming Using Microservices, explores the power of real-time data streaming within a microservices ecosystem. This chapter covers the concept of streaming, its benefits, and how to implement stream processing microservices using Node.js. It also demonstrates how to integrate these services with Apache Kafka to build a real-time data pipeline.

Chapter 9, Securing Microservices, focuses on the fundamental aspects of securing microservices by implementing robust authentication mechanisms. It covers the use of JSON Web Tokens (JWT) for stateless authentication, discusses centralized and decentralized approaches to security, and demonstrates how to build a dedicated authentication microservice. Additionally, best practices for ensuring your microservices' confidentiality, integrity, and availability are provided, offering a solid foundation for secure microservice architectures.

Chapter 10, Monitoring Microservices, focuses on equipping your microservices with robust observability and monitoring practices. This chapter covers the importance of logging and monitoring in microservice architectures, ensuring that you can effectively track the health and performance of your system. It introduces essential observability concepts such as logs, metrics, and traces and explores centralized logging with the ELK Stack (Elasticsearch, Logstash, and Kibana). By the end of this chapter, you'll have a strong foundation for implementing logging and monitoring strategies to keep your microservices resilient and responsive.

Chapter 11, Microservices Architecture, provides a deep dive into advanced architectural patterns for microservices. This chapter explores the **API gateway**, **event-sourcing**, and **Command Query Responsibility Segregation (CQRS)** patterns to separate reads and writes.

Chapter 12, Testing Microservices, emphasizes the importance of testing in maintaining microservices' stability and reliability. This chapter covers essential testing strategies, including unit tests and integration tests, ensuring that your microservices can withstand any demand and work seamlessly together.

Chapter 13, A CI/CD Pipeline for Your Microservices, unveils the process of automating microservices development through **Continuous Integration (CI)** and **Continuous Delivery (CD)**. This chapter covers the essentials of CI/CD processes, working with GitHub Actions, building a robust pipeline that streamlines the transition from development to production and deploying your application to Azure Cloud.

To get the most out of this book

To fully benefit from this book, you should have a foundational understanding of JavaScript and basic programming concepts. Familiarity with Node.js, including its runtime environment and asynchronous programming model, will be advantageous as you dive into microservices development. Additionally, a basic knowledge of web development and RESTful APIs will help you grasp the communication techniques and patterns discussed in the book. While not mandatory, experience with Docker, Git, and CI/CD processes will enhance your ability to follow along with the practical examples and deployment strategies covered in the later chapters.

Software/hardware covered in the book	Operating system requirements
Node.js (Windows version v20.12.1)	Windows, macOS, or Linux
Docker Desktop (Windows version 4.33.1)	Windows, macOS, or Linux
VS Code (Windows version 1.92.2)	Windows, macOS, or Linux
Postman (Windows version 11.8)	Windows, macOS, or Linux

While the aforementioned versions are specific to Windows, Node.js, Docker Desktop, Visual Studio Code, and Postman also work seamlessly on macOS and Linux. Users of these operating systems should download their appropriate versions from the official websites. The core functionality remains consistent across all operating systems, ensuring a similar experience regardless of your platform.

> **Important note**
>
> If you are using the digital version of this book, we advise you to type the code yourself or access the code from the book's GitHub repository (a link is available in the next section). Doing so will help you avoid any potential errors related to the copying and pasting of code.

For your convenience, you can download the source code to follow along with the book. However, most chapters also provide detailed instructions to guide you in writing everything from scratch, ensuring that you understand each step of the process.

Download the example code files

You can download the example code files for this book from GitHub at `https://github.com/PacktPublishing/Hands-on-Microservices-with-JavaScript`. If there's an update to the code, it will be updated in the GitHub repository.

We also have other code bundles from our rich catalog of books and videos available at `https://github.com/PacktPublishing/`. Check them out!

Conventions used

There are a number of text conventions used throughout this book.

`Code in text`: Indicates code words in text, database table names, folder names, filenames, file extensions, pathnames, dummy URLs, user input, and Twitter handles. Here is an example: "To track changes, we are going to add `createdAt` and `updatedAt` fields."

A block of code is set as follows:

```
{
    "name":"AccName1",
    "number":"Ac12345",
    "type":"root",
    "status":"new"
}
```

Any command-line input or output is written as follows:

```
$ cd transactionservice
```

Bold: Indicates a new term, an important word, or words that you see on screen. For instance, words in menus or dialog boxes appear in **bold**. Here is an example: "Go to the **Terminal** menu, select **New Terminal**."

> **Tips or important notes**
> Appear like this.

Get in touch

Feedback from our readers is always welcome.

General feedback: If you have questions about any aspect of this book, email us at `customercare@packtpub.com` and mention the book title in the subject of your message.

Errata: Although we have taken every care to ensure the accuracy of our content, mistakes do happen. If you have found a mistake in this book, we would be grateful if you would report this to us. Please visit `www.packtpub.com/support/errata` and fill in the form.

Piracy: If you come across any illegal copies of our works in any form on the internet, we would be grateful if you would provide us with the location address or website name. Please contact us at `copyright@packtpub.com` with a link to the material.

If you are interested in becoming an author: If there is a topic that you have expertise in and you are interested in either writing or contributing to a book, please visit `authors.packtpub.com`.

Share Your Thoughts

Once you've read *Hands-On Microservices with JavaScript*, we'd love to hear your thoughts! Scan the QR code below to go straight to the Amazon review page for this book and share your feedback.

https://packt.link/r/1-788-62540-4

Your review is important to us and the tech community and will help us make sure we're delivering excellent quality content.

Download a free PDF copy of this book

Thanks for purchasing this book!

Do you like to read on the go but are unable to carry your print books everywhere?

Is your eBook purchase not compatible with the device of your choice?

Don't worry, now with every Packt book you get a DRM-free PDF version of that book at no cost.

Read anywhere, any place, on any device. Search, copy, and paste code from your favorite technical books directly into your application.

The perks don't stop there, you can get exclusive access to discounts, newsletters, and great free content in your inbox daily

Follow these simple steps to get the benefits:

1. Scan the QR code or visit the link below

https://packt.link/free-ebook/978-1-78862-540-1

2. Submit your proof of purchase
3. That's it! We'll send your free PDF and other benefits to your email directly

Part 1:
Fundamentals of
Microservices Architecture

In this part, we will gain a comprehensive understanding of the foundational principles and internal workings of microservices architecture. We will explore what microservices are, how they compare to traditional monolithic architectures, and the various communication techniques and patterns that make microservices a robust and scalable solution. Additionally, we'll learn the essential JavaScript and Node.js concepts that are necessary to develop microservices.

This part contains the following chapters:

- *Chapter 1, Introduction to Microservices*
- *Chapter 2, Diving into Microservices Internals*
- *Chapter 3, What Do You Need Before Getting Started?*
- *Chapter 4, Stack Development Technologies*

1
Introduction to Microservices

As human beings, we all go through various stages of development. With each stage we reach, even if it seems like the best at the time, we later realize we still have a long way to go. Each period has its problems, and depending on their size and nature, they require different solutions.

We humans tend to simplify things. That is why we build our lives around problems and their corresponding solutions. Finding solutions to problems has been our main goal throughout history, perhaps due to our instinct to survive.

If we consider each piece of software as an individual, they also have problems to solve. Depending on the size and shape of the problems, software has a different structure, which we call **architecture**. The size and nature of the problems directly affect the architecture of the software. One of these architectural approaches we use is called microservices.

Microservices are important when it comes to building scalable distributed applications that respond to modern-day concerns. It is also a de facto requirement for most huge companies when they interview you as a developer. The vast majority of technologies we use nowadays try to support microservice development out of the box. So, being a software engineer without microservice knowledge doesn't make you an ideal candidate in the modern IT world.

Starting from this chapter, we're going to dive into the world of microservices. We will build strong theoretical knowledge before moving on to practical sections.

First, we will go back and try to understand what type of popular approaches were there before microservices. Microservices are important, but understanding the need to apply them is foremost.

In this chapter, we're going to cover the following topics:

- Introducing microservices
- Exploring the monolith approach
- What is service-oriented architecture?
- The differences between SOA and microservices

- Advantages of microservices
- Disadvantages of microservices

Introducing microservices

A microservice architecture decomposes an application into loosely coupled, independently deployable services that own their data and communicate through lightweight protocols. It breaks down large applications into smaller, self-contained business capabilities, enabling faster development, easier scaling, and better fault tolerance. Microservices enable continuous delivery and agile development by allowing teams to independently build, test, and deploy features. You can imagine an application as an orchestra, where each microservice is a musician playing their part, but in perfect harmony with the others, to create a beautiful symphony.

What we've just mentioned sounds like a *silver bullet* but as you know, nothing is free and there is no one-size-fits-all solution to the problems we face. The same applies to microservices.

We, as software developers, love to learn new trends and try to apply them to our practice. But after delving into the details, we understand that every trend is just an encapsulation of old knowledge. Before applying any architecture to software, it is always better to engage in careful planning, discussion, collaboration, and analysis.

Moving toward microservices

Creating software is more than just learning a programming language and applying syntactical elements of it to code, to build things. It's like wielding a hammer and nails; having them in your arsenal doesn't make you a skilled builder. Similarly, having all the tools doesn't make you a good software developer.

As you embark on creating a basic `hello world` type application, it remains just that – *basic*. However, it is important to understand that such simple applications don't warrant payment. If you want your application to have value, it must address tangible real-world challenges – in short, it should hold business value. Adding more business value also brings complexity. In most cases, more business means more complexity. After some time, you'll realize that instead of dealing with a business, you're starting to deal with the complexity that your business brought to your application.

In navigating complexity, we aim to break it down into smaller, maintainable, extensible, and reusable components. Only by doing so can we effectively handle the complexity and future changes. In programming, the only true constant is the need to embrace changes, a principle that remains as-is, not just during the process of creating the application, but until the end.

This constant change forces us to not only master the selected programming language but also to have an understanding of the business domain. Naturally, this leads to us adopting a design-oriented mindset. Without having good knowledge of business, it is almost impossible to develop valuable software.

Although the simple applications we write to learn a language may seem useless, when we connect the dots, we get closer to the truth. Isn't our whole life spent in search of truth? Soon, you'll realize that the software that meets the customer's business requirements is the software that matters, and that reflects the truth.

If you start your development process without carefully analyzing and designing, you're going to pay a higher price throughout the development itself. The earlier you start with design and analysis, the less likely you are to run into a bigger problem at a later stage. We call our first not properly analyzed and designed application **a big ball of mud** that uses *spaghetti-driven development*:

In software design, the phrase *a big ball of mud* is used to draw attention to an **anti-pattern** or a design approach that produces undesirable results. Let's understand this phrase in more depth.

Understanding a big ball of mud

The main issue with a big ball of mud is the lack of structure and organization. The absence of modularity and distinct issue separation in the code base leads to a complex network of interconnected files and functions. Imagine a house that is just a disorganized jumble of rooms and materials with no walls or other distinguishing features. Because everything in it is connected, changes that are made in one part could have a disastrous effect on other parts. It's like pulling on a loose thread in a badly tailored sweater – you run the risk of the entire garment coming apart. Similarly code fragments are dispersed throughout the code base, which causes inefficiencies when performing maintenance.

Due to the absence of structure and documentation, maintaining the code base and adding new features is challenging for developers. Imagine attempting to navigate a house devoid of layout or labels; it's nearly impossible.

Because of their close coupling, changes in one area can unintentionally disturb seemingly unrelated components. Because of its fragility, the software is prone to mistakes and regressions. Imagine a house built with weak, interconnected supports so that even a small outside force could result in serious harm.

A big ball of mud may seem like the right choice at first in small, simple projects, but as the project grows and develops, its complexity quickly increases. To guarantee long-term maintainability, scalability, and developer satisfaction, this design approach must be avoided at all costs.

Guess what? I already know that you've gone through this stage – the stage of applying and failing with a big ball of mud. These difficulties helped you learn more rather than learn from success.

Every difficulty teaches us something, right? Until one year in my life, I was always grateful for the good things in my life. But over time, I realized that it was those difficulties that made me who I am. After I changed my way of thinking, I began to thank the difficulties in my life and those who made me suffer. If you could go back and remove the difficulties in your life, believe me, you would also remove your present self. Difficulties strengthen you and make you a strong person.

Mankind is a creature that rarely listens to advice. We have to get into trouble – we have to experiment with trouble. I know that the downsides I mentioned about a big ball of mud in this section only make sense to those who have gone through this difficulty. In the end, we all learn through experimenting.

As a novice software developer, it's beneficial to experiment with a big ball of mud at some point. You'll quickly discover that while it provides a swift start, its efficiency dwindles over time.

Let's try to summarize the disadvantages of a big ball of mud:

- **Unplanned and chaotic**: The appearance of a big ball of mud is the result of poor design and coding techniques rather than a deliberate architectural decision.

- **Tight coupling**: The code is tightly interconnected; changes that are made to one section run the risk of having unexpected effects in unrelated areas.

- **Difficulty in understanding and maintaining**: The code base is messy and lacks documentation, making it hard for developers to grasp and modify.

- **Error-prone and fragile**: The code base leads to unpredictable errors and regressions with modifications. In a big ball of mud system, everything is tightly connected like a big mess of wires. This makes it hard to know what happens when you change one part, like trying to fix one loose wire in a tangled mess. This can easily lead to unexpected problems and things breaking, like causing a short circuit in the tangled wires, making it harder to develop and maintain the system in the long run.

- **Reduced developer productivity**: You spend more time on maintaining the code base instead of focusing on new features.

- **Limited scaling and growth**: A rigid code structure makes it difficult to introduce new features or adapt to changes:

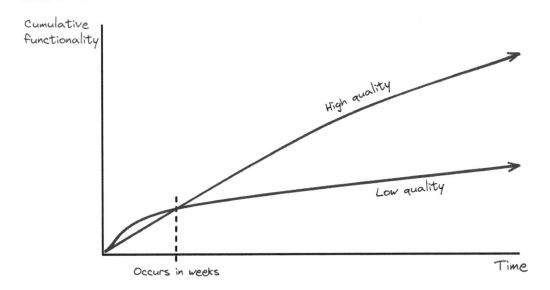

Figure 1.1: A quality diagram of a big ball of mud

When writing a program, we see that it becomes more of a problem than a solution within a short time (see *Figure 1.1*). The preceding graph tracks how a project progresses over time. Time is on the bottom (X-axis) and features added are on the side (Y-axis).

Starting a project without a clear plan, such as using the big ball of mud approach, might seem easy at first. Imagine building with blocks – no instructions are needed and you can put things together quickly. But for these projects, as they get more features (higher Y-axis value), the overall quality suffers (gets worse).

In the short term (a few weeks), both well-designed projects and big ball of mud projects might seem similar. But over time, the quality of the messy project goes downhill.

Overall, while a big ball of mud approach might seem faster initially, it ultimately creates more problems in the long run. It's like taking a shortcut that might save you time now but leads to bigger issues later on.

One of the factors that turned our code into a big ball of mud over time was a lack of planning and organization. Planning and organizational structure are the attributes we usually use when building microservice architecture.

Understanding the software development process

The development process not only covers coding – it is also about business, communication, discussion, analyzing, designing, testing, and deploying. Let's call these the **attributes** of the software development process (see *Figure 1.2*). Software development is much more than just writing code lines. While coding is certainly an important part, it's only one piece of the puzzle. Because of that, it is essential to understand the core needs and goals of the business:

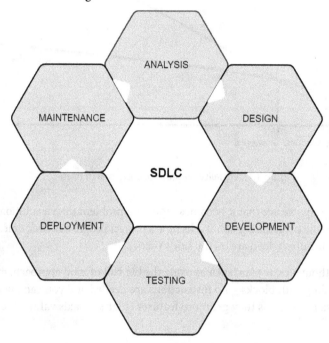

Figure 1.2: Software development life cycle

The following list provides comprehensive insights into the software development process:

- The need to solve specific problems and think in terms of the business landscape is what drives software development. For developers to create software solutions that are not only relevant, but also meaningful, they must have a deep understanding of market dynamics, industry, and user requirements.

- Effective collaboration and transparent communication are the backbone of success at every stage. Developers engage with a range of stakeholders, including business analysts, designers, testers, and clients. Clear communication ensures that everyone is on the same page regarding objectives, requirements, and project milestones.

- Discussing the ideas, obstacles, and potential solutions is very important. Effective brainstorming sessions, code reviews, and attentive user feedback all contribute to the quality of software. Open communication makes problem-solving more efficient.

- It is essential to carry out a thorough analysis of the requirements, user behavior patterns, and data insights. To create a solid software design strategy, developers must carefully analyze existing solutions, identify user needs, and break down complex problems.

- Careful consideration must be given to the architecture, functionality, and user interface of the software. Software that has been carefully designed is easy to use, effective, and maintain. A friendly user experience is the result of close collaboration between developers and designers.

- Strict testing procedures are essential to guarantee the functionality, dependability, and conformity of the software regarding user expectations. Different testing approaches address different areas, such as performance benchmarks and core functionality.

- Ensuring that end users can access the software is the last step. This is usually called **deployment**. This includes setting up the infrastructure, taking stringent security precautions, and, if needed, providing thorough user training to optimize usability and adoption rates.

Now that we understand the software development process, let's take a deeper look at the monolith approach to software development.

Exploring the monolith approach

Say we have an e-commerce site with a single code base that was developed years ago. Over time, features and functionalities were added randomly, leading to messy code that contains duplication, is hard to maintain, and is difficult to troubleshoot. Here is the first suggested transition so that you can make your application responsive or alive again:

- **Analyze the current state of your application**: You need to identify key pain points affecting developer productivity and user experience. Try to divide the problem into smaller pieces. Trying to cover everything at once will lead you to more difficulties. Focus on specific modules or functionalities within the larger code base for initial refactoring. You need to understand dependencies, duplication, and complexity in your application.

- **Communication and collaborative planning**: The next steps are identifying the areas for improvement and agreeing on common architectural principles. Emphasize the phased approach, starting with small, isolated modules and demonstrating progress before moving on.

- **Choose a monolith architecture**: Decide which architectural style and pattern (layered, tiered, MVC, MVVM, and so on) aligns best with your needs in the given context.

- **Start small and iterate**: Set small goals and apply iterative development.

- **Make improvements**: Eliminate code duplication, clean up spaghetti code (a term that's used for unstructured and difficult-to-understand programming code), and improve documentation.

- **Application**: After each refactoring step, it is better to apply unit, integration, and regression testing to ensure code functionality and identify potential regression in your application.

- **Feedback**: Gather feedback from developers and users throughout the process to adapt and refine the approach.

Welcome – you're in the world of monoliths! But what is the concept of monolith?

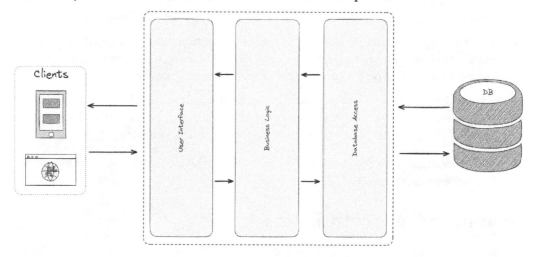

Figure 1.3: Monolith architecture

Many online articles delve into the specifics of monolith architecture but rarely touch upon the broader concept, called the monolith approach. This isn't surprising as the architecture has clear-cut characteristics. We love to be concrete and as developers, we are rarely theory lovers. However, it's important to keep in mind that the monolith approach covers a greater variety of options.

The **monolith approach** is a broader concept that refers to a general way of building software as a single, self-contained unit. It can be implemented using various architectures, not just the traditional monolith architectures we know. It highlights simplicity, rapid development, and tight integration. The monolith approach is architecture-agnostic, meaning it can be implemented using various architectural styles or patterns, or even without a specific architectural framework at all, so long as the core principle of consolidating components into a single unit is maintained.

On the other hand, **monolith architecture** (see *Figure 1.3*) is a specific software architecture where everything, from UI to business logic to data access, is built as a single, tightly coupled unit. It often uses a single code base, programming language, and database.

Monolith architecture refers to the specific architectural design or pattern that's used to implement the monolith approach. It includes all of the technological choices and structural design of the monolithic system, including the arrangement of modules, the interactions between components, and the data management process.

The monolith approach itself doesn't dictate a specific architecture. However, certain architectural styles and patterns naturally align with and support the monolith approach more effectively than others. Examples include the layered architecture, the MVC architecture, and the N-tier architecture. The monolith approach can also be implemented without strictly adhering to a specific architecture, especially for smaller projects. The key feature here is to maintain a single code base and deployment unit. Whether you choose a structured style or a more organic approach, the core principle remains: build a cohesive software unit. Understanding this distinction forces you to make informed decisions when navigating the vast world of software architectures. So, while the monolith approach promotes the development of software as a unified entity, the monolith architecture determines how that unity is achieved and maintained. Knowing this difference allows you to navigate the wide world of software architectures with knowledge and confidence.

While not without its drawbacks, the monolith approach offers several advantages, particularly for certain types of projects. These advantages are listed here:

- **Simplicity and speed**: Monolith architecture enables faster development and deployment cycles by consolidating the entire system into a single codebase, reducing the overhead of managing multiple services.

- **Maintainability and control**: Having everything in one place allows for easier management, control over application performance, and a unified approach to maintaining and securing the system

- **Performance and cost**: This architecture offers the advantage of reduced complexity, leading to lower infrastructure costs and optimized performance for applications with straightforward requirements.

- **Additional benefits**: It provides practical advantages for simpler projects, making it easier to manage data and application operations, especially for smaller teams.

Even though the monolithic approach has benefits, such as speed and simplicity, not all projects can benefit from it. To help determine whether the monolithic approach is right for your project, consider these general guidelines:

- **Simple and well-defined applications**: A monolith works well in applications that have a defined scope and few functionalities. Simple mobile apps, internal tools, and basic e-commerce sites are a few examples.

- **Quick product launches and idea testing**: This is made possible by the agility of a monolithic architecture, which is useful if your project requires for quick development cycles or frequent prototyping.

- **Small teams with limited experience**: Initially, managing and maintaining a monolith may be more manageable for teams that lack experience with distributed systems or microservices.

- **Tight data coupling and consistency**: Monolithic architectures are advantageous for applications that rely heavily on consistent data across multiple functionalities. It guarantees data integrity throughout the application and simplifies data management.

- **Limited scalability requirements**: Without the hassle of scaling microservices, a monolithic architecture might be able to satisfy your scalability requirements if your application expects stable user traffic and moderate growth projections.

The best architecture depends on your specific application's requirements. Here, you must consider factors such as scalability, complexity, technology needs, and development team structure. As we mentioned previously, there's no one-size-fits-all solution in software development.

While the monolith approach has its benefits, it's not suitable for every application. It's better not to use monolith when it comes to the following aspects:

- Building a highly scalable application

- Applications with constantly evolving features, modularity, and independent deployment

- If your application requires integrating diverse technologies or frameworks, also referred to as heterogeneous technologies

- If high availability and resilience are critical and one of the important attributes for your system is fault-tolerance

- If different teams work on distinct functionalities – that is, if there is independent development and deployment across teams

- When you have large teams and distributed development

Besides its pros and cons, Monolith is usually a preferable architecture for getting started but not the only architecture to build better applications. We have another preferable architecture called **service-oriented approach** (**SOA**) that we plan to dive into details starting from the next page.

What is service-oriented architecture?

A monolithic architecture unifies all of the components/elements – including the user interface and data access – into a single code base, promoting simplicity and quick development. Although it's not impossible, combining different technologies into *one system* can be difficult to maintain and unfeasible at times. In the absence of contemporary methodologies such as feature flags and blue-green deployment, it becomes necessary to deploy the entire application every time you want to update a monolithic application. There are difficulties with organizing and delivering the application smoothly, which could mess up its launch.

On the other hand, SOA (see *Figure 1.4*) focuses on modularity and reuse, breaking down functionalities into independent services that communicate with each other through **application programming interfaces (APIs)**.

SOA can be defined as multiple, smaller, and often coarser-grained services, each with a specific function. This modularity offers advantages such as flexibility and scalability. Services in SOA can be deployed and scaled independently, meaning you can update or scale one service without affecting others. This is a key benefit of SOA.

The analogy from moving from monolith to SOA can be described like this: You have a big method/ function that does everything (similar to a monolith). After some time, some other parts of your functionalities are required so that these functionalities can be reused. Instead of copying it, you're breaking this giant method into reusable parts (similar to SOA). In this case, the method calls are going to be our API calls:

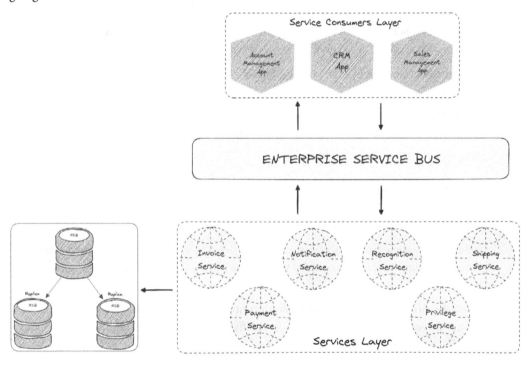

Figure 1.4: An overview of service-oriented approach

Consider multiple applications (as shown in *Figure 1.4* – account management, CRM, and sales management) that need to share common functionalities. Instead of duplicating them for every application, we provide a service-oriented approach. At first glance, it may look like they are *perfect* grained services, but our focus is just to *share* common behavior that supports scaling and reusing.

To encapsulate communication complexity, we may use a service bus, which allows us to write additional logic and move the complexity to the outside of the application, which acts as a mediator. This is one of the signs that we should use architectural mediators in applications.

Think of two functions within a single program and one directly calls the other. In SOA, each function becomes a standalone service, communicating through a defined interface. This enables independent deployment, updates, and even development by different teams.

Imagine building with Lego bricks instead of monolithic blocks. That's the essence of SOA: breaking down applications into reusable, independent services, each focused on a specific task. Instead of hard-coded connections, they communicate through standard protocols such as **REST** or **SOAP**, making them platform-agnostic and adaptable.

SOA offers numerous advantages that can significantly improve the flexibility, agility, and efficiency of your organization's IT infrastructure. Let's discover its key benefits:

- **Business agility**: SOA supports fast development and deployment, helping businesses quickly adapt to market changes and align their software with evolving business objectives.

- **Technical advantages**: SOA offers flexibility and scalability, allowing for easier integration, upgrades, and reuse of components across the system without disrupting the overall functionality.

- **Operational benefits**: SOA streamlines operations by reducing maintenance overhead and improving system reliability, while enhancing security through centralized management.

Although SOA has many advantages, there are drawbacks as well:

- **Enhanced complexity**: SOA introduces more complexity by requiring careful coordination between independent services, demanding skilled personnel, and detailed planning for development, testing, and maintenance.

- **Possible problems with performance**: SOA can introduce latency due to network-based service interactions, adding complexity when ensuring secure and efficient communication between services.

- **Other difficulties**: SOA comes with high upfront costs and requires skilled professionals, making it challenging to maintain service coordination, manage responsibilities, and ensure smooth integration as the system evolves.

SOA is one step toward microservices. Most of the core ideas of microservices come from SOA.

In the final section of this chapter, we'll understand the benefits and challenges of the microservices architecture.

The differences between SOA and microservices

Microservices architecture simplifies building distributed, flexible, and scalable software. Instead of one monolithic system, it divides an application into small, standalone services, each of them focused on a specific task. These services communicate through simple interfaces, allowing for independent deployment and easy integration. When developing properly designed microservices, we get loosely coupled, reusable, extensible, and easily maintainable applications.

When comparing microservices to SOA, they may seem similar in concept. SOA and microservices architecture are both architectural styles that are used for building distributed systems, but they have some key differences. Let's compare them:

- **Scope and granularity**: Services in SOA are like big boxes containing multiple functionalities that are meant to be reused across different applications. Microservices are like tiny, specialized tools, each focusing on one specific task or feature within an application.

- **Communication protocols**: Services in SOA mostly communicate using strict protocols, such as **SOAP, XML-RPC, WSDL**, and **UDDI**. Microservices prefer lightweight protocols such as **RESTful HTTP** or messaging queues, allowing for more flexible communication.

- **Technology stack**: SOA can work with different technologies and platforms. Microservices often use containerization tools such as **Docker** and orchestration tools such as **Kubernetes** for easier deployment and management.

- **Dependency management**: Services in SOA can have intricate dependencies that require careful coordination. Microservices strive for loose coupling, reducing dependencies between services to simplify development and deployment.

- **Deployment and scaling**: Services in SOA are often centrally deployed and scaled at the service level. Microservices are deployed separately, allowing individual scaling and better resource utilization.

- **Organizational impact**: Once SOA is implemented, significant organizational changes may be required for coordination and management. Microservices promote decentralization of management by giving small, cross-disciplinary teams the autonomy to control their services.

The difference between *approach* and *architecture*, especially regarding microservices, is important.

The microservice approach is all about how we think when designing software. It's like having a mindset or philosophy of breaking down big, complicated systems into smaller, easier-to-handle parts. Each of these parts focuses on one specific task. It's somewhat abstract and emphasizes concepts such as **modularity** (allowing for simple replacement), **scalability** (allowing for increased work), and **flexibility** (allowing for change adaptation):

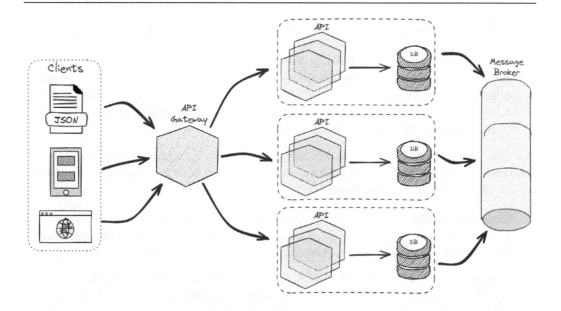

Figure 1.5: Microservices architecture

Every approach has its pros and cons. Nothing is ideal. To identify it from the Microservices perspective, let's talk about the advantages and disadvantages of Microservices.

Advantages of microservices

In this section, we'll look at the many reasons that make microservices an important part of software development:

- **Scalability**: You can scale each microservice independently based on demand, ensuring resources are allocated where needed for optimal performance and cost-effectiveness.

- **Flexibility and agility**: Teams can work on different services simultaneously, speeding up development and making updates easier. Being agile is essential to adapting to the ever-shifting demands and markets of businesses.

- **Fault isolation**: If one microservice fails, it doesn't necessarily affect others, thanks to their independence. This isolation improves system reliability by minimizing downtime.

- **Technology diversity**: Multiple programming languages and technologies can be used in a single application thanks to microservices. Teams are encouraged to explore and be creative by selecting the finest tools for each service.

- **Easy maintenance and updates**: Compared to huge monolithic programs, smaller services are easier to comprehend, manage, and update. Risks are decreased because modifications to one service won't inadvertently affect others.

- **Scalable development teams**: Small, cross-functional teams can now own separate services thanks to microservices. This configuration promotes creativity, accelerates decision-making, and heightens accountability.

- **Improved fault tolerance**: Microservices make it simpler to implement redundancy and failover techniques at the service level. This increases the system's ability to withstand setbacks.

- **Improved deployment practices**: **Continuous integration** and **continuous deployment (CI/CD)**, two contemporary deployment techniques, mesh nicely with **microservices** architecture. Time to market is shortened by the release process being streamlined by automated deployment pipelines for every service.

- **Improved use of resources**: Resource allocation based on the unique requirements of each service is made possible by granular scaling, which maximizes resource efficiency and reduces costs.

- **Encouragement of cooperation**: Encouraging cooperation between the development and operations teams through microservices makes it easier to implement DevOps principles. At the service level, feedback loops, automation, and monitoring can be put into place to improve overall quality and efficiency.

- **Huge and complicated systems**: Microservices can help you simplify huge and complex applications as you can divide them into smaller, more manageable parts.

- **Handles many users**: Because microservices allow you to scale each component individually to effectively handle the load, they are ideal for apps that experience high traffic or a large number of users.

- **Requires frequent updates or new features**: Microservices allow you to swiftly react to changing needs by allowing you to change individual components without affecting the entire application.

- **Uses different technologies**: Microservices let you use different tools and programming languages for different parts of your app so that you can pick the best one for each job.

- **Built by many teams**: If your app is being worked on by lots of different teams, microservices let each team work on their part, without getting in each other's way.

- **Needs to stay running**: Microservices help your app stay up and running, even if one part fails. This is because each part is separate. As a result, problems in one area don't crash the whole thing.

- **Works in the cloud**: Microservices are a good fit for apps that run in the cloud because they're designed to work well with cloud technology. Plus, tools such as containers and orchestrators make it even easier to manage them in the cloud.

In summary, microservices provide a modern, flexible method for developing software, allowing businesses to innovate rapidly, grow effectively, and release high-caliber software products into the market more quickly. However, don't attempt to use them for every kind of application you're creating.

Although microservices offer many advantages, you should be aware that they also come with some additional complexity, such as having to manage several moving components and more communication being required between services.

Disadvantages of microservices

Throughout this chapter, we learned that the main reason for having various architectures in software development is a sign that there is no single truth and that depending on the requirements, architecture may vary. Every approach in design has its disadvantages and before applying any architecture, you should carefully analyze and understand them.

Here are some important disadvantages of microservices:

- **Increased complexity in development**: Breaking down a system into smaller services can lead to increased complexity in development, deployment, and testing.

- **Interservice communication**: Managing communication between microservices can become complex, requiring careful design and implementation of APIs and protocols.

- **Infrastructure complexity**: Managing and deploying a large number of microservices can introduce operational overhead, including the need for sophisticated orchestration and monitoring tools.

- **Infrastructure cost**: The overhead of managing multiple services and the associated infrastructure can lead to increased costs, particularly in terms of hosting and operational expenses.

- **Security issues**: A larger number of services means a larger attack surface, potentially increasing the security risk.

- **Communication security**: Securing communication between microservices requires additional attention to prevent unauthorized access.

- **Coordination and communication**: Teams need to coordinate effectively to ensure that changes in one service do not adversely affect others.

- **Data consistency**: Maintaining consistency across microservices can be challenging, especially when dealing with distributed databases. Ensuring data integrity and consistency becomes a complex task.

- **Team expertise**: Developers need expertise in both the domain and technology stack of their specific microservice, potentially limiting flexibility in task assignments.

Therefore, we should carefully consider if microservices are the correct choice for our project based on the expertise of our team, the requirements of our application, and the readiness of our organization for the shift.

Summary

This chapter introduced you to microservices. We talked about coding without proper design and analysis, which brings us to a big ball of mud. Having no clear architecture is similar to having no map in the middle of the ocean.

Our first step was starting with monoliths. We talked about the advantages and disadvantages of the monolith approach and tried to understand the differences between approach and architecture.

Nowadays, requirements for applications are broader and more complex, and always trying to deal with them using a monolith approach may not be a good solution. To add important attributes, such as "distributed," to the architecture, we considered SOA while discussing its pros and cons.

The final destination for us was microservices. We provided a clear definition for it and tried to understand the advantages and disadvantages of using them.

Microservices bring a lot of interesting challenges to our lives and one of them is communication. Dividing a big problem into smaller chunks is good but making proper communication between the chunks isn't easy. When you're ready, turn to the next chapter to explore it with me.

2

Diving into Microservices Internals

Microservices aren't just about breaking down a large application into smaller, more manageable ones. They also introduce challenges, one of which is communication between services. Monolithic applications, which we discussed in the previous chapter, make communication between elements relatively straightforward. However, in microservice architecture, we have physical isolation between services. Even though we want microservices to be independent, as well as easy to reuse, maintain, and grow, getting them to talk to each other effectively becomes a major challenge.

Effective microservice communication is crucial for the overall success of architecture. It enables services to exchange data, coordinate actions, and trigger events. If microservices can't communicate effectively, they become like isolated islands, stopping the application from working properly and keeping it running slowly. Well-designed communication patterns ensure that microservices can collaborate effectively to deliver the desired functionality. This communication strategy also promotes loose coupling, which means that changes in one service have minimal impact on others, thereby making the application more resilient and easier to maintain.

This chapter is about establishing a strong foundation for the next practical chapters, along with providing comprehensive information about microservice communication. A solid understanding of microservices communication will help you build reliable, consistent, scalable, and fault-tolerant microservice applications.

In this chapter, we're going to talk more about the following topics:

- Microservices communication techniques
- Synchronous microservice communication
- Asynchronous microservice communication
- Essential communication patterns

Solidifying the communication

As your application grows, managing its complexity becomes increasingly challenging. To tackle this, developers rely on best practices, design patterns, and various approaches. In traditional software design, techniques like abstraction, encapsulation, and decomposition help us deal with complexity.

The microservice architecture offers a provides a powerful solution to complexity through the **Separation of Concerns (SOC)** principle. This principle breaks down a complex system into smaller independent parts, each with a well-defined responsibility. Imagine a monolithic application as a mountain; microservices allow us to break it down into smaller, more manageable hills through bounded contexts. However, this freedom comes at the cost of somehow figuring out how to establish communication between microservices. Of course, it is not as easy as it was with the monolithic approach, because with that, everything was inside one codebase. Creating a connection between elements of a monolith was as simple as calling any method.

The best way to explain the relationship between monoliths and microservices is by using the first two principles of **S.O.L.I.D**, the **Single Responsibility Principle (SRP)** and the **Open-Closed Principle (OCP)**, as metaphors.

The SRP's core principle of dividing a large problem into smaller, more focused units aligns with the microservices approach. We break down the big picture into smaller, manageable modules, each with well-defined responsibilities and reasons for change. This mirrors the SRP's aim of splitting classes and modules into manageable pieces.

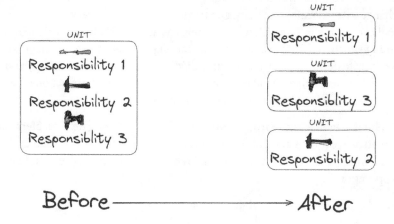

Figure 2.1: Applying the SRP

The main idea behind the SRP is the SoC, which is also adopted in microservice architecture. It promotes dividing a system into independent parts based on functionality. This improves maintainability, reduces complexity, and allows for independent development and deployment of each part

Metaphorically, the SRP's abstract idea is to break down the big module into smaller one (see Figure 2.2) that are similar to what we get when we divide a monolith into smaller services called microservices.

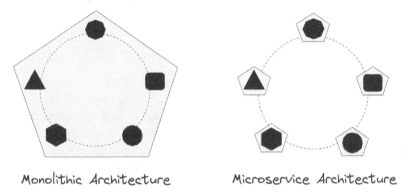

Figure 2.2: Monolithic architecture to microservice architecture

The final results of splitting up your monolithic application are microservices; they are software entities for us in this comparison. Making them open for an extension means that there is a team that works on them. This team can extend and modify them without depending on other teams or modules. Having loose coupling between services allows us to independently work on services.

However, there's a catch: *communication*. With multiple smaller entities instead of one monolithic class, the application relies on communication to function as a whole. While the SRP creates independent subsystems, it doesn't address the challenges of enabling communication between them. In fact, the SRP itself can contribute to this complexity. The SRP can leave you with multiple smaller subsystems without solving communication issues between them.

This is where the OCP comes in. The OCP states that software should be open for extension but closed for modification. From a metaphorical perspective, in the context of microservices, this means designing communication mechanisms that are flexible and adaptable to future changes without requiring modifications to existing services.

When one microservice (we'll call it *Microservice A*) asks for some resource from another microservice (*Microservice B*), it doesn't need to know the internals of Microservice B. In exchange for that, Microservice B may use a different implementation form of the same endpoint without notifying Microservice A

Microservice communication techniques

The biggest communication challenge with microservices is establishing reliable and scalable connections between them. We use different techniques to handle microservices communication. It is worth mentioning that there are multiple techniques to achieve proper communication between microservices. However, in this chapter, we will only focus on the most popular ones, as well as the ones that we think are most important. Let's explore these techniques together.

Introduction to APIs

In software development, **Application Programming Interfaces** (**APIs**) are important tools that help us avoid doing the same tasks over and over. APIs protect us from the complexities of our working environment and area of expertise, making it easier to manage complicated processes and ignore detailed domain knowledge. They encapsulate complexity, making it unnecessary to understand the underlying implementation details. APIs by themselves are black boxes that provide only the required information. This means that we don't have to worry about the nitty-gritty technical stuff and can focus on using the provided interfaces to interact with our environment. For example, when we use a framework, we see all the DLLs (packages) as APIs that give us the functions that we need.

A web-based API is just a type of API. It's used to help different programs share information over the internet using standard web rules and methods. Usually, these APIs are seen as REST APIs or **Simple Object Access Protocol** (**SOAP**) services and rely on client-server architecture. This allows for creating connections between various online resources such as websites or services, which can help in building big systems like microservices or just in sharing data.

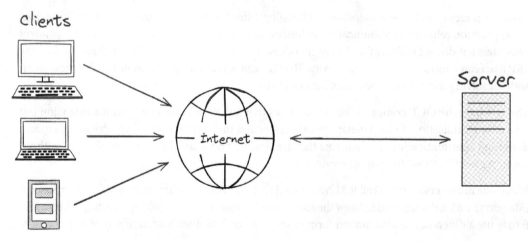

Figure 2.3: Client-server architecture

We talked about REST here, but what does it mean? Let's discuss this in the next section.

What exactly is REST?

Representational State Transfer (**REST**) is a style of architecture that is used for building applications that are loosely connected over the HTTP protocol. It's important to note that REST is primarily a design approach rather than a strict architectural pattern. When I consider the differences between architectural style and pattern, I always perceive abstraction and implementation.

An architectural *style* defines a set of principles and guidelines for organizing a system's structure. It provides a high-level abstraction of how different components should interact and communicate with each other. Architectural styles are broad, conceptual approaches to designing software systems.

An architectural *pattern*, on the other hand, is a specific solution to a recurring architectural problem. It's a reusable design blueprint or template that describes how to solve a particular design problem within a given architectural style. It provides a concrete blueprint for implementing a particular aspect of the style.

Many call REST a protocol. However, REST itself isn't a standardized protocol, although it's commonly implemented using web standards today. While it's often associated with HTTP, it's not limited to this protocol; REST can work with other protocols too.

To simplify, think of REST as a blueprint for how systems should communicate. It outlines how a client (such as a web browser) can request information from a server, and how the server responds, potentially changing the client's state.

The core ideas behind REST are resource, representation, state, and transfer. When a client requests a resource from a server, the server sends back a representation of that resource, which is essentially a copy. If the state of the resource changes later, the client can request it again to get the latest version. The process of sending this resource from server to client is the transfer part of REST.

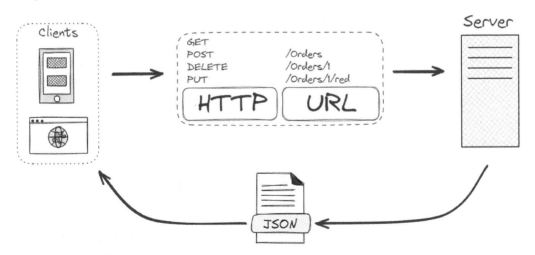

Figure 2.4: An overview of REST

So, why is REST important?

- It separates the client and server, breaking their direct reliance on each other.

- It's **platform-independent**, meaning that it's not restricted to any particular system.

- It's **language-agnostic**. Whether you're coding in PHP, C#, Node.js, or any other language, you can implement REST services.

- It's flexible with data formats, supporting both XML and JSON, among others.

- It facilitates building distributed systems, enabling components to be spread across different locations.

- It offers discoverability, making it easy to identify and access resources.

- It's straightforward to use, simplifying the process of integrating services.

- It leverages **HTTP cache**, improving performance by storing frequently accessed data locally.

With this understanding, let's look at some of the constraints of REST.

What are some REST constraints?

The key indicator that a service follows REST principles lies in the constraints it follows. REST adheres to six constraints, five of which are mandatory.

- **Uniform-interface constraint**: This is perhaps the most critical aspect of REST. This states that devices and programs should access resources using the same URL. A URL can offer different representations, such as XML or JSON, via content negotiation. Both GET and POST requests can be made to the same URL.

  This brief overview doesn't cover the entirety of the uniform-interface constraint, which consists of four sub-parts:

  - **Identification of resources**: Resources should be identifiable via URL. For instance, if the URL is `https://website.com/api/students`, `students` is the resource.

  - **Manipulating resources through representation**: If a client can modify a resource, metadata about how to do so should be included with the returned representation.

  - **Self-descriptive messages**: Each request should contain all necessary information, which is typically conveyed via HTTP headers.

  - **Hypermedia As the Engine of Application State (HATEOAS)**: Requests should provide documentation, enabling clients to discover other resources easily.

- **Client-server constraint**: This constraint separates the client and server. Here, a client and server facilitate data exchange. They evolve independently and remain ignorant of each other's architecture.

- **Stateless constraint**: This ensures communication without maintaining session data. The servers don't retain client session data, and each request is independent of others.

- **Cacheable constraint**: To improve speed and efficiency, responses should be cacheable, and the caching should be managed via headers. Instead of fetching data from the server every time, we should use the cached version that helps reduce load to the server and speed up response times.

- **Layered system**: To reduce complexity, the server architecture is organized hierarchically, and each layer only interacts with the one adjacent to it.

- **Code on demand constraint**: Servers can provide executable code examples to clients, though this is not mandatory due to security concerns.

The most popular implementation based on REST is called **RESTful services**. RESTful services heavily rely on REST principles. However, this doesn't mean that using RESTful service creation tools will always ensure that you end up with REST-based services. You should learn and apply these principles to make your API more **RESTable**.

Think of RESTful APIs as a common language for microservices. One service can send an HTTP request (such as `get user data`) to another and get the information it needs. This keeps things simple and avoids messy situations wherein services need to understand each other's inner workings

RESTful APIs act like messengers between microservices, ensuring they work together smoothly, even though they're separate components.

How does a RESTful API work?

Imagine information such as pictures, text, or data stored online. This information is like a resource. When an application needs this resource, it sends a message, which is called a request, to the server to ask for it. Think of the request as a polite way to ask for something.

To make sure that the server understands the request, the application follows a set of instructions, like a recipe. These instructions are called documentation and are provided by the server creator.

Depending on how sensitive the information is, the server might check the application's identity, similar to checking your ID before entering a secure place. This is called authentication. Once the server has received and understood the request, it processes it and finds the information. Then the server sends a response back to the application.

HTTP-based REST implementation

Developers often build RESTful APIs using a special language for web communication called HTTP, which is like a language for talking to websites. In this language, there are special words called **HTTP methods** that tell the server what to do with the information (the resource). Let's discover the most used HTTP methods together in the next few subsections.

GET

We as developers use the GET method when we want to ask for some representation of the given resource without changing it.

The HTTP GET method is a request for the server to retrieve a specific resource without modifying it. It's like saying "Please give me this information."

Here's a breakdown of how it works:

1. You (the client, like your web browser) send a request to the server using the GET method. This request is like a message asking for the resource you want.

2. The website (server) receives the request and understands what you're asking for because of the GET method.

3. The website (server) finds the information that you requested and sends it back to you in response. This response might include things like text, images, or other data.

Think of it like asking a friend to show you a picture on their phone. You wouldn't just grab it; you'd politely ask to see it. Similarly, the GET method allows you to get information politely from a website.

It's important to note that the GET method is used for retrieving information and shouldn't be used for changing or modifying anything on the website. Think of it like borrowing a book from the library, not writing in it.

POST

The POST method is used to create a resource on the server.

Think of the POST method as a secure way to send information to the website (server). It's like filling out a form and clicking *submit* to send your data.

Here's how it works:

1. You (the client) fill out a form with the information you want to send (such as your name and email).

2. Your tool (usually a browser) sends a request to the website (server) using the POST method. This request includes the information you entered on the form.

3. The website (server) receives the request and understands the information because of the POST method.

4. The server processes the information you send which may involve actions like creating an account, storing a comment, or sending an email.

5. The website (server) might then send a response back to you, such as a confirmation message or a new page to see.

Think of it like sending a package to a friend. You wouldn't just leave it on their doorstep; you'd package it and send it through a reliable service. Similarly, the POST method allows you to securely send information to a website.

It's crucial to remember that the POST method is primarily used for sending and processing information, not just for viewing it. Unlike GET, which retrieves information, POST typically triggers actions on the server.

PUT

We use the HTTP PUT method to update the existing information on the server.

Think of PUT as a way to carefully update existing information on a website (server). It's like carefully revising a document or updating your profile details.

Here's a breakdown of how it works:

1. You (the client, like your web browser) prepare the updated information, for example, changes to your profile picture or edited text in a document.

2. Your browser sends a request to the website (server) using the PUT method. This request includes the updated information you prepared.

3. The website (server) receives the request and understands what needs to be updated because of the PUT method.

4. The server carefully replaces the existing information with the updated version that you sent. This is similar to carefully replacing a page in a book with a revised version.

5. The website (server) might then send a response back to you, such as a confirmation message or the updated information itself.

It's important to remember that using PUT requires caution and accuracy because it directly modifies existing information. Think of it like carefully editing a document; making a mistake could result in changing or losing important information.

The PUT method is typically used when you know exactly what information needs to be updated and you want to replace it completely. It's not for retrieving information like GET or creating new information like POST.

DELETE

The HTTP DELETE method acts like a digital eraser, carefully removing a specific piece of information from a server. You can think of it as deleting a single item from your shopping list, leaving the rest untouched.

Here's how it works:

1. You (the client), like your web browser, decide to remove something specific, such as an old photo or an outdated article.

2. Your browser sends a DELETE request to the server, pinpointing the exact item that you want to remove. This is like pointing your finger at the item on your shopping list.

3. The server receives the request and understands the intention because of the DELETE method.

4. The server carefully removes the specified item from its storage, similar to crossing off the item on your list.

The server might reply with a confirmation message letting you know that the deletion happened successfully, or simply remain silent.

You should remember that using DELETE is like using an eraser: it's permanent. Once something is gone, it's usually gone for good. So, be sure that you truly want to remove the item before sending the DELETE request.

DELETE is different from other methods. Unlike GET (used for getting information) or POST (used for creating new information), DELETE specifically removes something.

It's important to be precise with DELETE requests, as they target a specific item and cannot be undone easily.

PATCH

The PATCH method acts like a touch-up tool for information on a server. It's similar to the PUT method, but PATCH lets you update certain parts of the information, like editing specific sections of a document without changing the whole thing.

Imagine that you have a shopping list with items like bread, milk, and eggs. You realize that you need more milk, but everything else is fine. Instead of rewriting the entire list, you can use PATCH to update just the milk quantity. This way, the rest of the list stays the same.

Here's the breakdown:

1. You (the user) decide to change a specific part of something, such as updating the price of an item online.

2. You send a PATCH request to the server, pointing out the exact part you want to modify, such as the price in our example.

3. The server understands the request because of the PATCH method.

4. The server carefully updates only the chosen part, leaving the rest untouched, similar to editing just one section of a document.

5. The server might then send confirmation or simply show the updated information.

Take note that PATCH is a method for making targeted updates, modifying only specific parts of a resource. It's useful when you only want to change specific parts of something, keeping the rest the same. This makes it more flexible and efficient than completely rewriting everything like with the PUT method.

Now that we understand the HTTP verbs, let's move onto the HTTP status codes.

HTTP response status codes

HTTP uses client-server architecture. Sending requests always ends with a response. Depending on the request, you may end up with different response status codes that indicate the result of the operation.

HTTP status codes are responses from the server indicating the success or failure of your request. These codes are organized into five main groups:

- Informational responses (100 – 199)
- Successful responses (200 – 299)
- Redirection messages (300 – 399)
- Client error responses (400 – 499)
- Server error responses (500 – 599)

Let's cover the most used HTTP response status codes:

- **Success** (codes starting with 2):

  - **200 OK**: This is the best message you can get! It means that the server understood your request and did what you asked.

  - **201 Created**: This code means that your request resulted in creating something new, such as a new document or account.

- **Redirects** (codes starting with 3):

  - **301 Moved Permanently**: This tells you that the requested item has been moved to a new location permanently. The server usually gives you the new address.

  - **302 Found**: This code means that the requested item is temporarily at a new location. The server also provides the new address.

- **Client Errors** (codes starting with 4):

  - **404 Not Found**: This is a common code indicating that the server couldn't find the item you requested, like a missing book in a library.

- **401 Unauthorized**: This code indicates that you are not allowed to access the requested item, like trying to enter a locked room.

- **403 Forbidden**: This code means that you are authorized but don't have permission to access the specific item, like having a key but not being allowed into a specific room.

- **413 Request Entity Too Large**: This code indicates that the data you sent in your request is too large for the server to handle, like trying to fit too many books into a small box.

- **429 Too Many Requests**: This code means you've made too many requests in a short period of time, like trying to borrow too many books at once.

- **Server Errors** (codes starting with 5):

  - **500 Internal Server Error**: This code means that the computer encountered an internal problem and couldn't fulfill your request, like a library experiencing technical issues.

  - **503 Service Unavailable**: This code indicates that the computer is temporarily unavailable due to maintenance or overload, like a library being closed for renovation.

Remember, these are just a few examples but understanding them can help you decode the messages from websites and navigate the online world more smoothly.

Introduction to GraphQL

The two main ways in which we design and work with APIs nowadays are using REST and **GraphQL**.

Usually, when developers begin their journey in API development, they start by making a REST API. However, as they dive deeper into the specifics, they realize that the REST approach doesn't always work perfectly for every situation. GraphQL then steps in to help when REST isn't the best fit.

Even though Facebook started using GraphQL in real projects as early as 2012, when it was still called SuperGraph, it wasn't shared with the public until 2016.

Today, GraphQL has become the preferred method for designing and interacting with APIs, surpassing REST in popularity.

The primary reason for adopting GraphQL was to tackle the issues that arose when both the mobile and desktop versions of an application utilized the same API, specifically the REST API. Say you're using a website on your mobile device. The desktop version can handle larger amounts of data, so it receives a more comprehensive dataset from the server. Unlike desktop versions, mobile apps have limits on data use because of slow connections and less processing power, making it impossible to handle large data sets.

Here's an example of a REST response that contains excessive data for mobile needs, where we only require a portion of the information:

```
{
    "user": {
        "id": 5,
        "name": "username",
        "surname": "surname",
        "rank": 56,
        "email": "example@gmail.com",
        "profilephoto": "....................."
    }
}
```

So, when the user data is loaded for the first time, we only need a part of this data in the mobile version. For this reason, the resource-based distribution of the data (using REST) seems to be an ideal choice for design. Since there is no problem with internet availability for most desktop users, there is no problem with receiving data from different resources and displaying them as a single piece of information.

To ensure that we get only the required information, we filter the data based on its **ID**. In doing so, we conduct a kind of synchronous operation.

However, we are not suggesting an ideal solution for mobile data retrieval. Instead, we propose either developing a separate API specifically for mobile devices or implementing a more flexible and dynamic resource fetching mechanism by adopting an alternative approach to RESTGraphQL offers a more efficient approach to API interaction and design, especially when considering mobile and other resource-constrained devices. Originally intended for mobile use, GraphQL has evolved to support dynamic and effective data exchange across various platforms. Unlike traditional REST API design, GraphQL enables the synchronous retrieval of information from multiple resources in a single query, eliminating the need to fetch data resource by resource.

In addition to its application in mobile development, GraphQL is now extensively utilized in microservice design, further showcasing its versatility and widespread adoption in modern software development practices.

Understanding the differences between REST and GraphQL is important when it comes to applying them in practice. Let's define the main differences between these two powerful communication techniques:

- Mobile apps need slim and efficient data compared to desktop apps. REST APIs, which are often used for desktops, can be bulky for mobile. GraphQL solves this by letting you request only the specific data your app needs, avoiding unnecessary downloads while reducing over-fetching and under-fetching.

- REST works by focusing on individual pieces of information such as *users* or posts. To get related details, such as information about a specific user's posts, you need to make separate requests for each piece. This can feel slow because you have to wait for one request to finish before making the next. Long story short, REST APIs typically deliver one set of information for each access point. In contrast, GraphQL allows you to request various data combinations from a single point, making it more flexible and adaptable.

- Gathering information from multiple sources in REST requires separate requests, which can sometimes cause delays. GraphQL, however, lets you grab data from various sources in one go, presenting it to the user as a single unit. This reduces the number of requests and makes your app feel smoother.

- Updating a REST API often involves versioning it to avoid breaking existing apps. GraphQL avoids this complexity by allowing additions without requiring changes on the app side, making it easier to keep things up to date.

- Unlike REST, which focuses on managing specific pieces of data, GraphQL is built with mobile and frontend experiences in mind. This means it allows you to do the following:

  - Get only the data your app needs, reducing the amount of information transferred (smaller payload size)

  - Avoid unnecessary requests by fetching everything in one go, making your app faster and more efficient

- REST APIs struggle with frequent changes because their structure is fixed. Imagine an endpoint that can receive many different instructions or give answers in various formats. This can cause issues with REST. GraphQL, however, handles these situations much better.

- In microservice architectures, where each service manages its own data, GraphQL shines. It allows you to combine information from multiple services in a single request, presenting it as one unified piece of data to the user. This makes building and managing complex applications much easier.

- When developing a single-page or native mobile app, GraphQL's principles of "give only the information that the user needs" and "focus on a single unified resource" allow us to develop frontend-heavy applications.

- Under GraphQL, the frontend team can work on their tasks (user stories) without waiting for the backend team to create specific REST endpoints. This allows for faster progress and quicker app updates.

- RESTful APIs employ HTTP methods like PUT, DELETE, POST, and PATCH for data modification, collectively termed mutations in GraphQL. On the other hand, GraphQL utilizes a Query operation for retrieving data.

In most scenarios, having REST and GraphQL will be enough for you. However, they are not the only communication mechanisms for your microservices. We have another interesting communication protocol called a **Remote Procedure Call** (**RPC**). Let's dive in.

Remote Procedure Call

Another communication protocol that we can use when establishing communication between microservices is RPC. Using RPC, one microservice can request a service from another microservice that is located in another computer on a given network without understanding the network details.

RPC is a method for these microservices to talk. It's like one program asking another program on a different computer to do something, even though they aren't directly connected. This makes it easier for the microservices to work together.

Let's define the core RPC flow:

1. Imagine a microservice asking another microservice on a different computer to run a specific function (such as a task). This request is disguised as a normal function call, even though it's happening over a network.

2. A middleman service (called a proxy) intercepts this request and takes care of the complex network communication behind the scenes.

3. The proxy sends a message containing the details of the function and any required data to the target microservice.

4. The target microservice receives the message, understands the function request, and executes it.

5. Once it is done, it sends a response message back through the proxy.

6. Finally, the proxy delivers the response to the requesting microservice, making it seem like a regular function call.

This flow sounds familiar, doesn't it? That is because it is just a simple client-server mechanism. With the meaning and flow of RPC made clear, it's time to understand some of its other important aspects.

Benefits and considerations of RPC

What about the benefits of RPC for microservices? Let's emphasize the main points:

- **Easier development**: Using RPC is like making normal function calls, which programmers are already familiar with. This makes it simpler to build microservices because developers don't need to worry about the technical details of network communication.

- **Potentially faster**: RPC can be faster than other methods because it uses pre-defined data formats specifically designed for these calls, instead of needing to interpret complex formats like JSON or XML.

What are some important things that you need to consider with RPC?

Let's see here:

- **Tight connections**: RPC can make microservices more reliant on each other. If one microservice changes the way its functions work (their interface), it can affect all the other microservices that rely on it.

- **Limited flexibility**: Choosing a specific RPC framework might make it harder to switch to a different one later.

In conclusion, RPC is a powerful tool for microservices to talk to each other. It simplifies development and can be fast, but you should keep in mind the potential downsides of tighter connections and limited flexibility when deciding whether it's the right choice for your project.

Tools for RPC

There are special programs called RPC frameworks built specifically to make communication between microservices smoother. These frameworks act like toolkits that simplify the process. Here are a few popular ones:

- **gRPC**: This framework focuses on making things fast and efficient. It uses a special format called **Protocol Buffers** to package data in a way that's compact and easy to transmit.

- **Apache Thrift**: Another popular option, Thrift is known for working with many different programming languages and can handle various data packaging formats.

- **SOAP**: Provides a standardized way to encode messages using XML and transport them using mostly HTTP and HTTPs protocols . We can use SOAP to implement RPC. This allows applications to call procedures on remote servers as if they were local procedures. But we should take into account that SOAP is not limited to RPC and can be used for more general message exchange processes as well.

- **Windows Communication Foundation** (WCF): WCF is a framework developed by Microsoft for building service-oriented applications. It can be used to implement various communication mechanisms, including RPCs. WCF provides a lot more functionality than just RPC. It offers features such as data contracts, service hosting, and security. So, while WCF can be used for RPC, it's not limited to that specific approach.

RPC is a powerful way for microservices to communicate. It makes development easier and can be faster than other methods. However, remember the potential drawbacks of tighter connections and limited flexibility when deciding whether it's the best choice for your project. Weigh the pros and cons carefully to make the right call for your specific needs.

After discussing the general idea behind the communication protocols, it is time to talk about communication methods for microservices. Understanding the strengths and weaknesses of each approach is essential for designing robust and scalable microservice architectures.

Synchronous microservice communication

To exchange some information between microservices, they need to be able to talk to each other. In microservice communication, we mostly use two main patterns to establish communication between microservices. They are **Synchronous Communication** (**sync**) and **Asynchronous Communication** (**async**).

Sync is the easiest of the two communication patterns.

When one microservice needs information from another, it makes a direct request and waits for an answer before moving forward. The communication by itself is simpler and more reliable. It is just a function or method call if you compare it to a monolith application)

Here's a breakdown of the steps:

1. The calling microservice sends a message to another microservice.
2. The calling microservice pauses its work and waits for a reply.
3. The other microservice processes the request and sends a response back.
4. Once the calling microservice has received the response, it can continue its task.

We mostly use REST, GraphQL, and gRPC when implementing sync between microservices that rely on HTTP.

This image shows a simple synchronous communication between Order API and Stock API.

Figure 2.5: Synchronous microservice communication

Let's now see some important aspects of sync.

Some of its advantages are as follows:

- **Simple and predictable**: The flow of execution is straightforward.
- **Immediate feedback**: The requestor receives the response immediately, making it suitable for interactive applications.

Of course, as we learned before, nothing is without its downsides. This communication form also brings some disadvantages to the table:

- **Blocking**: The requestor is blocked until the response arrives, which can lead to performance issues if the receiving service takes a long time.

- **Coupling**: Services become tightly coupled, making them more difficult to change and scale independently.

- **Single point of failure**: If the responding microservice is unavailable, the entire process gets blocked.

After having understood the flow of this communication and some of its advantages and disadvantages, it's also important to see how we might apply this to some real-world situations.

Here are some real-world examples of sync in microservices:

- **Shopping cart**: Imagine you fill your cart online and hit pay. The cart service (like your shopping list) talks directly to the payment service (like the cashier) to confirm payment before creating the order. This way, you know right away whether the payment went through.

- **Catching cheaters**: When you place an order online, the order service (like the order taker) asks the fraud checker (like security guard) to see whether it's okay. The checker says yes or no right away, so only real orders go through.

- **Live chat support**: When you type a message in a chat, your message goes to a service that finds an agent (like finding a helper). The agent gets your message and replies directly, so you can chat back and forth quickly.

- **Online games**: In online games, your actions are sent to a game server (like the game referee). The server updates the game world (like changing the score) based on your actions and sends it back to everyone playing, keeping the game smooth for all.

- **Stock trading**: When you buy or sell stocks on an app, it talks directly to a service at your brokerage (like your investment person). This service makes the trade right away, tells the app that it's done, and updates your account balance. This gives you quick confirmation so you can manage your money.

These are just a few examples, and in general, you should understand that sync is ideal when you need any of the following:

- Immediate feedback and interaction

- Real-time dialogue

- Real-time decision-making and execution

- Just-in-time analysis and implementation

- Tightly coupled workflows with high dependency

Asynchronous microservice communication

Sync is like having a direct conversation, but async is more like leaving a message. Microservices don't wait for a reply, they just send the information and move on.

In asynchronous communication, the requesting service sends a message to the receiving service without waiting for an immediate response. The response is delivered later, either through a callback or through a separate channel.

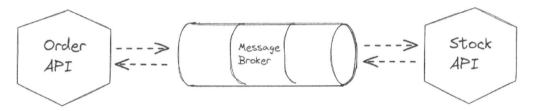

Figure 2.6: Asynchronous microservice communication

Here's a breakdown of the steps:

1. **Send a message:** The calling microservice sends a message with the information to another microservice.

2. **Move on:** The calling microservice doesn't wait for a reply. It continues its own task.

3. **Process later:** The other microservice receives the message and works on it whenever it's free.

4. **Reply:** The other microservice might send a response back later, but that's not required.

Think of it like leaving a note for someone – they can get to it when they have a chance.

In most cases, we use a message broker to handle async between microservices.

For complex communication patterns, high message volume, or critical tasks, a message broker is a good choice. For simpler scenarios where reliability is less crucial, direct queues or event sourcing can be better alternatives to a message broker.

Let's cover the most important advantages of using async between microservices:

- **Non-blocking:** The requester can continue processing without waiting for the response, improving performance and scalability.

- **Decoupling:** Services are loosely coupled, making them easier to change and scale independently.

- **Resilience:** Async can handle failures and retries more gracefully than sync.

- **Independent work:** Microservices can focus on their own tasks without worrying about others being busy.

However, it also has some drawbacks:

- **Delayed results**: You might not know whether the message was received or processed right away.
- **More complex**: Setting up async can be trickier than sync. Sync doesn't require an additional layer when establishing communication. However, as I mentioned before, for true async you mostly need to use a message broker as middleware between communicated services.

Next, let us look at some practical applications of this type of communication:

- **Sending emails**: The order service can send an order confirmation email without waiting for it to be sent.
- **Updating inventory**: When a sale is made, the order service can send a message to update the inventory. It can keep processing other orders in the meantime.
- **Long-running tasks**: A microservice can send a message to another service to do a time-consuming job, such as video encoding, without being stuck waiting.
- **Social media feed updates**: Post service publishes a message to the feed queue. The feed service subscribes to the queue and updates user feeds in the background.

It is better to choose to use async between microservices when any of the following conditions apply:

- An immediate response is not essential
- Background tasks or long-running processes are needed
- Decoupling and scalability are key considerations

Async is great for tasks that don't need immediate answers, but sync might be better for things that need a quick response.

Essential communication patterns

When building microservices, we mostly need a single point of entry for our clients to consume the services that we develop. You may think about it like a decorator or wrapper over your services. Clients talk to your app through a simple door (API gateway) instead of needing to know the messy inner workings (microservices). The gateway intelligently routes incoming requests to the appropriate microservices based on factors such as URL patterns, path variables, or headers.

An important component of microservice architecture is an API gateway. This API offers several features to help manage and expose common functionalities across multiple microservices. Often, a client request might require data from multiple microservices. The gateway acts as an orchestrator, fetching data from relevant services, aggregating it (if necessary), and returning a cohesive response to the client. In short, API gateways are essential components of microservice architecture. They provide a single point of entry for clients, enhancing security and manageability, as well as the overall effectiveness of your microservices)

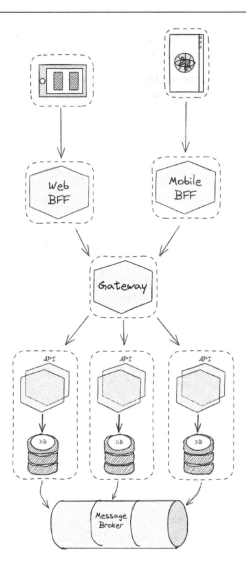

Figure 2.7: An API gateway

Now, let's try to summarize the benefits of API gateways:

- **Single entry point**: There is no need to understand the internals of microservices. Using an API gateway helps you to be isolated from such details.

- **Request routing**: An API gateway acts as smart middleware to route queries from the users to the exact microservices

- **Aggregator**: The gateway acts as an orchestrator, fetching data from relevant services, aggregating it (if necessary), and returning a cohesive response to the client.

- **Security**: The gateway can be a central hub for authentication, authorization, and rate limiting. It verifies client identities, enforces access controls, and prevents potential abuse.

- **Transformation**: The gateway can manipulate requests and responses to match the expected formats of backend services or tailor responses for clients. This includes tasks such as content negotiation, protocol translation, and data validation.

- **Common tasks**: The gateway can handle common tasks such as request validation, caching, and logging, reducing the burden on individual microservices.

- **Load balancing**: When there's a lot of work to be done (heavy traffic), load balancing acts like a traffic director. It cleverly distributes incoming requests across multiple copies (instances) of the same microservice. No single microservice gets overwhelmed, making the best use of all available resources.

- **Circuit breaker**: An API gateway often contains a circuit breaker for resiliency, cascading failure, and protecting system's stability. A circuit breaker in microservices is like a switch that automatically stops sending requests to a service if it's not responding well, helping prevent system-wide failures.

Message brokers

In a direct communication model, microservices would have to be aware of each other's locations and availabilities. This creates a tightly coupled system that's difficult to maintain and update.

By introducing a message broker, microservices become loosely coupled. They simply send messages to the broker, which handles the routing and delivery. This allows microservices to operate independently without needing to know the specifics of other services.

With message brokers, communication becomes asynchronous. A producer (microservice) can send a message without waiting for a response from the consumer (another microservice). This improves performance and scalability as microservices don't have to wait on each other.

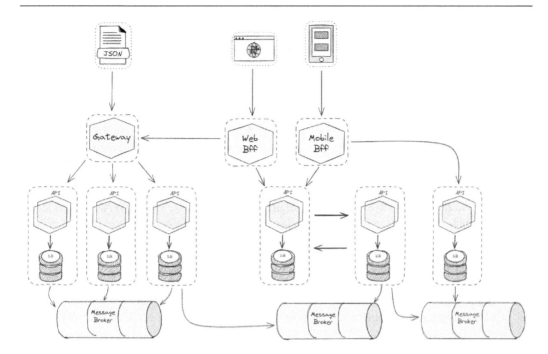

Figure 2.8: Message brokers

Message brokers use different message storage models. The most popular ones are **Message Queues** (**MQs**) and **Topic.** Message brokers store messages in an MQ until they are received by consumers. MQs are a crucial part of message brokers that act as storage for the data. Unlike Topic, they delete data after the consuming process.

Let's try to understand the components of a typical message broker:

- **Producer (Publisher):** This is the one that sends a message.

- **Consumer (Subscriber):** This is the one that reads a message.

- **MQ (or Topic):** This is the one that stores the message. Topic allows for a publish-subscribe model, whereby multiple consumers can receive the same message. On the other hand, MQ queue follows a **First-In, First-Out** (**FIFO**) approach, ensuring messages are processed in the order in which they are received.

There are a lot of popular message broker implementations out there. In practice, we will use Apache Kafka, one of the most popular message brokers. Let's talk about the most popular message broker implementations:

- **RabbitMQ**: This is an open source message broker that is widely known for its flexibility and ease of use. It supports different messaging patterns, including point-to-point (only one specific application receives a message) and **Publisher and Subscriber (pub/sub)**. It acts as a central post office for your applications. Apps can send and receive messages without needing to know each other's exact addresses. It helps us to have tightly coupled communication. It is flexible, easy to use, and has a large community.

- **Apache Kafka**: It is a powerful option to implement a message broker. It has crucial attributes such as high throughput, durability, scalability, fault tolerance, real-time processing, and many others. Apache Kafka is more than a message broker with data storage and stream processing integration. We will talk more about the internals of Kafka in the next chapters.

- **Amazon Simple Queue Service (SQS)**: Like other message broker implementations, it provides decouple and scale microservices. SQS acts as a queue where you can send messages (data), store them securely, and then retrieve them via other applications or services. SQS decouples applications by enabling them to communicate asynchronously. The sender doesn't need to wait for the receiver to be available, improving overall application responsiveness and scalability.

If you need real-time stream processing, Apache Kafka might be a better option for you rather than RabbitMQ and SQS. On the other hand, if you like to have advanced features such as message filtering or priority queues, use RabbitMQ over SQS.

Summary

This chapter was about microservice communication. We talked about different communication techniques such as REST, GraphQL, and RPC.

We discussed the fact that we mostly use two types of communication forms between microservices: synchronous and asynchronous. Sync is simple and has immediate feedback, but it is a blocking operation with attributes such as a single point of failure and coupling. We talked about the advantages and disadvantages of sync and discussed when to and when not to use it in practice.

On the other hand, we learned that async is non-blocking and comes with delayed responses. It is mostly preferable (depending on the task) but brings additional complexity. To make async happen, we learned that we mostly need additional layers like message brokers.

The last part of the discussion was centered around the most used patterns such as API gateway and message broker.

API gateway, as an orchestrator, provides a single point of entry with additional functionalities such as security, transformation, load balancing, and so on. It is an essential part of microservice communication.

We further learned about establishing async. Using message broker, we mostly establish async between microservices. It is an additional layer between services that handles common tasks (depending on message broker implementation). It has multiple implementations such as RabbitMQ, Apache Kafka, Amazon SQS, and so on.

Starting from the next chapter, we will cover JavaScript and NodeJS essential you need to know before diving into details of microservice development. Stay tuned!

3

What Do You Need Before Getting Started?

The microservice approach does not inherently depend on any specific programming language. You can implement it using different programming languages. The concept of microservices supports using different languages for different services within a single application. This means the choice of programming language for each service can be based on its specific needs and functionalities. For example, you're able to implement *microservice A* using C# but *microservice B* using JavaScript. That is the beauty of microservice development, which allows us to bypass programming language barriers.

This book is about writing microservices in JavaScript. As in any programming language, before implementing the microservice approach, it is best to understand the basics of the given language, which will help us to build better and more effective microservices. The focus of this chapter is to provide the foundation, rather than a comprehensive guide, for the language, along with Node.js. There are a few topics, especially in JavaScript, that need to be reviewed before implementing any microservice applications using the language itself.

In this chapter, we're going to explore the following topics:

- JavaScript essentials
- Node.js essentials

Technical requirements

For this chapter, you need the following:

- A browser (select your favorite one)
- Visual Studio Code (or you can use your OS's default text editor): Simply go to `https://code.visualstudio.com/` and install it

- **GitHub**: Go to `https://github.com/PacktPublishing/Hands-on-Microservices-with-JavaScript/tree/main/Ch03`

  The next chapter will explain the required software installation processes in detail. For now, you can download the GitHub repository source code without using any GitHub commands and experiment with it.

JavaScript essentials

JavaScript is a popular, single-threaded, synchronous programming language that helps us mostly to build interactive web applications. Its strength is its ability to mix different programming methods. This mix lets you write code in several ways: focusing on objects, using functions like building blocks, reacting to events, or giving step-by-step instructions, making your code clear and easier to handle. The JavaScript you use in the browser or in Node.js is not completely *native*. That is why we need to differentiate between the concepts of the *JavaScript engine* and the *JavaScript runtime*.

JavaScript engine

A JavaScript engine is a special type of program that reads, parses, and translates our JavaScript code into computer-understandable language (machine instructions) – see *Figure 3.1*. We don't have one single JavaScript engine for all browsers. For instance, Google Chrome, Opera, and the latest Microsoft Edge browsers use the *V8 engine*, Firefox has *SpiderMonkey*, and Safari uses the *JavascriptCore engine*. Anyone with the ability to follow ECMAScript engine standards can create their own JavaScript engine.

But how can we have compatible JavaScript across the browsers? How do we make sure that the JavaScript code will work for all browsers? That is why we need a standard that will tell us exactly what we need to do to make sure that JavaScript will work for all browsers. Thankfully, we have a combination of rules that allows us to ensure consistency across different web browsers. This essential rulebook for scripting is called **ECMAScript** (**ES**). Of course, ES isn't just for JavaScript; it applies to other scripting languages as well, but JavaScript is the most well-known implementation of it.

Figure 3.1: JavaScript translation process

Let's look at the JavaScript engine in depth in the next few subsections.

Call stack and memory heap

JavaScript engine consists of multiple elements, and two of them are the **call stack** and the **memory heap** (*Figure 3.2*).

Figure 3.2: Call stack and memory heap

When we run our JavaScript application, code is executed in the call stack. Think of it as a series of steps that your code can walk through in a given order. On the other hand, the heap is about data storage. It is unstructured memory that stores the objects.

JavaScript translation process

The **translator** is a program that can translate human-readable source code into machine-readable instructions. It has two main parts. The first part is the **compiler**. In the compilation process, the program converts the entire code into machine code at once. The second part is the **interpreter**. In the interpretation process, the interpreter goes through the source code and runs it line by line, converting it into machine instructions. Several years ago, JavaScript used to be a purely interpreted language, but fortunately, some modern JavaScript engines work in a hybrid mode of translation. Modern JavaScript engines use a combination of interpretation and JIT compilation, where the interpreter runs code line by line, while the compiler converts frequently used code to machine code to optimize performance. The V8 engine, for instance, combines the compiler and interpreter, which is called the **Just-in-Time (JIT)** compilation process.

Interpreters are fast in terms of getting up and running. There is no need to convert the source into another language, which means there is no compilation step. For options such as executing something right away, interpreters are a better option than compilers. The major problem here is that if you run the same code (say, the same JavaScript function) again and again, it can get really slow. Interpreters don't apply any optimization to your code. That is when the compiler comes in. It takes a bit more time than interpreters because it converts your code into another language, but it is smart, and when it sees the same code again, it just optimizes it in order to not interpret it again.

In terms of translation, JavaScript uses the advantages of interpreter and compiler together.

A classical compilation means that the machine code is stored in a portable file and can be executed at any time, but for the JIT compiler, it is a bit different. The machine code should be executed as soon as possible before compilation ends.

Let's try to understand how JavaScript-specific JIT works over Google's V8 engine. As a JavaScript runtime, Node.js also relies on the V8 engine, and understanding its internals will help us a lot from the Node.js perspective.

When you execute your source code written in JavaScript, the JavaScript engine parses it. The *parser* is a sub-element of the JavaScript engine that takes your source code and outputs tokens. That is how the JavaScript engine understands whether there is an error. It acts as a **lexical analyzer** and the final output is called an **Abstract Syntax Tree (AST)**. To witness the beauty of the AST, you can just navigate to the AST explorer (`https://astexplorer.net/`), type any JavaScript code, and see the parsing process.

An AST is an engine-specific data structure that is generated by splitting up each line of your JavaScript code into pieces that are understandable to the language. The engine uses it to generate machine code. The AST is then taken by the *interpreter* and converted to byte code.

Byte code is a special type of collection of instructions that is approximately similar to machine code but acts as a wrapper and abstracts us from the complexities of the machine code. The default interpreter in V8, called **Ignition**, outputs byte code; on the other hand, the compiler, **Turbofan**, optimizes this bytecode into efficient machine code

Turbofan also acts as a JIT compiler. In the middle of the interpreter and compiler, there is a *profiler* that profiles the interpretation process (Ignition) and forwards the code that needs to be optimized to the compiler (Turbofan). (See *Figure 3.3*.)

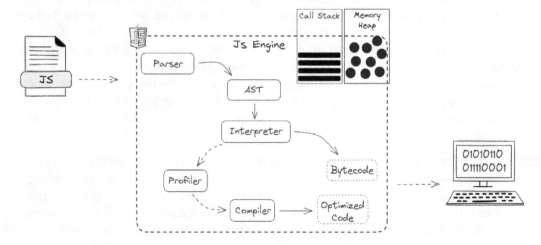

Figure 3.3: JavaScript engine internals

Okay, but you might be asking yourself why we need to understand under-the-hood operations in the JavaScript engine. Well, that actually will help you to write better, faster code with optimized microservices. That knowledge will help you to write optimization-friendly code. The JavaScript engine is not always able to apply optimization and, in some cases, it depends on your writing style. It is possible to write deoptimization code that might be difficult for your JavaScript engine to optimize. That is why it is better to always understand the internals. For instance, using the `delete`, `evals`, `arguments`, and `with` keywords and mechanisms such as *hidden classes* and *inline caching* may slow down code optimization. These concepts are beyond our book, but you can learn about them by checking the open source JavaScript tutorials and documentation.

The next thing we need to talk about is the single-threaded nature of JavaScript, and believe me, things get interesting when we dive into the threading details.

Threading in JavaScript

As we mentioned before, JavaScript is a single-threaded, blocking, synchronous programming language that has only one call stack. JavaScript is "single-threaded," but it's not necessarily "blocking." It is synchronous by default but can handle asynchronous code execution using callbacks, promises, and async/await. But what does this mean and why do we need to understand it? Well, most programming languages support multithreading out of the box. This means it is possible to run multiple independent operations at a given time. But when it comes to JavaScript, things are a bit different. It is possible to run only one set of instructions at a given time for JavaScript natively, and this is a big problem in the world of multithreading, especially for long-running tasks. Fortunately, when you deal with JavaScript, you're not dealing with only a JavaScript engine but also something called a **JavaScript runtime**.

JavaScript runtime

The browser, by its nature, is a wrapper and a runtime for the JavaScript engine. The responsibility of the runtime is to provide *additional* support to implement all the required functionalities for the given context. Here, in browsers, the context is a web-based interactive application. Node.js is also a runtime based on Google's V8 engine. Engines help you to extend native JavaScript engine functionalities even more and add an async nature to them. These functionalities together in the browser are called **web APIs**. To see browser-based, important web APIs, just do the following steps:

1. Open your favorite browser (in our case, it is Google Chrome).
2. Right-click and select **Inspect**.
3. Go to the **Console** tab and type `window`.
4. Hit *Enter*.

You can also see this in *Figure 3.4*:

```
> window

<· ▼ Window {window: Window, self: Window, document: document, name: '', location:
      ▶ IJ_values: {eG8Zqf: 1, IvNqzc: true, qgwOed: false, qjWw6c: true, XFWgg: fal
      ▶ WIZ_global_data: {QrtxK: '0', GWsdKe: 'en-AZ', w2btAe: '%.@."","","0",null,r
      ▶ W_jd: {BI8SUE: Array(0), BI8SUI: Array(0), BI8SUQ: Array(13), BI8SUY: Array(
      ▶ addEventListener: ƒ (a,c,d)
      ▶ alert: ƒ alert()
      ▶ atob: ƒ atob()
      ▶ blur: ƒ blur()
      ▶ botguard: {m: 41, bg: ƒ, a: ƒ, kwi_: ƒ}
      ▶ btoa: ƒ btoa()
      ▶ caches: CacheStorage {}
      ▶ cancelAnimationFrame: ƒ cancelAnimationFrame()
      ▶ cancelIdleCallback: ƒ cancelIdleCallback()
      ▶ captureEvents: ƒ captureEvents()
      ▶ chrome: {loadTimes: ƒ, csi: ƒ}
      ▶ clearInterval: ƒ clearInterval()
      ▶ clearTimeout: ƒ clearTimeout()
      ▶ clientInformation: Navigator {vendorSub: '', productSub: '20030107', vendor:
```

Figure 3.4: window global object

The elements of the `window` object (its properties and methods) that you can see are in addition to your JavaScript engine, which is built into the browser you use. Browsers have web APIs that are approximately similar for all of them. Most core web APIs are designed to be standardized so that websites can function similarly across different browsers. However, there can be minor differences in implementation or features between browsers, and some APIs might be specific to a particular browser. Most popular API functions, such as `fetch`, `settimeout`, `setinterval`, and `document`, are part of this huge API called `window`. It means they are not native JavaScript functions but engine-based functions for us in the given context. Web APIs decorate our JavaScript code with async behaviors.

When you write code that has these functions (`fetch`, `document`, etc.), the JavaScript engine will forward them to the web APIs. Web APIs are written in low-level languages (in most cases in C/C++) and after execution, your callback, which is provided in the given instruction, will be added to the *callback queue*. All native JavaScript functions will be executed directly in the call stack, but non-native instructions need to be executed first in the web API and the result of the execution, as a callback, will be added to the callback queue (*Figure 3.5*).

There is also the *event loop*. The responsibility of the event loop is just to check the call stack and to push callback queue elements there only if it is empty.

To make sure all the terms we mentioned are understood well, let's consider a simple example. Look at *Figure 3.5*:

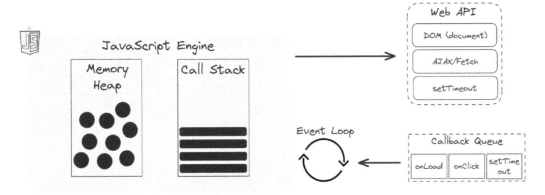

Figure 3.5: JavaScript event loop with a callback queue

Open your favorite web browser, right-click on the page, select **Inspect**, select the **Console** tab, and paste the following code. You can find event_loop.js in the Ch03/js folder of the book's GitHub repository:

```
function print(message) {
    console.log(message);
}
setTimeout(() => {
print("Message from Timeout");
}, 0);
print("Message 1");
print("Message 2");
```

Here in our code, you might expect to see setTimeout's message first and then other messages in the given order. Because we have specified 0 for setTimeout, it should immediately execute our code. But the output is different, as we can see in *Figure 3.6*.

```
> function print(message) {
      console.log(message);
  }

  setTimeout(() => {
      print("Message from Timeout");
  }, 0);

  print("Message 1");
  print("Message 2");

  Message 1

  Message 2

< undefined

  Message from Timeout
```

Figure 3.6: The call stack executes a queue item at the end

As you might guess, if the executed function is non-native, which means it is a web-API-based function, then the JavaScript engine will forward it to the web API, and after execution, its callback will be added to the callback queue. Meanwhile, setTimeout is going to be a non-blocking, asynchronous operation, and that is why we see the result of print functions first.

So, it doesn't matter if you have set 0 or more as the second argument to setTimeout; it goes through the pipeline we explained anyway. The event loop will check whether the call stack is empty and when both print functions are done, it does become empty, so we're able to see the result of setTimeout only after the event loop pushes it to the call stack.

Now let's talk about the asynchronous nature of JavaScript in more detail.

Callback-based asynchronous JavaScript

Callback is a common term in programming that is used when you want to send a function as an argument to another function. A function can accept not only simple data but also an expression. Callbacks are actively used by a web API. When you add some event listeners, or start setTimeout or setInterval, you usually rely on callbacks.

Callbacks are indispensable, but sometimes their usage makes your code less understandable and less maintainable, especially from an asynchronous code perspective. To prove that, go to callback_hell.html and run it in any browser. (You can find callback_hell.html in the Ch03 folder of the book's GitHub repository. For the sake of simplicity, all the GitHub repository references will contain only the path, i.e., Ch03/callback_hell.html.)

The file contains callback-based multiple asynchronous actions that we call *callback hell*.

```
addScript("js/app.js", (script, error) => {
      if (error) {
        addErrorMessage("main", error.message);
      } else {
        setTimeout(() => {
          let message = execute();
          addSuccessMessage("main", message);
          setTimeout(() => {
            message = "operation completed successfully";
            addSuccessMessage("main", message);
            setTimeout(() => {
              message = "ready for another execution";
              addSuccessMessage("main", message);
            }, 2000);
          }, 3000);
        }, 4000);
      }
    });
```

Here is what this script does:

1. Dynamically adds the provided script to the head of the HTML file.

2. Runs a function that belongs to that script (in our case, it is an `execute` function).

3. Runs the `operation completed successfully` message after `three` seconds.

4. `Three` seconds after the preceding message runs, it outputs the `ready for another execution` message to the console. If the loaded file doesn't exist, then the error message will be printed as an output.

As you can see, the code is hard to read, understand, and maintain this code due to its nesting. In software development, *maintaining* refers to the ongoing process of keeping software functioning properly, secure, and up to date. It might be more complex if you have more operations to do.

The way to promises

While callbacks are still a main part of JavaScript, promises are the preferred way to handle asynchronous operations in modern JavaScript development due to the benefits they offer in readability, error handling, and code maintainability.

Promises were added in JavaScript with the **ECMAScript 6 (ES6)** specification, which was released in 2015. Before ES6, callback hell was a common way to handle asynchronous operations in JavaScript. Thanks to promises, now we have a clean and more manageable approach for asynchronous programming. We actively use promises in Node.js development, so it is crucial to understand and properly use them.

To create a promise, we use a `Promise` object. It has a single callback argument, which is called `executor`. It runs automatically when the promise is constructed successfully. The executor consists of two callbacks:

- `resolve`: We use this to inform a user about a successful operation
- `reject`: We use this to indicate that something went wrong

When a promise is done, it should call one of the functions, either `resolve` (value) or `reject` (error).

The promise is initially in a `pending` state. It will be moved to a `fulfilled` state if `resolve` happens; otherwise (if rejected), the state will be moved to `rejected`.

The promise's result is initially `undefined`. It will store `value` if `resolve` is executed; otherwise (if rejected), it will store `error`.

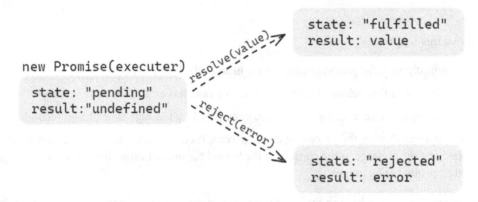

Figure 3.7: Promise state and result

It is completely okay to use only `resolve` or `reject` for `executor` if you want to provide only one path for your execution.

Let's try to implement the callback example in *Figure 3.7* using promises.

File: Ch03/js/promise_chaining.js

```javascript
addPromisifiedScript ("js/app.js")
        .then(() =>
            new Promise((resolve) => {
              setTimeout(() => {
                let message = execute();
                addSuccessMessage("main", message);
                resolve();
              }, 4000);
            })
        )
        .then(() =>
            new Promise((resolve) => {
              setTimeout(() => {
                let message = "operation completed successfully";
                addSuccessMessage("main", message);
                resolve();
              }, 3000);
            })
        )
        .then(() =>
            new Promise((resolve) => {
              setTimeout(() => {
                let message = "ready for another execution";
                addSuccessMessage("main", message);
                resolve();
              }, 2000);
            })
        )
        .catch((error) => addErrorMessage("main", error.message));
```

Now, instead of nested callbacks, we have promise chaining. So, why should you choose promises over callbacks? Consider the following benefits:

- Thanks to their linear syntax, promises help us to make code easier to follow

- We have .catch(), which provides a central way to handle errors

- Promises allow you to chain multiple asynchronous operations together in a more readable way

- async/await builds on top of promises and provides an even more synchronous looking way to write asynchronous code (we'll learn about async/await in this chapter too)

How about making the promise-based code more readable?

File: Ch03/js/promise.js

```
function delay(ms) {
      return new Promise((resolve) => setTimeout(resolve, ms));
    }

    addPromisifiedScript("js/app.js")
      .then(() => delay(4000))
      .then(() => {
        let message = execute();
        addSuccessMessage("main", message);
      })
      .then(() => delay(3000))
      .then(() => {
        let message = "operation completed successfully";
        addSuccessMessage("main", message);
      })
      .then(() => delay(2000))
      .then(() => {
        let message = "ready for another execution";
        addSuccessMessage("main", message);
      })
      .catch((error) => addErrorMessage("main", error.message));
```

As you can see, adding a simple delay function can make our code more readable, instead of having nested callbacks.

A promise acts as a producer. If you want to handle the response of your promise, you need to register a consumer. This registration is mainly done by using a .then instruction. It is a continuation of a promise that gets the result of the previous promise. This instruction can handle both responses (success and failure).

Check the code here to see how we can handle success and error cases. When the operation succeeds in addPromisifiedScript, the resolve part of the code will be triggered; otherwise, reject will be triggered:

```
addPromisifiedScript("js/app.js").then(
      (resolve) => {},//success continuation
      (reject) => {}//error handling
    );
```

We often use .then() with only resolve mode. If you want to have one centralized way of handling errors, it is better to use .catch(), which is the equivalent of applying .then(null,reject=> {}).

You can set up a promise to handle online book orders (an async operation). You might get a confirmation email for the order (a resolved promise) or encounter an error (a rejected promise), but either way, you're still finished interacting with the bookstore's website (the finally block). You can put code in the finally block to clean things up after the promise is done, win or lose. This could be things such as turning off a loading wheel on your screen, closing a connection you don't need anymore, or anything else that needs to happen regardless of the outcome.

Promise API

Instantiating a promise object using a new keyword is not the only way of using it. The Promise API has several useful static methods that we can use in practice. Let's take a look at them in the following subsections.

Promise.all()

If you have multiple promises that need to be executed in parallel, and you need to wait for all of them to be ready, then Promise.all() might be a good choice. It returns an array of results if all promises resolve successfully or rejects as soon as one of the promises fails.

Open github_avatars.html in the GitHub chapter repository and run it by double-clicking on it:

```
const usernames = ["TuralSuleymani", "rasulhsn"];
    const url = "https://api.github.com/users/";
    let requests = usernames.map((name) => fetch(url.concat(name)));
    Promise.all(requests)
        .then((responses) => Promise.all(responses.map((r) =>
          r.json())))
        .then((gitusers) =>
          gitusers.forEach((user) => createAvatar(user.avatar_url))
        );
```

Promise.all() waits for all promises to be executed in parallel and be ready and then returns multiple promises.

In our example, we use it in two scenarios:

- Fetching data from GitHub in parallel (*line 25*)
- Getting data as JavaScriptON from all promises (*line 27*)

For `Promise.all()`, we wait for all promises to be successfully executed. If even one promise fails (doesn't work out), `Promise.all()` immediately stops and gives up entirely. It forgets about all the other promises in the list and completely ignores their results.

The code we just looked at should render two GitHub users' avatars as images in an `.html` file.

Imagine you have several tasks to run, such as fetching things from the internet. If one task fails, the others might still keep going. But `Promise.all()` won't care about them anymore. They might finish eventually, but their results won't be used. (`Ch03/js/promiseAPI.js` contains all Promise API examples demonstrated.)

The following sample code shows that `Promise.all` accepts multiple promises as an array:

```
Promise.all([
    new Promise((resolve, reject) => setTimeout(() => resolve("success
      resolve"), 500)),
    new Promise((resolve, reject) => setTimeout(() => reject(new
      Error("Something went wrong!!")), 1000)),
    new Promise((resolve, reject) => setTimeout(() => resolve("another
      success resolve"), 1500))
  ])
  .then((success) => console.log(success))
  .catch(alert); // Error: Something went wrong!!
```

`Promise.all()` doesn't try to stop the other tasks because there's no way to cancel promises once they've started.

Promise.allSettled()

Unlike `Promise.all()`, `Promise.allSettled()` is more patient. Even if one promise fails, it waits for all the promises to finish before giving you the results.

Imagine a similar scenario with the tasks. This time, `Promise.allSettled()` will wait for all the tasks to be completed, regardless of whether one fails.

In the end, it will give you a report on all the tasks, telling you whether each one succeeded (`success resolve`) or failed (`Something went wrong!!`):

```
Promise.allSettled([
    new Promise((resolve, reject) => setTimeout(() => resolve("success
      resolve"), 500)),
    new Promise((resolve, reject) => setTimeout(() => reject(new
      Error("Something went wrong!!")), 1000)),
    new Promise((resolve, reject) => setTimeout(() => resolve("another
      success resolve"), 1500))
  ])
```

```
  .then(results => {
     // 'results' is an array containing information about each promise
  (resolved or rejected)
     console.log(results);
  });
```

This way, you get a complete picture of what happened with all your tasks, even if some failed.

Promise.race()

`Promise.race()` is like a race between promises. You provide it with a bunch of promises, and it waits for the very first one to either succeed or fail.

Whichever promise finishes first (wins the race), its result (a success or error value) becomes the result of `Promise.race()`. The rest of the promises are completely ignored, regardless of whether they eventually succeed or fail:

```
Promise.race([
    new Promise((resolve, reject) => setTimeout(() => resolve("success
       resolve"), 2500)),
    new Promise((resolve, reject) => setTimeout(() => reject(new
       Error("Something went wrong!!")), 1000)),
    new Promise((resolve, reject) => setTimeout(() => resolve("another
       success resolve"), 3500))
  ])
  .then(result => {
    console.log(result);
  }).catch((err)=>console.log('Error detected', err));
```

You need to be careful when you use `Promise.race` for the following reasons:

- It's useful when you only need the result from the fastest promise
- It stops listening to other promises as soon as one finishes
- It returns the result (success value or error) from the winning promise

Promise.any()

`Promise.any()` waits for any of the promises to succeed, not necessarily the first one.

As soon as one promise resolves successfully, `Promise.any` immediately stops waiting for the others and returns the success value.

However, if all the promises in the list end up failing (rejected), `Promise.any` itself rejects with a special error called `AggregateError`. This error contains information about why all the individual promises failed:

```
Promise.any([
    new Promise((resolve, reject) => setTimeout(() => resolve("success
      resolve"), 2500)),
    new Promise((resolve, reject) => setTimeout(() => reject(new
      Error("Something went wrong!!")), 1000)),
    new Promise((resolve, reject) => setTimeout(() => resolve("another
      success resolve"), 3500))
  ])
  .then(result => {
    console.log(result);
  }).catch((err) => console.log('Error detected', err));//will not be
executed
```

We also have `Promise.resolve()` and `Promise.reject()`, but they are rarely used due to the `async/await` keyword.

Async/await in JavaScript

Promises are so popular that there is a special syntax to work with them. This combination is called **async/await**. You can find all examples related to the `async/await` keyword in the `async_await.js` file in the chapter's repository.

You're able to add an `async` keyword to any function, even just a simple function. But what is the value of using the `async` keyword before your functions? Well, the `async` keyword is a syntactical sugar that helps us to wrap our function to a promise. Check out this function:

```
async function sayHello() {
    return "hello user";
}
```

It is exactly the same as this:

```
function sayHello() {
    return Promise.resolve("hello user");
}
```

The async version of the function, behind the scenes, will generate a promise (*Figure 3.7*). This means that using this syntax, you're able to add continuations such as `.then()`, `.finally()`, and `.catch()` to that function. It is just a promise-based function.

```
> async function sayHello() {
      return "hello user";
  }

  sayHello();
< ▶ Promise {<fulfilled>: 'hello user'}
> sayHello().then((response)=>console.log(response));
  hello user
< ▶ Promise {<fulfilled>: undefined}
```

Figure 3.8: The async function is promise-based

So, the responsibility of async is to ensure that the functions always return a promise. But that is not all. There is another keyword in this pair that is called await. If you need to wait for your promise to be settled, then you're able to use this keyword. Say we have a simple delayedMessage() function that returns exactly the same message as provided by the arguments but with some delays:

```
function delayedMessage(msg) {
    return new Promise((resolve)=> {
        setTimeout(() => {
            resolve(msg);
        }, 3000);
    });
}
```

Instead of getting data by chaining (using .then), you can simply apply a synchronous programming technique. This means just waiting for functions to return data, get the data, and then continue:

```
let message = await delayedMessage("hello");//wait here for the
Promise to be settled
```

That is simple. So, instead of working with then, catch, and finally, you can interact with promise-based functions using just async-based syntax. Put simply, await is just a more elegant way of working with promises.

Here is a simple example of fetching data from multiple URLs using promises:

File: Ch03/js/getdata_promise.js

```
const url = "https://jsonplaceholder.typicode.com";
const paths = ["/posts","/comments"];
let promises = Promise.all(paths.map(path=> fetch(url.concat(path))));
promises.then(responses=> Promise.all(responses.map(t => t.json())))
.then(data=> {
    data.forEach(element => {
```

```
            console.log(element);
        });
    })
```

In our preceding example, we fetch data from /posts and /comments of the JavaScript onplaceholder URL using promises.

Using async/await, we're able to simplify it, like this:

File: Ch03/js/getdata_async.js

```
const url = "https://jsonplaceholder.typicode.com";


const paths = ["/posts","/comments"];


let getData = async function() {
    const responses = await Promise.all( paths.map(path=>fetch(url
      .concat(path))));
    constJavaScriptons = await Promise.all( responses
      .map(response=>response.json()));
    JavaScriptons.forEach(element => {
        console.log(element);
    });


}
getData();
```

Instead of using .then() every time, we are now able to use synchronous-programming-based syntax.

You might be wondering how to handle exceptions in this code? If we are free to not use .catch(), then how will we be able to catch exceptions? The answer here is also really simple: just use try.. catch.

We have talked enough about promises. It is time to see how JavaScript internally handles promises.

Microtask queue

We've talked about promises and async/await. It is now the exact time to talk about the related topic of the **microtask queue**. The callback queue is not the only queue used by the JavaScript runtime. There is another important queue that is used by Node.js and classical, browser-based JavaScript. This is called the microtask queue (also known as an event queue or PromiseJobs) – see *Figure 3.8*. To better manage asynchronous tasks in JavaScript, the ECMA standard added this internal queue. It has approximately the same behavior as a callback queue in terms of the call stack because the execution of these tasks is possible only when nothing else is running in the call stack.

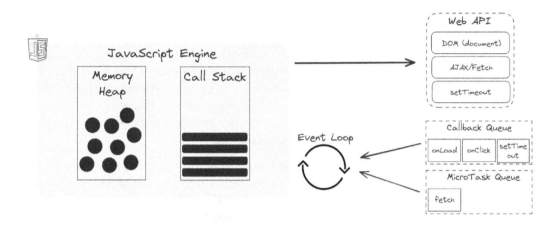

Figure 3.9: Microtask queue

So, when a given promise is ready, the continuations, such as then/catch/finally handlers, are put into the queue. When the call stack is empty, the JavaScript engine will take these tasks in a **First in, First out** (**FIFO**) order and execute them.

Here is a simple example (Ch03/js/microtasks.js):

```
let promise = Promise.resolve();
promise.then(() => console.log("planning to see this message first"));
console.log("but this message will be seen first");
```

The order of the output is seen in *Figure 3.10*.

```
but this message will be seen first
planning to see this message first
```

Figure 3.10: The output of the preceding code

Because, when the JavaScript engine detects a promise, it moves its .then() to the microtask queue. It is an async operation, so we directly switch to the next line. It is possible to execute a promise only if the call stack is empty.

Of course, the topics we discussed are not the whole list of topics you need to work with Node.js. We bypassed some simple and middle-level topics and covered only some important ones we think might help you when working with Node.js. JavaScript skills are essential, and you need to be aware of its syntax. Having better JavaScript skills will be a guide for you throughout the learning process of the book.

Node.js essentials

Node.js is not a separate programming language. It is a runtime over Google's V8 engine. This simply means that the creator of Node.js just took the V8 engine out of the browser and put it into another runtime. Node.js is a wrapper over the V8 engine and extends it by adding networking, APIs for I/O, and other operations. A key aspect of Node.js is its non-blocking I/O model. This means Node.js can handle multiple requests simultaneously without being blocked by slow operations. The event loop and callback queue become even more important in this context.

Node.js has different dependencies under the hood, but the most interesting one for us to discuss is **Libuv**. Libuv provides a thread pool for handling certain tasks, with four threads by default, but this can be configured based on the application's requirements. This is the main magic that provides I/O-based non-blocking operations. It is written in C, and it provides an event-driven asynchronous I/O model. It is possible to perform blocking operations using a thread pool to distribute CPU loads. We have four threads to use in Libuv by default. For network-based async operations, Libuv relies on the OS itself, but for some other async functions, such as reading something from a file, Libuv relies on its thread pool. The concept of a thread pool allows us to do some important operations in a separate thread and not block others.

Node.js primarily focuses on asynchronous I/O and aims to minimize blocking operations. The thread pool is mainly used for tasks that cannot be efficiently handled asynchronously by the OS, such as intensive calculations or filesystem operations requiring significant processing.

Like in browsers, we have different queues to be used when it comes to the Node.js async nature. The general concept is the same. They both use an event-loop-based model, but for Node.js, we have some more queues.

The event loop is a mechanism that continuously operates while your Node.js application is running. It's responsible for handling different asynchronous events. The event loop utilizes queues to organize these events, ensuring they are processed in the proper order. The event loop consists of six different queues.

The event loop utilizes several queues to manage different types of asynchronous operations (*Figure 3.9*). These queues ensure tasks are processed in a specific order, as follows:

- **Timer queue**: This queue holds callbacks scheduled with `setTimeout` and `setInterval` functions. These callbacks are executed after a specified delay or at regular intervals. (Technically, it's a min-heap for efficient scheduling.)

- **I/O queue**: This queue contains callbacks associated with asynchronous I/O operations like those found in `fs` and `http` modules. The event loop processes these callbacks when the I/O operation completes.

- **Check queue**: This queue holds callbacks scheduled with `setImmediate`. These callbacks are considered a high priority and are executed before other tasks in the next loop iteration.

- **Close queue**: This queue contains functions meant to run when an asynchronous resource is closed, ensuring proper cleanup.

- **Microtasks queue**: These are further divided into two sub-queues:

  - **nextTick queue**: This queue holds callbacks scheduled with `process.nextTick`. These are also a high priority and get executed immediately after the current operation finishes.

  - **Promise queue**: This queue contains callbacks associated with resolving or rejecting promises. These are processed whenever the event loop encounters a resolved or rejected promise during its execution.

It's important to note that the first four queues (timers, I/O, check, and close callbacks) are managed by Libuv. The microtask queues (`nextTick` and `Promise`) are separate but still play a crucial role in determining the order of callback execution within the event loop.

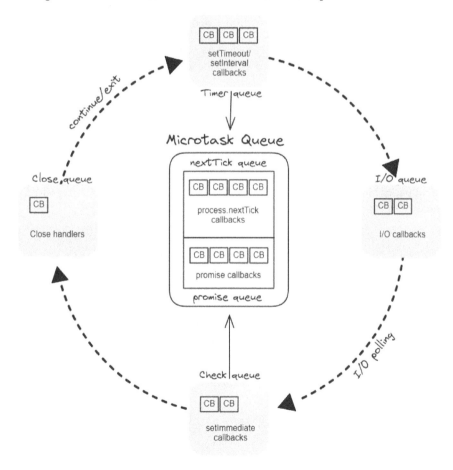

Figure 3.11: Node.js queues

Let's talk about the priority order of the queues. First things first, it is important to understand that user-written, synchronous JavaScript code has the highest priority over all of these queues. This simply means that these queue elements will be executed only if the call stack is empty. However, what about these six queue orders? We will discuss them in more detail now:

- **Microtask queue:** The event loop first checks for any callbacks in the microtask queue. It prioritizes the `nextTick` queue, executing those tasks first, followed by any callbacks in the promise queue.

- **Timers:** After microtasks, the event loop processes callbacks from the timer queue. This includes functions scheduled with `setTimeout` and `setInterval`.

  After the timers queue, the event loop is going to check the microtask queue again. First, the `nextTick` queue will be executed, and then the `promise` queue will be executed.

- **I/O callbacks:** Next, the event loop handles callbacks from the I/O queue. These represent asynchronous operations, such as file I/O or network requests, which have completed.

- **Microtask check (again):** The event loop checks for microtasks again after processing the I/O. This ensures that any microtasks created during those operations are executed immediately.

- **Check queue** (`setImmediate`): The event loop then executes callbacks from the check queue, which holds functions scheduled with `setImmediate`. These are considered high-priority tasks and run before other callbacks in the next loop iteration.

  After the check queue, the event loop is going to check the microtask queue again. First, the `nextTick` queue will be executed, and then the `promise` queue will be executed.

- **Close callbacks:** Finally, the event loop processes callbacks associated with closing asynchronous resources, ensuring proper cleanup.

  Check the microtasks queue again and execute callbacks if they exist.

- **Microtasks throughout the loop:** The event loop keeps the party going as long as there are callbacks waiting to be invited. Once everyone's had their turn and there's nothing left to do, it gracefully exits the stage.

As you might notice, microtasks are checked multiple times within the event loop. This ensures that any microtasks created during the execution of other callbacks are handled immediately. This prioritizes tasks scheduled with `nextTick` and `promise` resolutions, keeping the event loop responsive.

Summary

This chapter was about JavaScript and Node.js internals.

First, we started our discussion with JavaScript internals. The main point was to understand the JavaScript engine and the JavaScript runtime. JavaScript is a single-thread language, but it has an async nature and we're able to use callbacks and promises to implement it. In async programming, callbacks are a bit old school nowadays thanks to promises. We also talked about the Promise API and learned a lot of interesting functions.

The popularity of promises brings other interesting features to JavaScript: async/await. Using examples, we tried to demonstrate how they make our code more readable, understandable, and similar to sync code.

For promises, we have a special queue in the JavaScript engine pipeline called the microtask queue.

Then we started a discussion around Node.js and learned that it is also a runtime and uses the JavaScript engine to read and translate JavaScript code. It takesJavaScript to another level, and using Node.js, we can build real-time applications, microservices, web APIs, streaming applications, command-line tools, and more.

Internally, Node.js heavily relies on Libuv and provides tons of functionalities that mostly can be categorized under asynchronous I/O and thread pooling. Libuv provides the core functionality for Node.js's asynchronous programming model, making it efficient and scalable for handling numerous concurrent connections and I/O operations.

The last discussion for this chapter was on Node.js queues and event loops. We have several queues in Node.js and they have special orders that we need to understand to build more effective applications.

In our next chapter, we will talk about the stack development technologies that you need to know before writing any lines of code.

Stack Development Technologies

Knowing what tools and apps to use can speed up your development process significantly. That is why we need to prepare our development environment first before typing lines of code. The development environment should make you feel comfortable and help you throughout the process of learning and writing your microservices.

It is like building a house. Choosing the right tools can speed up the process and save you time. Of course, having the right tools doesn't mean you will succeed, but it is better to fail with the right ones than to have the cause of failure be the choice of tools.

This chapter focuses on installing the required tools. The programming language and frameworks are also tools for us to build microservices. In one form or another, everything we use while writing software is a tool for us. It makes no sense to install all the tools we plan to use at this point, but at least understanding how to install most of them will help us to switch to coding faster.

We will also have a look at some of the Node.js frameworks that we plan to use in this book. Understanding them is crucial for fast and easy development.

In this chapter, we're going to cover the following topics:

- Node.js and its installation
- Node.js frameworks
- Choosing the right IDE
- Understanding and installing Docker
- Understanding and installing Apache Kafka
- Understanding and installing Git
- Installing Postman
- Installing MongoDB

Technical requirements

To follow along with this chapter, you only need a browser of your choice and an internet connection. Regarding the rest of the tools we plan to use, we will learn how to install them in this chapter.

Node.js and its installation

As we learned in the previous chapter, Node.js is a runtime environment built on Google's V8 engine. You can build a wide variety of applications using it:

- **Web applications**: Node.js is a popular choice for building both the backend and frontend of web applications. Its JavaScript-based environment makes it easy for developers to work on both sides.

- **Real-time applications**: Node.js's event-driven architecture and non-blocking I/O model make it ideal for building real-time applications such as chat apps, collaboration tools, and streaming services. These applications require constant communication between users and the server, and Node.js can handle this efficiently.

- **Single-page applications (SPAs)**: SPAs are web applications that load a single HTML page and update the content dynamically using JavaScript. Node.js can be used to build the backend API that provides data to the SPA client-side code.

- **API-driven applications**: Many modern applications rely on **application programming interfaces (APIs)** to access data and functionality from other services. Node.js is a great choice for building these APIs due to its ability to handle many concurrent requests efficiently.

- **Microservices**: Node.js is well-suited for building microservices because of its modular nature and asynchronous capabilities.

- **Command-line tools**: Node.js can be used to create command-line tools that automate tasks or interact with other systems.

- **Desktop applications**: While less common, Node.js can also be used to build desktop applications with frameworks such as Electron.

Of course, this is not the full list, but it gives you a good idea of the wide range of applications that can be built with Node.js.

Learning some technology or language mostly starts with installing the required tools. The same applies to Node.js. So, let's dive into its installation process.

Installing Node.js for Windows

You might be surprised but I'm a big fan of Microsoft and its products. This means I'm using a Windows **operating system (OS)**. All types of installations will be explained using mainly the *Windows OS,* but I will provide the relevant links to help non-Windows users be on the same level of progress.

When installing Node.js from the official page (`www.nodejs.org`), it automatically detects your OS and provides the exact OS instructions to install it.

We also have different ways of installing Node.js, even for the same OS. The most popular ones are prebuilt installers and installation via package manager.

Let's follow these step-by-step instructions to install Node.js:

1.   Go to `www.nodejs.org/en/download`. In my case, I'll be using Windows-based instructions.
2.   Select **prebuilt installer**.
3.   From the tab, select the required version of Node.js, along with the OS and CPU architecture to run it (*Figure 4.1*).

      You might be wondering which version of Node.js to choose – **LTS** or **Current**? Well, the answer is easy:

      •   For long-term use, where things need to stay stable and work well together, the **LTS** version is a safe bet. It's a reliable option.

      •   On the other hand, the **Current** version has all the latest bells and whistles, which is great for programmers who want to try out new features.

      For our code examples, the LTS version is sufficient. Select it and continue.

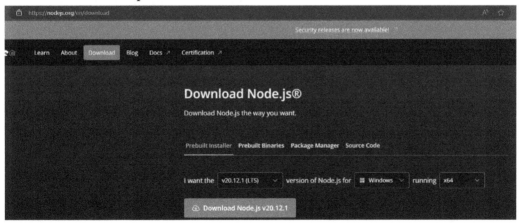

Figure 4.1: The Node.js installation page

These same instructions are applicable for *non-Windows* users. You need to select your appropriate OS and its platform and click the green **Download Node.js v<version_number>** button. Depending on the selected version, the version on the button will automatically be updated. We'll look at this installation in depth in the next section.

4. When installing, just accept the license and follow the wizard's instructions without any custom setup configuration. In the middle of the installation, the wizard will require you to select how the app will behave when compiling native modules. It is preferable to select the checkbox shown in (*Figure 4.2*):

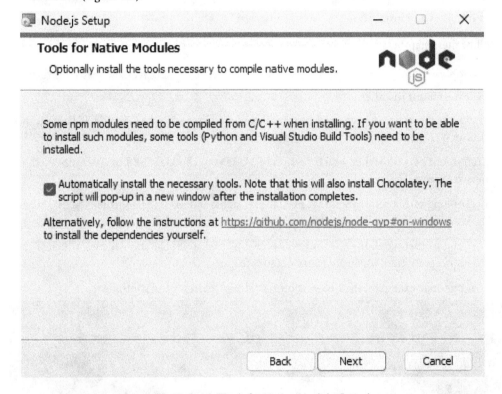

Figure 4.2: Node.js's "Tools for Native Modules" window

If you select the **Automatically install** checkbox (*Figure 4.2*), it will install additional tools like Chocolatey, Python, and Visual Studio Build Tools.

5. After installation, just press the *Win + R* combination and type node in the window that opens:

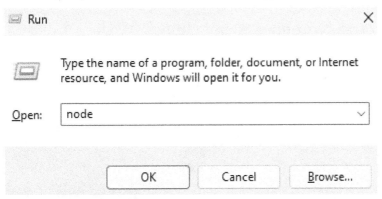

Figure 4.3: The input window for running your commands

6. After typing node, hit *Enter*. You should see the following app:

```
C:\Program Files\nodejs\node.exe                          —  □  ✕

Welcome to Node.js v20.12.1.
Type ".help" for more information.
> ▄
```

Figure 4.4: Node command line

The window shown in *Figure 4.4* is a **read-eval-print loop** (**REPL**), which serves as a programming language environment, akin to a console window (*Figure 4.5*). It accepts a single expression as input from the user, processes it, and then displays the result in the console. It is a handy method for promptly experimenting with basic JavaScript code.

```
C:\Program Files\nodejs\node.exe            —    □    ✕

Type ".help" for more information.
> 4+5
9
> "Hello"+" from" +" NodeJS"
'Hello from NodeJS'
> ▄
```

Figure 4.5: Node.js REPL

Now, let's continue our discussion of installing Node.js in terms of macOS and Linux.

Installing Node.js for macOS and Linux

One of the easiest options for macOS and Linux users is to use a package-manager-based installation. Select your OS and go to the **Package Manager** section. From the **using** section, you can select the active management tool (*NVM*, *Brew*, *Chocolatey*, or *Docker*) and follow the instructions provided in that window (*Figure 4.6*):

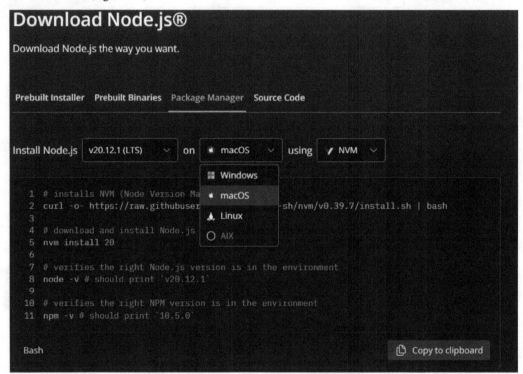

Figure 4.6: Node.js installation for different OSs

If you want to download Node.js for Linux distributions using NVM, you should follow the instructions provided here:

```
# installs NVM (Node Version Manager)
curl -o- https://raw.githubusercontent.com/nvm-sh/nvm/v0.39.7/install.
sh | bash
# download and install Node.js
nvm install 20
# verifies the right Node.js version is in the environment
node -v # should print `v20.12.1`
```

```
# verifies the right NPM version is in the environment
npm -v # should print `10.5.0`
```

Please note that Node.js versions may differ while you read this book. For more up-to-date installation instructions, please read Node.js's official page.

While Node.js is our primary tool while developing microservices, throughout the learning process, we will also use some of Node.js's frameworks to make our lives easier. The most popular ones that we'll use in this book are *NestJS* and *Express.js*.

Node.js frameworks

Node.js has a lot of interesting frameworks. We'll be using *NestJS* and *Express.js* (we look at more on these frameworks shortly) but of course, more frameworks rely on Node.js, and it is impossible to use all of them in a single book and even if possible, it doesn't make too much sense to do it.

First things first, Node.js is not a framework but a runtime environment that executes JavaScript code outside the browser. Some developers call it a framework but that is not true. We need to understand the term framework to understand whether something is a framework or not. In programming, a **framework** is essentially a pre-built structure that serves as a foundation for creating software applications. It's like a blueprint that you can customize to fit your specific needs, rather than having to start entirely from scratch. Frameworks come with pre-written code for common functionalities, such as handling user input, database interactions, or security. These components act as building blocks that you can leverage to save time and effort.

Frameworks often have a defined way of organizing your code, which ensures consistency and makes it easier for other developers to understand and maintain the code base.

A key aspect of frameworks is an *inversion of control*. Instead of your code calling into the framework, the framework calls your code at specific points. This allows the framework to manage the overall flow of the application.

With that information, you can tell Node.js is not a framework. It is just a runtime, but we have frameworks that are built on *top* of Node.js. The most popular ones are *NestJS*, *Express.js*, *MeteorJS*, and *SailsJS*. Oh, by the way – many popular frameworks, such as *Sails*, *NestJS*, *Kraken*, *poet*, and *Item API*, are built on Express. As mentioned previously, we'll be using NestJS and Express.js, so let's look at them closely.

Express.js

Express.js simplifies the web development process. By using Express.js effectively, you can create dynamic and interactive web experiences for your users. Because Express.js is lightweight, it's a great choice for creating web applications that need to perform well under heavy traffic. One of the key features of Express.js is its ability to handle different routes, which are essentially paths users take to access specific parts of your web application.

Imagine Node.js as the building blocks and tools, like bricks and mortar. Express.js is like prefabricated walls and plumbing – it gives you a structured way to assemble those blocks to create a web application faster. Building a complex web application with just Node.js can get messy. Express.js provides a framework so that you can organize your code into routes, middleware, and views, making it more maintainable and easier for others to understand.

While you can build everything from scratch with Node.js, Express.js offers built-in features for handling routes, handling HTTP requests and responses, and creating APIs, saving you time and effort.

Express.js is a popular framework with a vast community of developers. This means you have access to a wealth of resources, tutorials, and additional libraries to streamline development. While there are other Node.js frameworks available, Express.js is a strong choice due to its simplicity, flexibility, and large community support.

NestJS

NestJS is a framework built on top of Node.js that is specifically useful for building robust and scalable server-side applications.

NestJS enforces a clear and organized architecture for your application. This makes complex projects easier to manage and maintain, especially for teams of developers. It integrates seamlessly with TypeScript, a superset of JavaScript that adds static typing for improved code reliability and fewer errors. It also promotes a modular approach, where you break down your application into smaller, reusable components. This makes your code base more organized and easier to scale as your application grows.

> **Note**
> Another piece of good news is that if you're familiar with *Angular*, a popular frontend framework that NestJS borrows many concepts, it makes it easier to learn and use for Angular developers.

NestJS goes beyond basic web applications. You can build RESTful APIs, GraphQL APIs, WebSockets applications, and even command-line interfaces using this framework.

It also utilizes **dependency injection**, a powerful technique for managing dependencies between different parts of your application. This promotes loose coupling and makes your code more testable.

Long story short, NestJS provides a structured and feature-rich toolkit on top of Node.js, allowing you to build scalable and maintainable server-side applications efficiently.

Choosing between Express.js and Node.js

This book is not about Node.js frameworks, and our aim is not to provide full information about them. However, having fundamental knowledge about the differences between these two will help us to have a broader understanding. Let's outline some situations where either of these frameworks would be a good fit. With this understanding, you'll be able to make a more informed decision and pick the right framework for your project:

- **Use Express.js in the following situations**:

  - If your project is small or medium-sized. For simpler web applications or APIs, Express.js's lightweight and flexible nature might be ideal.

  - If you prioritize flexibility. Express.js offers more control over your application's structure, allowing you to tailor it to your specific needs.

  - If you're familiar with JavaScript. If you're comfortable with vanilla JavaScript, the learning curve for Express.js is gentler.

- **Use NestJS in the following situations**:

  - If your project is large or complex. NestJS's structured architecture and features are beneficial for managing and maintaining bigger applications with multiple developers.

  - If you value scalability. NestJS's modular design makes it easier to scale your application as it grows in terms of features and complexity.

  - If you want built-in features. NestJS offers features such as dependency injection and support for TypeScript out of the box, improving code maintainability and reliability.

  - If your team is familiar with Angular. If your developers have experience with Angular, NestJS's similar structure can ease the learning curve.

After installing Node.js, we need to prepare our **integrated development environment** (**IDE**) for development.

Choosing the right IDE

Choosing the right IDE may help you do fast development. For Node.js development, especially to follow our code examples, we don't have strict requirements related to IDE. You can use your favorite text editor or built-in text editor for your OS. Choosing the right IDE is a taste and functionality preference. An IDE helps you in syntax highlighting, autocompletion, and refactoring, and also easily interacts with important libraries. You can use different IDEs, such as *Visual Studio Code*, *Eclipse Che*, *Sublime Text*, *WebStorm*, and *IntelliJ IDEA*.

We prefer Visual Studio Code because it is free, easy to use, can be extended using extensions, is cross-platform compatible, easily configurable, and supports multiple programming languages.

Let's install Visual Studio Code. To install it, just follow these instructions:

1. Go to https://code.visualstudio.com/download.

2. Click on your OS version and wait for the download to be completed.

3. Click on the file you've downloaded and follow the default instructions.

As you learn microservices development, you'll become familiar with the classical application installation process. For that reason, we haven't provided detailed screenshots and won't be spending too much time on installation details. For more information, you can simply search for the relevant application installation instructions on Google.

Visual Studio Code provides a rich extension library for all needs (*Figure 4.7*). You can download anything you want to help you do fast development, refactor, highlight your code, and more:

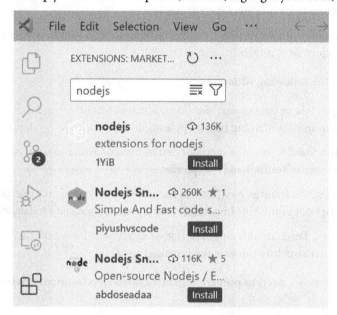

Figure 4.7: Visual Studio Code's EXTENSIONS section

After installing our IDE, it is time to install Docker. It is a must-have tool, especially nowadays for microservice application development. We'll be actively using Docker in our development, so let's dive in.

Understanding and installing Docker

Before installing Docker, we need to understand its value and purpose.

Docker is like a shipping container for your software. It packages everything your application needs to run – the code, libraries, and settings – and bundles them together. This ensures your application runs everywhere, in any OS without any issues. It guarantees that if the application works locally, it will work globally.

Docker guarantees your application runs exactly how you built it, every time. No more surprises due to different computer setups.

The main concepts in Docker are images and containers. **Containers** are lightweight and start up quickly, making testing and development cycles much smoother. You can simply ship the Docker container to any environment, cloud-based or not, and be confident it will work. Containers share the underlying OS, so you can run more applications on a single machine without bogging it down.

In the world of Docker, an **image** is like a blueprint for a Docker container. It's a set of instructions that specify what goes inside the container, including the software, libraries, and configurations needed for your application to run. You build an image once, and you can use it to create many containers, saving you time and effort. Images can be shared and downloaded easily, allowing you to run your application on any machine with Docker. One of the advantages of images is that everyone using the same image gets the same environment, reducing surprises and ensuring reliable application behavior.

If you don't want to install some applications to your computer *forever* and easily remove them after development is done, it would be better to not directly install them but use Docker for your installation.

In the end, Docker simplifies the process of building, shipping, and running applications. It's like having a universal box for your software, ensuring it runs flawlessly wherever it goes.

That's enough theory – let's dive into the Docker installation process.

You can install Docker for almost all popular OSs, such as Windows, Linux, and Mac. It may have specific requirements for your OS, which you can learn about by navigating to `https://docs.docker.com/engine/install/`. Then, you can select your OS to install it.

Note that requirements may vary by the OS's internal version. In the **System requirements** section, you'll see prerequisites based on the internal version of the selected OS (*Figure 4.8*). For instance, for Windows, we have **WSL 2 backend** and **Hyper-V backend and Windows containers** system requirements:

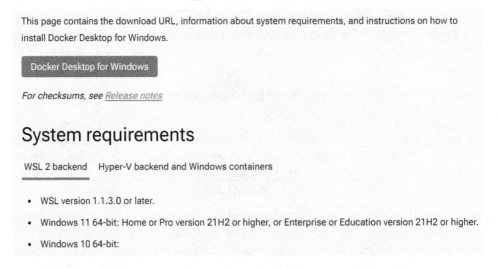

Figure 4.8: Docker's System requirements section

If your OS meets the provided system requirements, you'll be able to install Docker Desktop (*Figure 4.8*). For Windows, **WSL 2** is recommended over **Hyper-V**.

The installation is a straightforward process and doesn't require any additional configuration:

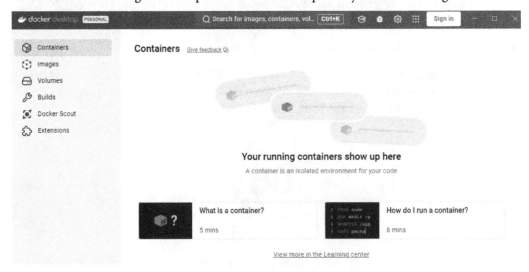

Figure 4.9: Docker Desktop

Docker is not the only powerful tool that we need to use when building microservices. We have another great tool that helps us have real-time communication between our microservices: Apache Kafka.

Understanding and installing Apache Kafka

Apache Kafka is an open-source platform that handles real-time data streams. Originally designed as a messaging queue, it has evolved into a robust system for streaming data and building event-driven architectures. Communication between microservices is crucial, and that's where Kafka shines.

Kafka itself is a huge concept that needs a different book. In this book, we're going to provide enough information that we'll be able to integrate and use it for our microservices. For more detailed information, you can follow my *Apache Kafka for Distributed Systems* course on the Udemy platform (`https://www.udemy.com/course/apache-kafka-for-distributed-systems/`).

Kafka uses a **publish-subscribe** messaging model. Services, acting as producers, publish events to specific channels known as **topics** within Kafka. Other services, functioning as consumers, subscribe to relevant topics and receive these events asynchronously.

This approach beautifully decouples services from one another. Producers don't need to wait for consumers to be available, and consumers can process events at their own pace. This improves scalability and flexibility.

Kafka also acts as a buffer, storing events until consumers are ready. This enables asynchronous processing, which prevents bottlenecks and improves overall system responsiveness.

Kafka is built for reliability. It replicates data across multiple nodes, ensuring that messages aren't lost even if a server fails. This enhances fault tolerance within the microservices architecture.

It's important to know that Kafka scales horizontally. You can easily add more nodes to handle increasing data volumes without impacting existing services. This caters perfectly to the dynamic nature of microservices.

As mentioned previously, a key feature of Kafka is its ability to handle real-time data streams. This is valuable for microservices that need to react to events promptly, such as in fraud detection or stock trading applications.

Kafka is flexibly related to programming languages and integrates seamlessly with various programming languages, making it adaptable to diverse microservice environments.

Kafka Streams, a powerful API within Kafka, empowers you to perform real-time computations and transformations on data streams within the Kafka cluster itself. This stream processing capability adds significant value to microservice architectures.

Long story short, by integrating Apache Kafka, microservice development benefits from increased scalability, resilience, and agility. It fosters a loosely coupled, event-driven approach that empowers microservices to communicate and react to changes effectively. This translates to a more robust, adaptable, and high-performing application architecture.

Apache Kafka's installation varies by OS, and you need some additional configuration per OS.

Also, along with Apache Kafka, we may use Zookeeper and Kafka UI. Starting from Apache Kafka v4, you won't need Zookeeper. However, this feature is still in development, so it makes sense to understand it also. Zookeeper has multiple responsibilities and plays a critical role as the coordinator.

Kafka itself is a CLI-based tool, so if you want to see things graphically, you'll need additional tools, such as Kafka UI, Offset Explorer, and more.

But I have good news for you. If you have Docker installed, there is no need to dive into the details of the installation process. We can create a `docker-compose` file to combine the required tools and install them together. You can download files one by one, but `docker-compose` helps you to create a special YAML file where you can define all the tools and application dependencies and install them together. Here is our `docker-compose` file's content:

```
services:
  zookeeper:
    image: bitnami/zookeeper:3.8
    ports:
      - "2181:2181"
    volumes:
      - zookeeper_data:/bitnami
    environment:
      ALLOW_ANONYMOUS_LOGIN: "yes"

  kafka1:
    image: bitnami/kafka:3.6
    ports:
      - "9092:9092"
    volumes:
      - kafka_data1:/bitnami
    environment:
      KAFKA_CFG_ZOOKEEPER_CONNECT: zookeeper:2181
      KAFKA_CFG_LISTENERS: "PLAINTEXT://:9092"  # Use only
        one listener
      KAFKA_CFG_ADVERTISED_LISTENERS:
        "PLAINTEXT://kafka1:9092"
    depends_on:
      - zookeeper
```

```
kafka-ui:
  image: provectuslabs/kafka-ui:latest
  ports:
    - 9100:8080
  environment:
    KAFKA_CLUSTERS_0_NAME: local
    KAFKA_CLUSTERS_0_BOOTSTRAPSERVERS: kafka1:9092
    KAFKA_CLUSTERS_0_ZOOKEEPER: zookeeper:2181
    KAFKA_CLUSTERS_0_JMXPORT: 9997
  depends_on:
    - kafka1

volumes:
  zookeeper_data:
    driver: local
  kafka_data1:
    driver: local
```

To install Apache Kafka, you need to follow these instructions:

- Open Docker Desktop.

- Go to Ch04/docker-compose.yml and download it to your computer.

- Open the command line from the folder and type docker-compose up -d.

Docker should start pooling the images and create containers based on these images (*Figure 4.10*):

Figure 4.10: Docker with running containers

Now, we are ready to move forward and understand how to install Git, an essential tool under a developer's belt.

Understanding and installing Git

Git is a powerful **version control system** (**VCS**) for software development. Imagine it as a time machine for your code. It tracks every change you make to your project, like a detailed logbook.

With Git, you can easily revert to a previous version of your code, essentially undoing any errors.

It makes collaboration easy. Working with a team? Git lets everyone collaborate seamlessly. Each team member can work on their part of the project, and Git helps merge their changes smoothly, avoiding conflicts.

It also keeps a detailed history of all the changes, allowing you to see exactly what modifications were made and by whom. This is crucial for tracking progress and understanding the project's journey.

Git is one of the most important tools that we use in our day-to-day development process. You can install Git for any popular OS, particularly for Linux, Windows, and Mac:

- For more detailed instructions for *Linux*, go to `https://git-scm.com/download/linux`. There, you can find a Linux-distribution-based installation for Git.

- As with other popular tools, we have multiple options to install Git on *macOS*. Go to `https://git-scm.com/download/mac` to learn more about it.

- For *Windows*, I prefer to use the **Git for Windows** tool. You can download it from `https://gitforwindows.org/`. This application provides Git Bash and Git GUI mechanisms (*Figure 4.11*). You can use any of them throughout your development:

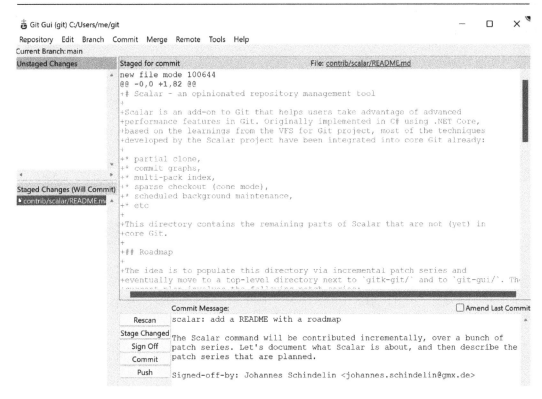

Figure 4.11: Git for Windows

There's another tool we need to install. Let's continue our installation journey with Postman.

Installing Postman

The penultimate tool we'll cover in this chapter is Postman. We'll build a lot of APIs, and we need some tools to rapidly and easily test them. It's a tool that helps developers interact with and test APIs.

Here's what Postman helps you do:

- **Build APIs**: You can design and plan out your API using Postman's tools.

- **Test APIs**: Send requests (such as asking for information) and see the responses (the information you get back) from the API. This helps ensure the API works as expected.

- **Work with APIs**: Postman lets you easily send different kinds of requests to APIs and see the results. It's like having a remote control for the API.

Here's how you can install it:

1. Go to https://www.postman.com/downloads/.

2. Click on your OS's name and download the relevant file.

3. Install it.

After installing Postman, open it. At this point, you can insert any URL into the URL section. There, you can also select the HTTP method (GET, POST, PUT, and so on) for that URL and send the request (*Figure 4.12*):

Figure 4.12: An overview of Postman

With that, let's move on to the final tool in this chapter: MongoDB.

Installing MongoDB

MongoDB is a popular NoSQL database. We will use it when we develop microservices and it might be a good choice for you in the future when you build microservices.

You may consider MongoDB based on the following characteristics:

- **Document-oriented**: Unlike traditional relational databases, which store data in tables with rows and columns, MongoDB stores data in flexible JSON-like documents. This makes it easier to represent complex data structures.

- **Scalable**: MongoDB can handle large datasets and high-traffic applications by scaling horizontally. It does this by adding more servers to the database cluster.

- **Flexible schema**: MongoDB allows for flexible schema design. Documents within a collection can have different structures. This is useful for storing data that doesn't fit neatly into rigid table structures.

- **Cross-platform**: MongoDB runs on various OSs, including Windows, Linux, and macOS.

- **Open source**: The core MongoDB server is open source and free to use, with a variety of commercial licenses available for additional features and support.

To install MongoDB Server, just navigate to `https://www.mongodb.com/docs/manual/installation/` and select your platform. At the time of writing, you can install it on Linux, macOS, Windows, and Docker. MongoDB has two available editions: Community and Enterprise. To experiment and test it, the Community edition will be enough.

Another useful product for interacting with MongoDB is the MongoDB Compass application. It can be found at `https://www.mongodb.com/try/download/compass` and is free. You can install it for different platforms:

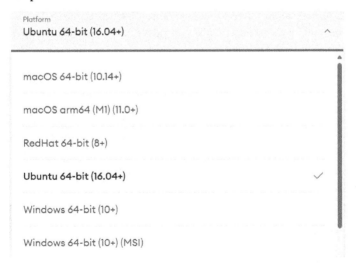

Figure 4.13: MongoDB Compass supports different platforms

MongoDB Compass is a free, **graphical user interface (GUI)** tool specifically designed for interacting with MongoDB databases. It essentially acts as a user-friendly client application that simplifies managing and working with your data.

You can use it for the following purposes:

- **Visualizing data**: Compass allows you to browse collections, view documents in a clear and organized format, and explore the structure of your data.

- **Querying**: You can write and execute queries directly within Compass to filter and retrieve specific data from your MongoDB databases.

- **Building complex queries**: Compass provides a visual interface for building aggregation pipelines, which are powerful tools for transforming and analyzing your data.

- **CRUD operations**: Compass allows you to easily

- **create, read, update, and delete (CRUD)** documents within your collections.

- **Schema analysis**: Compass helps you understand the structure and relationships within your data by providing schema visualization.

- **Index optimization**: Compass can recommend and assist with creating indexes on your collections to optimize query performance.

- **Connection management**: Compass allows you to connect to various MongoDB deployments, including local servers, cloud instances, and containers.

Overall, MongoDB Compass offers a user-friendly and intuitive way to interact with your MongoDB databases. It's a valuable tool for database administrators, developers, and anyone who needs to explore, analyze, and manage their MongoDB data.

Summary

Having a well-prepared development environment is crucial for a smooth and efficient software development process. By installing the necessary tools and programs beforehand, you eliminate the need to scramble for them mid-development, saving valuable time. A configured environment ensures a consistent workflow. You know exactly where your files are located, how to run them, and what commands to use. This reduces cognitive load and lets you focus on coding.

Using the same tools throughout the project helps maintain code style and consistency. This makes the code easier to read, understand, and maintain for yourself and others.

When everyone on the team uses the same development environment, collaboration becomes smoother. They can easily share code, troubleshoot issues, and understand each other's work.

In this chapter, we talked about the tools we need to install before starting our development journey. Of course, we haven't installed all the tools, but the main ones are here. We'll introduce additional tools as needed in future chapters, ensuring the installation process is straightforward.

If you're here, then congratulations! Starting from the next chapter, we will dive into the details of microservice development in practice.

Part 2:
Building and Managing
Microservices

In this part, we will dive into the practical aspects of building microservices with JavaScript. We'll start by creating a basic CRUD (Create, Read/Retrieve, Update, Delete) microservice and then move on to more advanced concepts, such as synchronous and asynchronous communication between services. We will also cover real-time data streaming, which is essential for creating responsive and dynamic applications.

This part contains the following chapters:

- *Chapter 5, Basic CRUD Microservices*
- *Chapter 6, Synchronous Microservices*
- *Chapter 7, Asynchronous Microservices*
- *Chapter 8, Real-Time Data Streaming Using Microservices*

5

Basic CRUD Microservices

Our previous chapters are proof that microservices development is not just about implementation. You need to at least have a clear understanding of the pros and cons of using microservices compared with other approaches we looked at in the previous chapters – monolith and service-oriented – and you need to have an essential understanding of the technologies you want to apply when building microservices.

Applying all theoretical knowledge you have in practice is also not an easy task. This chapter will help us to apply microservices in practice and is one step forward to real-world microservices implementation. In this chapter, we plan to provide a solid foundation for further practical chapters.

Implementing a microservice approach in your project means that you mostly have a complex business domain and the conceptual boundary of your microservice requires you to implement a part of this complex logic. It indicates that microservice development is more than **Create**, **Retrieve/Read**, **Update**, **Delete** (**CRUD**) but to have a basic understanding of the microservice application structure, this chapter is a good starting point.

We're going to explore the following topics:

- Understanding business requirements
- Tools to develop a basic microservice
- Preparing our first project
- Defining the internal architecture of our microservice
- Hands-on account microservice development
- Running and testing our first microservice

Let's get into it!

Technical requirements

To develop and test our first microservice, we'll need the following tools:

- An IDE of your choice (we prefer Visual Studio Code)

- Postman

- MongoDB

- A browser of your choice

It's recommended that you download this book's GitHub repository from `https://github.com/PacktPublishing/Hands-on-Microservices-with-JavaScript` folder to easily follow our code snippets.

Understanding business requirements

Before you jump into building microservices with JavaScript, it's important to clearly understand what your services need to do. Then, based on what your project requires, you can pick the right tools to help you create those microservices.

The team doesn't consist of only developers. The business domain people are also an integral part of the team when it comes to building business valuable applications. In software development, the final and main artifact is code and it should reflect the real business. Applying domain language that everyone speaks will make your code a valuable source of truth and it is only possible if you have zero translation between business and developers. The most popular approach to developing such types of microservices with a single language that everyone speaks is **Domain-driven Design** (**DDD**). Everyone in a team should use the same language that describes the business in a given boundary. This is called **Ubiquitous Language** (**UL**). Using UL, everyone in a team will speak the same language and the language will be reflected in your code. It means business helps your design and developers help businesses to have more clearer understanding.

Throughout our learning process, we'll mention some ideas from DDD, despite this not being a DDD book. Please refer to *Implementing Domain-Driven Design*, by Vaugh Vernon, and *Domain-Driven Design: Tackling Complexity in the Heart of Software*, by Eric Evans, to learn more.

This book is not about analyzing and gathering the business requirements. There are really good sources out there that focus exactly on this topic. To make things simple and less theoretical, we'll start with distilled requirements with clear boundaries.

We will build an account building microservice that requires the following *core functionalities*:

- Create account

- Update account

- Get all account information

- Get an account for the given ID

- Delete unused account

Then, we have the following *non-functional* requirements:

- **Scalability**: The microservice should be able to handle more and more requests as it gets used by more people.

- **Performance**: The microservice should respond to requests quickly to keep users happy.

- **Resilience**: The microservice should be able to bounce back from problems and keep working properly.

- **Easy testing**: The microservice should be simple to test to make sure it's working correctly.

- **Stateless**: The microservice shouldn't rely on remembering past interactions with users, and should instead store any important information in a database.

- **Easy updates**: The microservice should be straightforward to put to use and update whenever needed. Of course, usually, you'll have more non-functional requirements than these. However, for getting started, these should be more than enough.

Tools to develop a basic microservice

Developing an application is not just a coding process. In this chapter, to develop our microservice, we also need to select the Node.js framework and store information in our database:

- **Database**: We need to store information somewhere. It's better to keep the service itself simple and store the information in a separate database:

  For this service, we'll be using *MongoDB*, a popular database that works differently than traditional SQL databases. MongoDB is a popular choice for building web services with Node.js technology.

  It's designed to handle situations where users mostly read information, and it can store a lot of data efficiently. MongoDB can be easily expanded by adding more servers as needed.

- **Node.js framework**: You can build a fully functional microservice using just Node.js but it takes some time and a lot of lines of code. Nowadays, most developers use the Node.js frameworks to build services fast with a minimal amount of code lines. Node.js on its own is a low-level environment. Frameworks provide a predefined structure and organization for your code, making it easier to manage and maintain as your project grows. They often come with common functionalities such as *routing* (handling different URL requests), *templating* (generating web page content), and database interaction already built-in. This saves you time from writing those parts yourself.

Popular Node.js frameworks have large communities of developers. This means you have access to a wealth of resources, tutorials, and solutions online if you encounter problems. There's also a bigger pool of developers familiar with the framework for potential collaboration.

Frameworks can help mitigate security vulnerabilities by providing established coding practices and features to prevent common attacks.

For this chapter, we're going to use *Express.js*, one of the most popular Node.js frameworks for building microservices.

Preparing our first project

Our focus in this chapter is to create a microservice that provides really simple CRUD operations. So, it's going to be mostly domain-centric. That's why we start our application from the database.

To follow our examples, open the Ch05 folder in this book's GitHub repository and open it using your favorite text editor.

There's a difference between knowing the path and walking the path.

We prefer that you don't just download and explore the repository and that you also try to write some code with us. This will help you gain valuable practice.

Understanding the concept of packages

Building software doesn't mean that you should implement everything from scratch and this fact doesn't depend on programming languages. It is also applicable for Node.js development. Our main focus should always be solving business problems and making this process fast, easy, secure, and reliable. Almost every popular programming language provides a collection of libraries. In Node.js, these are called **packages**. Node.js development mostly starts with package configuration.

When you install Node.js, you automatically install the **Node package manager** (**npm**) tool. This tool allows you to find, build, and manage packages. You can find almost any package for your daily-basis needs. People use, test, maintain, and fix bugs and that makes npm a great and reliable source for development. For example, if you need validation for your application, you shouldn't build everything from scratch. Why not use popular practices that have already been implemented in popular libraries? We mostly build only business-specific functionalities by ourselves. Other relevant functionalities, such as connecting to the database, validation, security, logging, and more, can be installed as packages and reused.

Here's how you can interact with npm and configure it:

1. Open your favorite text editor (we're using Visual Studio Code).
2. Create a folder (in our case, Ch05).

3. Navigate to that folder using your terminal (Use **Terminal | New terminal** from Visual Studio Code and run the `cd folder_name` command to navigate to your empty folder – that is, use `cd Ch05`).

4. Type `npm init` and follow the instructions provided (*Figure 5.1*):

```
package name: (cp5) accountmicroservice
version: (1.0.0)
description: simple account microservice with crud functionalities
entry point: (index.js)
test command:
git repository: https://github.com/PacktPublishing/Hands-on-Microservices-with-JavaScript
keywords:
author: Suleymani Tural
license: (ISC)
```

Figure 5.1: Creating a package.json file

5. Hit *Enter* to generate **package configuration** (*package.json*).

6. At this point, we have a special file called `package.json` in our project with the following JSON content:

```
{
    "name": "accountmicroservice",
    "version": "1.0.0",
    "description": "simple account microservice with crud
functionalities",
    "main": "index.js",
    "scripts": {
      "test": "echo \"Error: no test specified\" && exit 1"
    },
    "repository": {
      "type": "git",
      "url": "git+https://github.com/PacktPublishing/Hands-on-
            Microservices-with-JavaScript.git"
    },
    "author": "Suleymani Tural",
    "license": "ISC",
    "bugs": {
      "url": "https://github.com/PacktPublishing/Hands-on-
            Microservices-with-JavaScript/issues"
    },
    "homepage": "https://github.com/PacktPublishing/Hands-on-
            Microservices-with-JavaScript#readme"
}
```

7. For learning purposes, it is also OK to use the npm init -y command instead of npm init as it will generate a minimal package.json file for you to get started with (*Figure 5.2*). After generation, you can manually update any line you want:

```
{
  "name": "ch05",
  "version": "1.0.0",
  "description": "",
  "main": "index.js",
  ▷ Debug
  "scripts": {
    "test": "type your test command here like this"
  },
  "keywords": [],
  "author": "",
  "license": "ISC"
}
```

Figure 5.2: Generated package.json file

Let's learn more about the package.json file.

Understanding the package.json file

The package.json file is a vital component in Node.js projects. It acts like a project manifest, storing crucial information about your project.

Let's summarize the role of the package.json file in our Node.js projects:

- It lists all the external modules (dependencies) your project relies on to function.

- Along with the names, it specifies the required versions using semantic versioning for compatibility. This ensures that everyone working on the project uses the same compatible versions of dependencies.

- It serves as a central location for project metadata, such as the project's name, version, description, license, and author information (see *Figure 5.2*).

- You can define custom scripts in the package.json file to automate repetitive tasks within your project. These scripts can do anything from starting the development server to running tests or building the project for deployment.

- If you plan to publish your project as a reusable package for others to use, package.json becomes even more important. It provides essential information for the package manager (such as npm) to understand how to install and use your project effectively.

Long story short, `package.json` keeps your project organized, ensures consistent dependencies, and simplifies collaboration among developers.

Understanding index.js files

Throughout this chapter, you'll encounter files named `index.js`. These files play a couple of important roles.

By convention, `index.js` acts as the entry point for our Node.js application. When we run our application using node, the `index.js` file is the starting point where the application's execution begins.

Inside `index.js`, you can typically find code that imports necessary modules and libraries using the required statements to configure your application (for example, setting up a web server and connecting to databases) and defines the main logic or event listeners for your application.

These files can also serve for namespacing and organization within your project. Consider a folder containing multiple JavaScript files with related functionalities. An `index.js` file inside that folder can act as a central point for importing those related files and re-exporting specific functions or classes from those files, making them accessible outside the folder using a single import statement.

> **Note**
>
> It's important to note that `index.js` is a convention, not a strict requirement. You can name your entry point file differently (for example, `app.js` or `main.js`). So long as you specify the correct filename when you're running your application with node, it will work.

In summary, `index.js` files serve as a common entry point and a way to organize code within folders in your Node.js projects. They provide a clean and consistent approach to structuring your application's starting point and managing related functionalities.

Installing the required packages

By itself, `package.json` doesn't contain any required package that we plan to use by default. It is just boilerplate for getting started. Here's a list of packages that we'll be using in this chapter, along with their installation commands:

- Express (`npm install express`)
- Joi (`npm install joi`)
- mongoose (`npm install mongoose`)
- dotenv (`npm install dotenv -save`)

Here's what the `package.json` file's dependencies and `devDependencies` look like:

```
"dependencies": {
    "dotenv": "^16.4.5",
    "express": "^4.19.2",
    "joi": "^17.12.3",
    "mongoose": "^8.3.2"
}
```

You've probably already realized that, when installing our first package, the node automatically generates another file called `package-lock.json`. Let's summarize its roles:

It acts as a lock file, specifying the exact versions of packages and their dependencies that were installed. This guarantees that regardless of who installs the project or on what machine, the same set of versions will be used, leading to consistent behavior.

By locking down versions, `package-lock.json` enables developers to reproduce the project's environment exactly. This is essential for maintaining stability and avoiding unexpected issues during deployments or across different development machines.

When shared within a team or used in **Continuous Integration/Continuous Delivery (CI/CD)** pipelines, `package-lock.json` ensures everyone involved is working with the same dependencies. This streamlines collaboration and automates reliable builds.

It works in conjunction with `package.json`. While `package.json` specifies the desired dependencies and their version ranges, `package-lock.json` pins down the exact versions that are used during installation.

Overall, `package-lock.json` is important for maintaining consistent and reproducible Node.js project environments across installations and team workflows.

You may have noticed that we have one more folder: `node_modules`. In Node.js projects, the `node_modules` folder is a special directory that stores all the third-party libraries and dependencies your project relies on. These libraries provide pre-written code for functionalities you don't need to build from scratch, saving you time and effort.

Node.js projects often depend on external code from various sources. The `node_modules` folder keeps all these dependencies organized in one place. Each project can have its own set of dependencies specific to its needs. This way, different projects can use different versions of the same library without conflicts.

At this point, we have an initial skeleton for our application. So, it's time to start the actual development process.

Defining the internal architecture of our microservice

Imagine that after carefully analyzing, we decided to have a special microservice that's responsible for working with account information and we called it the *account microservice*. Our account consists of an *ID*, *account name*, *account type*, *account status*, and *account number*. To track changes, we're going to add `createdAt` and `updatedAt` fields.

The microservice approach has been applied to our whole project and now we have multiple services. However, the internal design of our concrete microservice depends on the requirements and it's up to the team regarding which architectural pattern to apply. One of the most popular and classical architectural patterns in software development is **Model-View-Controller** (**MVC**). To make things simple and understandable, we will apply it to our microservice design.

MVC architectural pattern

The MVC architectural pattern is a popular choice for structuring Node.js APIs due to its emphasis on separation of concerns.

It has the following main components:

- **Model**:

  - Represents the data layer of your API.

  - Encapsulates data access logic and interacts with databases (for example, MongoDB, MySQL, and so on).

  - Handles data persistence and retrieval.

- **View** (not directly used in Node.js APIs):

  - Traditionally deals with UI presentation in web applications.

  - Not directly applicable in Node.js APIs as they are data-centric.

  - Note that the concept of *view* can be extended to represent the response format (JSON, XML) for the API.

- **Controller**:

  - Acts as the central coordinator of your API.

  - Receives incoming HTTP requests from clients (for example, `GET`, `POST`, `PUT`, and `DELETE`).

  - Interacts with the model to fetch or manipulate data based on the request.

  - Prepares the response data in the desired format (JSON, XML).

  - Returns the response to the client.

But why it is beneficial to use MVC for Node.js APIs?

- **Separation of concerns**: Makes code more organized and maintainable by dividing functionalities.

- **Improved testability**: Each layer (model, view, and controller) can be tested independently.

- **Flexibility**: Easier to modify or update specific parts of the API without affecting others.

- **Scalability**: Easier to scale the application by adding more controllers or models.

Now that we have enough theoretical knowledge about MVC, it's time to apply it in practice.

Integrating MVC into our Node.js project

While Node.js doesn't have a built-in MVC framework, popular web frameworks such as *Express.js* can be used to implement the pattern. Express.js handles routing (mapping URLs to controllers) and simplifies request-response handling.

You'll typically structure your project with separate folders for models and controllers.

We'll use the *N-Layered Architecture* to structure our code. This architecture is popular because it promotes the separation of concerns, making the application more modular, maintainable, and scalable.

Since we don't have complex requirements, getting started with it is a good initial point. Using both MVC and the N-layered architecture in your Node.js Express project can lead to a well-structured and maintainable API. The following are some common layers you'll encounter:

- Presentation Layer (UI or API)

- Business Logic Layer (core application logic)

- Data Access Layer (interaction with databases)

The model, representing data and its logic, aligns with the data access layer's responsibilities. Scripts in the `services` folder will store our business logic. The controller, which handles requests and manipulates data, shouldn't contain any business logic. Instead, it should act as a bridge that forwards the user's request to the business logic layer.

Now that we've defined a general architecture for our application, we're ready to focus on the implementation details. Starting from the next section, we'll implement the functional behaviors of our first microservice.

Hands-on account microservice development

To start from scratch, let's create a folder called `src`. We plan to organize our main application structure under this folder. This is going to be a data-centric application, so it's better to start development from the database segment.

In the end, we plan to build the following project structure for our application:

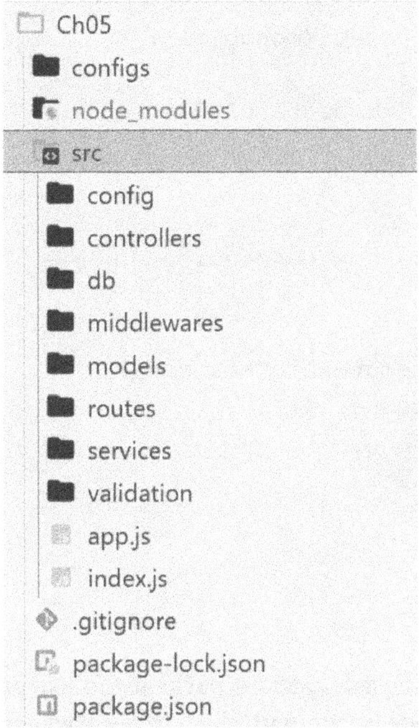

Figure 5.3: The final project structure

To follow along with ease, don't forget to download the source code from our repository.

Implementing our data-access functionalities

We always store data somewhere. The most used storage for data is a database. The data access that we plan to implement relies on MongoDB and isolates us from the difficulties of querying a database using SQL. It's like using arrays or lists but under the hood, it interacts with a database.

To start creating our account microservice, do the following:

Create a db folder under src.

1. Add the index.js file to the db folder.

2. First, we need to handle the database communication process. That's why our current file (index.js) will serve connection and disconnection functionalities:

```
const db = require('mongoose');

let mongoUrl;
async function connect({ mongo: { url } }) {
```

```
        mongoUrl = url;
        try {
            await db.connect(mongoUrl);
        } catch (err) {
            setTimeout(connect, 8000);
        }
    }
}

const dbConnection = db.connection;

function disconnect() {
    dbConnection.removeAllListeners();
    return db.disconnect();
}

module.exports = {
    connect,
    disconnect,
};
```

We've already mentioned the mongoose package. To use packages like this, we have the required command. Node.js automatically handles packages from the node_modules folder without specifying any relative or full path.

Here, we've implemented two main functionalities. They mostly act as wrappers over existing functionalities:

- The connect function tries to connect to the given database. In case of errors, we have one more attempt to try to connect to the database after 8 seconds. It is up to you to configure this but having a connection attempt after an unsuccessful operation makes sense.

- The disconnect function handles the disconnection case. Here, we're removing all listeners of our database via db.disconnect() manually.

Node.js has a file-based module approach. This means that every file, by itself, can be treated as a module and other modules can use it to build more complex modules. One of the ways you can make some functionalities of your module accessible to others is by using exports. You should only provide the required functions with the following proper encapsulation. If some of your functions are used by other functions in the same module and they are not part of your module's contract, it's better not to specify them in the exports list. In our case, we have two functions – connect and disconnect – that we're providing outside to be consumed by other modules.

Implementing the M in MVC

In our project, the responsibility of models is to act as a data access layer. This layer covers the main operations, such as INSERT, UPDATE, SELECT, and DELETE. We have account.js under the src/models folder; this is where all the database-related functionalities live. Here's what it looks like:

```
const mongoose = require('mongoose');

const { Schema } = mongoose;

const AccountSchema = new Schema(
    {
        name: {
            type: String,
            required: true,
        },
        number: {
            type: String,
            required: true,
        },
        type: {
            type: String,
            enum: ['root', 'sub'],
            default: 'root',
        },
        status: {
            type: String,
            enum: ['new', 'active', 'inactive', 'blocked'],
            default: 'new',
        },
        createdAt: {
            type: Date,
            default: Date.now,
        },
        updatedAt: Date,
    },
    { optimisticConcurrency: true },
);

module.exports = mongoose.model('account', AccountSchema);
```

Let's walk through this code:

- `const mongoose = require('mongoose');`: This line imports the Mongoose library, which is used for interacting with MongoDB databases in Node.js.

- `const { Schema } = mongoose;`: This line uses destructuring to extract the `Schema` class from the `mongoose` object. This makes the code more concise and easier to read.

- `new Schema({ ... })`: This line creates a new Mongoose schema object. The object that's passed as an argument defines the structure of the documents that will be stored in the account collection within your MongoDB database. Within the curly braces, `{}`, you define the properties (fields) of each document in the collection. Here's a breakdown of each property:

  - `name`:

    - `type: String`: This specifies that the name property should be a string.

    - `required: true`: This makes the name property mandatory. A document cannot be saved without a value for the name.

  - `number`: Similar to name, but also required.

  - `type`:

    - `type: String`: The status property is a string.

    - `enum: ['new', 'active', 'inactive', 'blocked']`: Similar to type, this defines a list of allowed values for the status: `'new'`, `'active'`, `'inactive'`, or `'blocked'`.

    - `default: 'new'`: If no status is specified, it will default to `'new'`.

  - `createdAt`:

    - `type: Date`: This property stores the date and time the document was created using the current time (`Date.now`).

  - `updatedAt`:

    - `type: Date`: This property is intended to store the date and time the document was last updated. However, it's not explicitly set to a default value here. You'll likely need to update this field manually in your application logic.

    - `{ optimisticConcurrency: true }`: This option is used for optimistic concurrency control, which is a mechanism that helps prevent data inconsistencies during updates (`https://mongoosejs.com/docs/guide.html#optimisticConcurrency`).

- `module.exports = mongoose.model('account', AccountSchema);`: This line creates a Mongoose model named `account` based on your defined `AccountSchema`. The model acts as a blueprint for interacting with `account` documents in your MongoDB database. By exporting the model, you make it available for use in other parts of your Node.js application.

Long story short, this code sets up a Mongoose schema for storing account information in a MongoDB collection. It defines properties such as `name`, `number`, `type`, `status`, `creation time`, and `last update time`, with validation rules and defaults. The code then exports a model that allows you to create, read, update, and delete account documents in your database.

Storing configuration

We need to store application-based configuration somewhere. For the current situation, we need MongoDB URL and port information. It isn't a good idea to hard-code this information directly into your code because of maintainability, reusability, and extensibility. Instead, we prefer to store it in a separate file. That's why we've installed the `dotenv` package.

The `dotenv` package in Node.js helps you manage environment variables for your project. It offers a way to store configuration settings, such as API keys or database credentials, outside of your code in a `.env` file. This improves security by keeping sensitive data out of your codebase.

Why use `dotenv`?

- **Security**: It keeps sensitive data out of your code base, reducing the risk of accidental exposure
- **Separation of concerns**: It separates configuration from code, making your code cleaner and easier to manage
- **Multiple environments**: You can create different `.env` files for different environments (development, staging, and production) with specific configurations for each

The `.env` file itself shouldn't be included in version control systems such as Git to avoid committing sensitive information. We can create a `.env.example` file with placeholder values to guide developers on how to set up their environment variables. However, for this book, we will include the .env file in our Git repository as is, to facilitate the learning process.

We have the `configs` folder under the `Ch05` folder. It is a root-level folder and contains a `.env` file without a name. Here's its content:

```
PORT=3001
MONGODB_URL=mongodb://localhost:27017/account-microservice
```

We need to validate and create a configuration object based on the configuration we've looked at. That's why we need one more folder called `config` under the `src` folder. So, let's create `config.js` with the following content:

```js
const dotenv = require('dotenv');
const Joi = require('joi');

const envVarsSchema = Joi.object()
    .keys({
        PORT: Joi.number().default(3000),
        MONGODB_URL: Joi.string().required().description('Mongo DB
url')
    })
    .unknown();

function createConfig(configPath) {
    dotenv.config({ path: configPath });

    const { value: envVars, error } = envVarsSchema
        .prefs({ errors: { label: 'key' } })
        .validate(process.env);

    if (error) {
        throw new Error(`Config validation error: ${error.message}`);
    }

    return {
        port: envVars.PORT,
        mongo: {
            url: envVars.MONGODB_URL,
        }
    };
}

module.exports = {
    createConfig,
};
```

Using the **Joi** package, we validate our configuration, and using the `createConfig` function, we're able to read and build config objects.

There are a lot of packages out there that can be used for data validation. We prefer to use Joi because it's popular and easy to use. Joi is a popular open source package that provides a declarative way to define data schemas and perform validation against those schemas.

it allows you to create JavaScript objects that represent the expected structure and data types for your application's inputs (request body, query parameters, and so on).

It offers a wide range of validation rules for common data types such as strings, numbers, arrays, and objects. You can define rules for presence, format, length, and more.

It integrates seamlessly with Express.js middleware, allowing you to validate data directly within your route handlers.

By separating validation logic from your route handlers, your code becomes cleaner and easier to understand.

Overall, Joi is a valuable tool for building robust and secure Node.js applications. By incorporating data validation with Joi, you can ensure that your application receives clean, reliable data, leading to a more stable and secure development experience.

We'll be using it in our application entry point (`src/index.js`).

Implementing the business layer

The business layer is the heart of an N-layered architecture. It's responsible for the core functionality of the application and implements the specific business rules that govern how the application operates. It translates user requests into actions and decisions based on the business rules. It also determines how data should be processed, validated, and manipulated to fulfill those requests. Furthermore, it acts as an intermediary between the presentation layer (user interface) and the data access layer (database). It receives data requests from the presentation layer, retrieves the necessary data from the data access layer, and then applies business logic before returning the processed data.

By separating business logic from the presentation and data access layers, the business layer promotes loose coupling and reusability. This makes the application easier to maintain, test, and modify as business needs evolve.

We have a `services` folder under `src` to physically locate service functionalities. We mostly have five functions in `account.js` to cover the main operations related to CRUD: `getAccountById`, `getAllAccounts`, `createAccount`, `deleteAccountById`, and `updateAccountById`. Let's look at the first four here:

```
const Account = require('../models/account');

//get account info by id
function getAccountById(id) {
    return Account.findById(id);
}

//get all account information
function getAllAccounts() {
```

```
        return Account.find({});
}

//create account based on name,number,type and status
function createAccount(name, number, type, status) {
        return Account.create({ number, name, type, status });
}

//delete account by account id
async function deleteAccountById(id) {
        const deletedAccount = await Account.findByIdAndDelete(id);
        if(deletedAccount)
         return true;
         else
         return false;
}
```

The first four functions are easy to understand. Using `require`, we import our account from models. Then, we wrap our data access operations with business functions. The biggest function in this module is `updateAccountById`. Let's take a closer look:

```
//'new', 'active', 'inactive', 'blocked'
const availableAccountStatusesForUpdate = {
        new: ['active', 'blocked'],
        active: ['inactive', 'blocked'],
        inactive: ['active'],
        blocked: ['active'],
};

//'root', 'sub'
const availableAccountTypesForUpdate = {
        root: ['sub'],
        sub: ['root'],
};

const NO_VALID_DATA_TO_UPDATE = 0;
const INVALID_STATUS_CODE = 1;
const INVALID_TYPE_CODE = 2;
const INVALID_ACCOUNT = 3;
const INVALID_STATE_TRANSITION = 4;
const INVALID_TYPE_TRANSITION = 5;

async function updateAccountById(id, { name, number, type, status }) {
        if (!name && !number && !type && !status) {
```

```
    return { error: 'provide at least one valid data to be
      updated', code: NO_VALID_DATA_TO_UPDATE };
}

if (status && !(status in availableAccountStatusesForUpdate)) {
    return { error: 'invalid status for account', code: INVALID_
      STATUS_CODE };
}

if (type && !(type in availableAccountTypesForUpdate)) {
    return { error: 'invalid type for account', code: INVALID_
      TYPE_CODE };
}

const account = await Account.findById(id);
if (!account) {
    return { error: 'account not found', code: INVALID_ACCOUNT };
}

//check for available status and transition
if (status) {
const allowedStatuses =
    availableAccountStatusesForUpdate[
        account.status];
    if (!allowedStatuses.includes(status)) {
        return {
            error: `cannot update status from '${account.status}'
              to '${status}'`,
            code: INVALID_STATE_TRANSITION,
        };
    }
}

//check for available type and transition
if (type) {
    const allowedTypes = availableAccountTypesForUpdate[account
      .type];
    if (!allowedTypes.includes(type)) {
        return {
            error: `cannot update type from '${account.type}' to
              '${type}'`,
            code: INVALID_TYPE_TRANSITION,
        };
```

```
        }
    }

    account.status = status ?? account.status;
    account.type = type ?? account.type;
    account.name = name ?? account.name;
    account.number = number ?? account.number;
    account.updatedAt = Date.now();

    await account.save();

    return account;
}
```

In the end, we need to export the required code blocks so that they can be used by other services:

```
module.exports = {
    getAccountById,
    getAllAccounts,
    createAccount,
    updateAccountById,
    deleteAccountById,
    errorCodes: {
        NO_VALID_DATA_TO_UPDATE,
        INVALID_STATUS_CODE,
        INVALID_TYPE_CODE,
        INVALID_ACCOUNT,
        INVALID_STATE_TRANSITION,
        INVALID_TYPE_TRANSITION,
    },
};
```

We have the following checks before updating our account information:

- Only allow an update to occur if one of the fields is provided.

- Return an error if an invalid status code is provided.

- Return an error if an invalid type is provided.

- If the account for the given ID doesn't exist, we need to return the error.

We have some rules to update the status. First, `availableAccountStatusesForUpdate` describes the rules: if the status is new, then it can be updated to `active` or `blocked`. For `active`, it is possible to update to `inactive` and `blocked`. If the status is `inactive`, then only `active` is allowed. The `blocked` status can only be transitioned to `active`.

These are not all the possible validations you can implement, but they show how you can apply check logic to update functionality. In the end, we expose functions with error codes outside to be used by the preceding layer.

Implementing the controller

In a Node.js project using the MVC pattern, the controller acts as the central nervous system, handling user requests and coordinating the application's response. It is the first point of contact for incoming requests from the user. It interprets the URL, HTTP method (GET, POST, and so on), and any parameters included in the request. The controller, by its nature, doesn't implement the business logic itself; instead, it directs the flow of the application based on the request. It might interact with the model to retrieve or manipulate data, or it could perform some basic validation or processing before moving on.

The controller interacts with the model to get the data needed to fulfill the user's request. This could involve fetching data from a database, performing calculations, or any other operations defined in the model layer.

Once the controller has the data or has processed the request, it selects the appropriate view to render the response for the classical UI application. It might also prepare the data so that it can be consumed by the view, such as formatting it into a specific template. In our case, we don't have a complete UI, and our JSON representation of data acts as a UI for us.

Finally, the controller generates the response that gets sent back to the user. This could be an HTML page, JSON data for an API, or any other format suitable for the request.

In essence, the controller acts as a middleman, managing the communication flow between the user (through the view) and the data layer (through the model). It keeps the view and model separate, promoting cleaner code and easier maintenance.

To implement a controller mechanism in our project, we need to create a folder called controllers under the src folder and add a new JavaScript file called account.js:

```
const accountService = require('../services/account');
const getAccounts = async (req, res) => {
    const result = await accountService.getAllAccounts();
    res.status(200).json({ success: true, account: result.map(x =>
      mapToResponse(x)) });
};

const createAccount = async (req, res) => {
    const { name, number, type, status } = req.body;
    const result = await accountService.createAccount(name, number,
      type, status);
```

```
    res.status(201).json({
        success: true,
        Account: mapToResponse(result),
    });
};

const deleteAccountById = async (req, res) => {
    const isDeleted = await accountService.deleteAccountById(req
        .params.id);

    if(isDeleted)
     res.status(204).json({
        success: true
     });
     else
     res.status(400).json({ success: false, message: 'No valid data to
        delete' });
};
```

Things are straightforward when it comes to implementing retrieve (get), create, and delete accounts. However, we should consider some additional factors when we update our account information:

First, getAccounts calls the getallAcccounts service function and returns 200 responses.

Then, createAccount calls the same named function from the service and returns 201, which means the resource has been created.

Finally, deleteAccountById calls the same named function from the service and returns 204, which means success with no content. If the delete operation fails, it will return a 400 status code.

Next, let's take a look at the update implementation:

```
const updateAccountById = async (req, res) => {
    const result = await accountService.updateAccountById(
        req.params.id, req.body);
    if (result.error) {
        switch (result.code) {
            case accountService.errorCodes.NO_VALID_DATA_TO_UPDATE:
                res.status(400).json({ success: false, message:
                    result.error });
                return;
            case accountService.errorCodes.INVALID_STATUS_CODE:
                res.status(400).json({ success: false, message:
                    'invalid status' });
                return;
```

```
                case accountService.errorCodes.INVALID_TYPE_CODE:
                    res.status(400).json({ success: false, message:
                        'invalid type' });
                    return;
                case accountService.errorCodes.INVALID_ACCOUNT:
                    res.status(404).json({ success: false, message:
                        'Account not found' });
                    return;
                case accountService.errorCodes.INVALID_STATE_TRANSITION:
                    res.status(400).json({ success: false, message:
                        result.error });
                    return;
                case accountService.errorCodes.INVALID_TYPE_TRANSITION:
                    res.status(400).json({ success: false, message:
                        result.error });
                    return;
                default:
                    res.status(500).json({ success: false, message:
                        'internal server error' });
                    return;
            }
        }

    res.status(200).json({
        success: true,
        Account: mapToResponse(result),
    });
};
```

Here, `updateAccountById` has a few more lines of code. Based on exported error codes, it prepares different HTTP status codes. If the provided data is valid, it returns a 200 success code.

We also have a simple function called `mapToResponse`. In Node.js, `mapToResponse` serves as a utility function to transform or map an account object to a specific format or structure that's suitable for sending as a response, typically in an API. Here's what it looks like:

```
function mapToResponse(account) {
    const {
        id, name, number, type, status,
    } = account;

    return {
        id,
        name,
```

```
        number,
        type,
        status
    };
}

module.exports = {
    getAccountById,
    getAccounts,
    createAccount,
    deleteAccountById,
    updateAccountById,
};
```

The only additional `private` function that we haven't exported is `mapToResponse`. As you know, the user may not need to retrieve the whole account data structure. Using this function, we only return the required fields to the user as a response.

The final piece of code is retrieving the account by ID (`getAccountById`):

```
const accountService = require('../services/account');
const getAccountById = async (req, res) => {
    const result = await accountService.getAccountById(req.params.id);

    if (result) {

        res.status(200).json({ success: true, account:
          mapToResponse(result) });
    } else {
        res.status(404).json({ success: false, message: 'Account not
          found' });
    }
};
```

Here, `getAccountById` redirects the query to the appropriate service and, based on the service's response, returns a success or not found message.

In the end, to use the main controller functions in the routing process, we must export them.

Simple data validation for your API

Unvalidated data can lead to unexpected behavior, errors, and security vulnerabilities. Validation helps ensure that data received from users or external sources conforms to your application's expectations.

Malicious users might try to inject invalid or unexpected data into your application. Validation helps prevent these attacks by rejecting data that doesn't adhere to the defined rules.

By defining validation rules upfront, you can catch errors early in the development process, reducing debugging time and improving code maintainability.

Let's create a validation folder under `src` with the `account.js` file that contains the following lines of code:

```
const Joi = require('joi');

const objectId = Joi.string().regex(/^[0-9a-fA-F]{24}$/);

const getAccountById = {
  params: Joi.object().keys({
    id: objectId.required(),
  }),
};

const deleteAccountById = {
  params: Joi.object().keys({
    id: objectId.required(),
  }),
};

const createAccount = {
  body: Joi.object().keys({
    name: Joi.string().required(),
    number: Joi.string().required(),
    status: Joi.string().valid('new', 'active', 'completed',
      'cancelled').optional(),
    type: Joi.string().valid('root', 'sub').optional(),
  }),
};
```

Let's take a closer look at the code:

- After installing the `Joi` package, it is enough to specify it in the `require` command.

- The regular expression defines a rule to validate the ID. We'll use this ID for GET, PUT, and DELETE operations.

- `const createAccount = { ... }`: This line declares a constant variable named `createAccount` and assigns an object literal to it. This object will hold the validation schema for creating an account.

- `body`: This property name specifies that the validation schema applies to the request body (typically, data sent in the body of a POST request).

- `Joi.object()`: This creates a Joi object schema that validates the structure (presence of specific properties) of the request body.

- `.keys({ ... })`: This defines the set of properties to be expected in the request body and their corresponding validation rules.

- `name: Joi.string().required()`: This validates the presence of a property named name and ensures it's a string value. The `.required()` part makes it mandatory.

- `number: Joi.string().required()`: Similar to name, this validates a required string property named `number`.

- `status: Joi.string().valid('new', 'active', 'completed', 'cancelled').optional()`: This validates an optional string property named `status`. The `.valid()` method restricts the allowed values to `'new'`, `'active'`, `'completed'`, and `'cancelled'`.

- `type: Joi.string().valid('root', 'sub').optional()`: Similar to `status`, this validates an optional string property named `type` with allowed values of `'root'` and `'sub'`.

- In general, the preceding code ensures that a request to create an account must include the following properties:

  - `name`: Required string value

  - `number`: Required string value

  - `status`: An optional string value that is either `'new'`, `'active'`, `'completed'`, or `'cancelled'`

  - `type`: An optional string value that is either `'root'` or `'sub'`

By using this schema, you can guarantee that the data that's received for creating an account adheres to the expected format and prevents unexpected or invalid data from entering your application:

```
const updateAccountById = {
  params: Joi.object().keys({
    id: objectId.required(),
  }),
  body: Joi.object().keys({
    name: Joi.string().required(),
    number: Joi.string().required(),
    status: Joi.string().valid('new', 'active', 'completed',
      'cancelled').optional(),
    type: Joi.string().valid('root', 'sub').optional(),
  }),
};
```

```
module.exports = {
  getAccountById,
  createAccount,
  deleteAccountById,
  updateAccountById,
};
```

The `updateAccountById` object specifies that the parameters must include an `id` parameter, which is required and must be a valid object ID. The `body` part of the request must contain `name` and `number` fields, both of which are required strings, and optionally a `status` field that can only be one of the specified values (`'new'`, `'active'`, `'completed'`, or `'cancelled'`) and a `type` field that can be either `'root'` or `'sub'`. This validation ensures that incoming requests to update an account adhere to the expected format and data types. In the end, to use these rules, we need to export them using `module.exports`.

We have another module related to data validation that's placed in the `middleware` folder under the `src` folder. **Middleware** refers to functions that can intercept and manipulate both incoming requests and outgoing responses before they reach their designated route handlers. Create the `validate.js` file with the following content:

```
const Joi = require('joi');

function take(object, keys) {
    return Object.assign({}, ...keys
        .filter(key => object.hasOwnProperty(key))
        .map(key => ({ [key]: object[key] })));
}

function validate(schema) {
    return (req, res, next) => {
        // Extract relevant parts of the schema based on request type
        const selectedSchema = take(schema, ['params', 'query',
          'body']);

        const objectToValidate = take(req,
          Object.keys(selectedSchema));
        // Perform Joi validation with improved error handling
        const { error, value } = Joi.compile(selectedSchema)
            .prefs({ errors: { label: 'key' }, abortEarly: false })
            .validate(objectToValidate);

        if (error) {
            const errorMsg = error.details.map(d => d.message).join(',
              ');
```

```
            return res.status(400).json({ success: false, message:
                errorMsg });
        }

        // Attach validated data to the request object
        Object.assign(req, value);
        next();
    };
}
```

If an error exists, the middleware extracts individual error messages using `error.details.map(...)` and joins them into a comma-separated string (`errorMessage`). A `400 Bad Request` response is sent with the error message in JSON format.

If validation passes (`!error`), the validated data (value) obtained from Joi is attached to the `req` object using `Object.assign`. This makes the validated data readily available in subsequent route handlers.

This middleware acts as a gatekeeper for your routes, ensuring that incoming requests adhere to the provided validation schema.

Implementing routing

Routing is a fundamental aspect of building web applications with Node.js and Express. It essentially directs incoming HTTP requests to the appropriate handlers within your application.

Routing allows you to define a clear separation between URLs (endpoints) and the code that handles them. This promotes modularity and makes your code base more readable and manageable.

It also enables you to define handlers specific to each HTTP method for a particular URL. This allows you to handle requests for retrieving data (`GET`), submitting data (`POST`), updating data (`PUT`), or deleting data (`DELETE`) appropriately.

By defining routes that map to resources and corresponding HTTP methods, you can establish a well-structured and predictable API that other applications can interact with.

As your application evolves, routing helps you easily add new features and functionalities.

You can create separate route handlers for new features, keeping your code base organized and scalable.

Routing also allows you to group related routes, promoting the reusability of code across different parts of your application.

In simpler terms, routing acts like a traffic controller for your application, directing incoming requests to the designated destinations (handlers) based on their URLs and HTTP methods. This keeps your code organized and maintainable and enables you to build robust and scalable web applications and APIs.

We have a `routes` folder under the `src` folder where we define all the routing rules for our application. Currently, it is our first version, so the `v1` folder indicates the first version of our API. **Versioning** allows you to introduce changes while maintaining compatibility with existing clients.

Let's add the `accounts` folder and the `index.js` file to our `v1` folder and define our routing rules.

The full path to the file will be `src/routers/v1/accounts/index.js`:

```
const { Router } = require('express');
const accountController = require('../../../controllers/account');
const accountValidation = require('../../../validation/account');
const validate = require('../../../middlewares/validate');

const router = Router();
router.get('/', accountController.getAccounts);
router.get('/:id',
  validate(accountValidation.getAccountById),
  accountController.getAccountById);
router.post('/',
  validate(accountValidation.createAccount),
  accountController.createAccount);
router.put('/:id',
  validate(accountValidation.updateAccountById),
  accountController.updateAccountById);
router.delete('/:id',
  validate(accountValidation.deleteAccountById),
  accountController.deleteAccountById);
module.exports = router;
```

Express.js provides routing functionality. Using it, we've defined the following:

- Users can *get* an account by ID using `/accounts/:id`

- Users can *create* a new account by sending a POST request to `/accounts`

- Users can *update* an account by ID sending a PUT request to `/accounts/:id`

- Users can *delete* an account by ID sending a DELETE request to `/accounts/:id`

The validation middleware ensures that requests adhere to the expected format before reaching the controller functions, which handle the actual account management logic.

As you might have guessed, we don't have any indicator for our route to be used with the `/accounts` prefix.

We need one more JavaScript file to handle this. Let's create `index.js` under the `routes/v1` folder with the following implementation:

```javascript
const { Router } = require('express');
const accountRouter = require('./accounts');

const router = Router();

router.use('/accounts', accountRouter);

module.exports = router;
module.exports = router;
```

Now, we'll be able to navigate to our resource using the `/accounts` prefix.

Constructing our web application

Now, it's time to define our basic structure for a Node.js application using the Express.js framework.

Let's create an `app.js` file under the `src` folder with the following code structure:

```javascript
const express = require('express');
const v1 = require('./routes/v1');

const app = express();

// service
app.use(express.json());

// V1 API
app.use('/v1', v1);

module.exports = app;
```

This code snippet defines a basic structure for building our web application:

- `const express = require('express');`: This line imports the Express.js framework, providing functionalities for building web servers and handling HTTP requests and responses.
- `const v1 = require('./routes/v1');`: This line imports a module named `v1.js` located in a folder named `routes/v1`. This module defines routes (URL paths) for version 1 of your application's API.
- `const app = express();`: This line creates an instance of the Express application using the `express()` function. This `app` object will be used to define routes and middleware, as well as handle application logic.

- `.use(express.json())`: This line registers a middleware function with the Express application. The `express.json()` middleware parses incoming JSON data in request bodies, making it accessible in your route handlers.

- `.use('/v1', v1);`: This line is crucial for routing. It mounts the routes defined in the imported `v1` module onto the `/v1` path of your application. Any requests to URLs starting with `/v1` will be handled by the functions in the `v1` module.

- `module.exports = app;`: This line exports the `app` object, which is the core of your Express application. This allows other modules in your project to import and use this application instance.

In essence, this code creates an Express application, configures middleware for JSON handling, mounts routes from a separate module for version 1 of your API, and makes the application instance available for import by other parts of your project.

Combining all the elements

The final step in our application is to construct everything together, like using Lego. This Lego is going to be a main runnable application that will help us to communicate between elements of our application.

Let's create an `index.js` file under the `src` folder that contains the following code:

```
const path = require('path');
const db = require('./db');
const app = require('./app');
const { createConfig } = require('./config/config');

async function execute() {
    const configPath = path.join(__dirname, '../configs/.env');
    const appConfig = createConfig(configPath);

    await db.connect(appConfig);
    const server = app.listen(appConfig.port, () => {
        console.log('account service started', { port: appConfig.port
            });
    });

    const closeServer = () => {
        if (server) {
            server.close(() => {
                console.log('server closed');
                process.exit(1);
            });
        } else {
            process.exit(1);
```

```
        }
    };

    const unexpectedError = (error) => {
        console.log('unhandled error', { error });
        closeServer();
    };

    process.on('uncaughtException', unexpectedError);
    process.on('unhandledRejection', unexpectedError);
}

execute();
```

This Node.js code defines an asynchronous function named `execute` that serves as the entry point for your application. Here's a breakdown of its functionality:

- **Importing modules**:

  - `const path = require('path');`: Imports the `path` module for manipulating file paths

  - `const db = require('./db');`: Imports the `db` module, likely containing functions for connecting and interacting with your database

  - `const app = require('./app');`: Imports the main application module, likely containing the Express application instance and your application logic

  - `const { createConfig } = require('./config/config');`: Imports the `createConfig` function from the `config/config.js` module, likely responsible for creating your application configuration

- **Configuration setup (async)**:

  - `async function execute() { ... }`: Defines an asynchronous function named `execute` that will be executed when the script starts

  - `const configPath = path.join(__dirname, '../configs/.env');`: Uses the `path` module to construct the absolute path to your configuration file (likely a `.env` file) two directories above the current script's location

  - `const appConfig = createConfig(configPath);`: Calls the imported `createConfig` function with the configuration file path, presumably to read and parse the configuration settings

- **Database connection (async):**

  - `await db.connect(appConfig);`: Attempts to connect to the database using the db module and the loaded configuration (`appConfig`) object. This line is asynchronous, so the function waits for the connection to be established before proceeding.

- **Starting the server:**

  - `const server = app.listen(appConfig.port, ...);`: Calls a method (likely `listen`) on the imported app object, which is probably an Express application. This starts the server listening on the port specified in the configuration (`appConfig.port`). The callback function logs a message when the server starts successfully.

- **Graceful shutdown:**

  - `const closeServer = () => { ... }`: Defines an arrow function named `closeServer` that gracefully shuts down the server. It checks whether the server object exists and then calls its `close` method. The callback function for `close` logs a message when the server is closed and exits the process with an exit code of `1`.

- **Error handling:**

  - `const unexpectedError = (error) => { ... }`: Defines an arrow function named `unexpectedErrorHandler` that handles uncaught errors or unhandled promise rejections. It logs the error message. It calls the `closeServer` function to gracefully shut down the server

- **Attaching event listeners:**

  - `process.on('uncaughtException', unexpectedError);`: Attaches the `unexpectedErrorHandler` function to the `uncaughtException` event of the `process` object. This ensures that any errors thrown outside of an `async` function or promise chain are caught and handled.

  - `process.on('unhandledRejection', unexpectedError);`: Attaches the `unexpectedErrorHandler` function to the `unhandledRejection` event of the `process` object. This ensures that any unhandled rejections from promises are caught and handled.

- **Running the application:**

  - `execute();`: Calls the `execute` function to start the application. Since `execute` is asynchronous, the entire application startup process becomes asynchronous, ensuring the database connection and server startup are completed before the application continues.

In summary, this code sets up the application configuration, connects to the database, starts the server, and implements error handling for a robust and graceful startup and shutdown process.

Running and testing our first microservice

We're not going to write any unit or integrate tests in this chapter. In *Chapter 11*, where we'll dive into the details of those topics. For this chapter, we'll do manual testing via Postman. To run our application, follow these steps:

1. Download Ch05 from our GitHub repository.

2. Open the project (Ch05) via Visual Studio Code.

3. Go to **Terminal** | **New Terminal**.

4. Run the npm install command from the Ch05 folder to load the required packages.

5. Change directories to src (using the cd src command).

6. Run the node index.js command. Mongo should be installed before you run this command. Check out *Chapter 4* for more information about the installation process for Mongo.

7. Open Postman.

In the next few subsections, we'll test our endpoints one by one.

Creating a new account

To create a new account, follow these steps:

1. Create a new tab in Postman.

2. Select POST from **HTTP verbs**.

3. Type localhost:3001/v1/accounts in the **URL** section.

4. Go to the **Body** section. Select raw and change Text to JSON. Add the following JSON to the text area:

```
{
    "name":"AccName1",
    "number":"Ac21345",
    "type":"root",
    "status":"new"
}
```

5. Click the **Send** button to send the request. You'll get the following response from the endpoint:

```
{
    "success": true,
    "Account": {
        "id": "662c081370bd2ba6b5f04e94",
        "name": "AccName1",
        "number": "Ac21345",
        "type": "root",
        "status": "new"
    }
}
```

Now, let's get the account by ID.

Getting an account by ID

To get an account with the given ID, follow these steps:

1. Create a new tab in Postman.

2. Select GET from **HTTP verbs**.

3. Type `localhost:3001/v1/accounts/{accountID}` in the **URL** section. In our case, **accountID** is `662c081370bd2ba6b5f04e94`.

4. Click the **Send** button to send the request. You'll get the following response from the endpoint:

```
{
    "success": true,
    "account": {
        "id": "662c081370bd2ba6b5f04e94",
        "name": "AccName1",
        "number": "Ac21345",
        "type": "root",
        "status": "new"
    }
}
```

Now, let's learn how to update our existing account.

Updating an account by ID

To update your given account, follow these steps:

1. Create a new tab in Postman.

2. Select PUT from **HTTP verbs**.

3. Type `localhost:3001/v1/accounts/{accountID}` in the URL section.

4. Go to the **Body** section. Select `raw` and change `Text` to `JSON`. Add the following JSON to the text area:

```
{
    "name":"updated account",
    "number":"AE33333"
}
```

5. Click the **Send** button to send the request. You'll get the following response from the endpoint:

```
{
    "success": true,
    "Account": {
        "id": "662c081370bd2ba6b5f04e94",
        "name": "updated account",
        "number": "AE33333",
        "type": "root",
        "status": "new"
    }
}
```

For most of the APIs, we usually want to retrieve all data. Next, we'll learn how to get all account information.

Gettings all accounts

To retrieve all accounts, follow these steps:

1. Create a new tab in Postman.

2. Select GET from **HTTP verbs**.

3. Type `localhost:3001/v1/accounts` in the **URL** section.

4. Click the **Send** button to send the request. You'll get the following response from the endpoint:

```
{
    "success": true,
    "account": [
```

```
        {
            "id": "662c081370bd2ba6b5f04e94",
            "name": "updated account",
            "number": "AE33333",
            "type": "root",
            "status": "new"
        }
    ]
}
```

The final endpoint involves deleting the account. Let's check it.

Deleting account by ID

Finally, to delete your already existing account by its ID, follow these steps:

1. Create a new tab in Postman.
2. Select DELETE from **HTTP verbs**.
3. Type `localhost:3001/v1/accounts/{accountID}` in the **URL** section. Provide the valid **accountID** value to delete the record.
4. Click the **Send** button to send the request. You'll get a `204 no-content` response from the endpoint.

With that, we have fully functional CRUD endpoints for accounts. We may not have a complex business case, but the purpose of this chapter was to show you how to implement endpoints for your microservices.

Summary

In this chapter, we created our first microservice. This was our first practical chapter about creating microservices. For this, having a clear understanding of your requirements is important. We provided simple requirements to make our first microservice more understandable and easy to follow. There, we learned how to set up our project. We talked about the tools we need to develop our first microservice; before every microservice development process can be undertaken, we need to define which tools and technologies we plan to use. We also created our internal structure using MVC and N-layered architecture. These are the most popular choices, so using them for your first development project is a great chance for you to learn popular techniques. The practical aspect of this chapter covered creating models, business logic, and controllers. There, we learned about the basics of validation using the JOI package. The application requires a separate file to store configuration, hence why we used the `dotenv` package. We also learn about routing, which is important if we wish to access our functionalities. Then, we integrated routing using Express.js.

In the end, we learned how to check our functionalities using Postman. In the upcoming chapters, we will delve into the development of a second microservice, focusing on establishing synchronous communication between microservices. We will introduce a new stack for the transaction microservice, using tools like NestJS, Prisma, and Axios, to demonstrate the versatility of JavaScript in microservice development.

6

Synchronous Microservices

We implemented our first microservice in the previous chapter, but to demonstrate microservice communication, we need to run at least one more service. To understand the beauty of JavaScript in microservice development, we will use a different Node.js framework called NestJS for the current chapter.

As we discussed earlier, microservice architecture consists of multiple services, and one of the complexities that this approach brings with it is communication. We already know that microservices, while offering advantages in scalability and development, introduce a layer of complexity in communication compared to monolithic applications. Unlike monolithic applications, where everything runs together, microservices communicate over a network. This introduces challenges in *latency* (the time it takes for a request to be processed and a response to be received), *reliability* (since network issues can disrupt communication), and *security* (since you need to secure communication between services).

In this chapter, we will delve into details of synchronous communication between microservices in practice and learn the use cases of synchronous communication between services.

This chapter covers the following topics:

- Understanding the requirements for the transaction microservice
- Tools to develop the transaction microservice
- Hands-on transaction microservice development
- Establishing synchronous communication with the account microservice

Technical requirements

To develop and test the second microservice, we need the following:

- IDE (we prefer **Visual Studio Code (VS Code)**)
- Postman
- Browser of your choice

It is recommended to download our repository from `https://github.com/PacktPublishing/Hands-on-Microservices-with-JavaScript` and open the `Ch06` folder to easily follow our code snippets.

Understanding the requirements for the transaction microservice

Everything starts from the requirements. Software requirements are basically instructions that tell programmers exactly what a software program needs to do. They're like a recipe for the program, outlining the ingredients (features) and steps (functions) needed. Before starting our development, we need to understand our requirements.

The system consists of two main microservices:

- **Transaction microservice**: This microservice will be responsible for processing transactions. It will receive transaction information, validate the account associated with the transaction, and process the transaction.

- **Account microservice**: This microservice will provide account information and validation functionality. We implemented this service in *Chapter 5*. It is responsible for verifying if an account exists and is in good standing.

The transaction microservice will communicate with the account microservice to validate the provided `accountId` value. The account microservice will verify if the `accountId` value exists.

The transaction should be successful only if the account exists and is in an *active* or a *new* state. For other states, we should add a new row to the transaction service with the *FAILED* state:

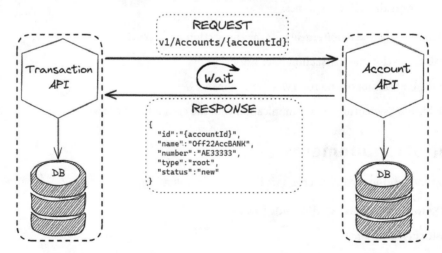

Figure 6.1: Communication between transaction and account microservices

First, we need to develop our transaction microservice. After having a proper working microservice, we will create synchronous communication between transactions and the previously built account microservice.

Tools to develop the transaction microservice

To build our second microservice, we plan to use completely different tools to show that we don't depend on concrete tools and technologies even in JavaScript. You can develop the same microservice using different technologies, and having multiple ones in your arsenal allows you to select the optimal stack tools for your development.

NestJS

As a Node.js framework, we plan to use NestJS. The official page describes it as "*A progressive Node.js framework for building efficient, reliable and scalable server-side applications*." Although Express.js has been the de facto standard for building web applications with a combination of Node.js, it doesn't force you to use Express.js for all types of web applications.

First things first – NestJS is another Node.js framework. Check out *Chapter 4*'s *Node.js frameworks* section to learn more about NestJS. Here's a summary of what it offers:

- It promotes a **modular architecture** that allows you to build scalable and easily organizable applications. You can easily organize your application into modules, components, controllers, and services.

- NestJS is built on top of **TypeScript** and uses TypeScript at its core. If you are a big fan of **strongly typed** tools/languages like me, then it is for you. Strongly typed languages enforce type safety, meaning compiler checks for operations. This can prevent unexpected crashes and incorrect results later.

- NestJS supports **validation** out of the box. It validates incoming data, which may be helpful when building APIs.

Installing all the required applications directly to your computer is not always the best choice. That is why we use Docker. While directly installing applications isn't inherently wrong, Docker provides a more efficient and manageable approach for certain situations.

Docker

Docker helps developers build things such as software programs more easily. Imagine a box that holds all the tools and parts a program needed to run. This box is like a Docker container. Docker lets you put your program and all its bits and pieces in this box so that it works the same way on any computer.

Check out *Chapter 4* to learn more about how to set up Docker on your computer.

Prisma ORM

Prisma is a next-generation **Object-Relational Mapper** (**ORM**). In the world of programming, an ORM acts as a bridge between two different ways of handling data: **object-oriented programming** (**OOP**) and relational databases.

Prisma, as an open source ORM, that simplifies database interactions in Node.js applications. It's like a set of helpful tools that take care of a lot of the complex stuff for you. The good news is, you don't need to deal with pure SQL queries. Here's what it offers:

- **Prisma Client**: This tool automatically builds code to access your database, making it safe and straightforward. It even checks your code for errors as you write it (if you're using TypeScript).
- **Prisma Migrate**: This tool helps you define how your database is structured and keeps it up to date as your application changes.
- **Prisma Studio**: This is a visual tool that lets you see and edit the information stored in your database directly, like a user-friendly dashboard.

Under the hood, you can use PostgreSQL, MySQL, SQL Server, SQLite, MongoDB, and more. When your application requires migrating from one database to another that Prisma supports, it will not affect your project source code because Prisma abstracts your code from internal details.

Prisma Client works well with many different ways of building Node.js applications:

- Traditional REST APIs
- Modern GraphQL APIs
- Efficient gRPC APIs
- Any Node.js project that needs to use a database

In short, Prisma simplifies interacting with databases in Node.js, saving you time and effort. It offers a variety of features to fit your project's needs.

Now, we are ready to develop our transaction service, and starting from the next section, we will dive into the details of the development process.

Hands-on transaction microservice development

The best way of learning from a technical book is by following its instructions. For all practical chapters, it is preferable to follow us along the journey and type every command with us. Downloading source code from the Git repository and investigating source code is also a good way of learning things in practice.

Getting started with NestJS is easier than Express.js. It has code generation steps and easy-to-use packages that help you to do a fast development. If you're looking for a better, modern template to get started, NestJS is one way of achieving it. NestJS provides a built-in command-line tool called the *Nest CLI*. It acts as a powerful assistant throughout your NestJS application's lifecycle. If offers interesting and useful functionalities such as the following:

- **Project initialization**: Quickly set up a new NestJS project with a well-structured directory layout following best practices.

- **Development support**: Run your application in development mode for hot reloading and streamlined debugging.

- **Production build**: Bundle your application for deployment in production environments, optimizing it for efficiency.

- **Code generation**: Generate various components such as controllers, services, modules, and more using schematics, saving you time and ensuring consistency.

Let's begin the development process:

1. Create a folder for your project (it is `Ch06` in our Git repo).

2. Open VS Code and open your folder from it.

3. Go to the **Terminal** menu, then select **New Terminal**.

4. Type `npm i -g @nestjs/cli` and hit *Enter*.

After the NestJS CLI is installed, we can create our project template with a single command. Just type `nest new transactionservice` and press *Enter* again.

If you encounter a `Cannot Be Loaded Because Running Scripts is Disabled on This System` error message while trying to run a script in Windows, follow these steps to resolve it:

1. **Open Windows PowerShell**: Press *Win + X* and select **Windows PowerShell (Admin)** to open it with administrator privileges.

2. **Set the execution policy**: In the PowerShell window, type the following command and press *Enter*:

   ```
   Set-ExecutionPolicy RemoteSigned
   ```

3. **Confirm the change**: When prompted, type `Y` (for Yes) and press **Enter** to confirm.

4. **Run your script again**: Try running your script once more. The issue should now be resolved.

You will get a prompt that asks you to select package manager during project setup (*Figure 6.2*). We have the following options:

- npm
- Yarn
- Pnpm

Our choice is npm for this project. It is a strong contender in the world of package managers, particularly for Node.js projects. It has a massive package registry, is the default for Node.js, and has a large community (*Figure 6.2*):

```
⚡  We will scaffold your app in a few seconds..

?  Which package manager would you  ♥  to use? npm
```

Figure 6.2: NestJS offers to select a package manager

After you've made your selection, the CLI will generate a project template for us (*Figure 6.3*):

Figure 6.3: CLI-generated folder structure for NestJS

The `src` and `test` folders are not empty and contain the initial project skeleton (*Figure 6.4*):

📁 Ch06 \ transactionservice
  📁 node_modules
  📁 prisma
  📁 src
    📄 app.controller.spec.ts
    📄 app.controller.ts
    📄 app.module.ts
    app.service.ts
    📄 main.ts
  📁 test
    📄 app.e2e-spec.ts
    📄 jest-e2e.json

Figure 6.4: CLI-generated src and test folders

To run the generated template successfully, take the following steps:

1. Navigate to the `transactionservice` folder from the terminal using the `cd transactionservice` command. For all types of commands, we need to navigate to this folder to run them properly. You can simply open the `transactionservice` folder directly from VS Code if you do not want to type the `cd` command every time.

2. Type `npm run start:dev`.

    This command starts a special server that helps you see changes quickly. It watches your files closely, and if it sees anything different, it automatically fixes things up and refreshes the server. This means you can see your updates right away without needing to restart everything yourself.

3. Open your favorite browser and navigate to `http://localhost:3000` (*Figure 6.5*):

Figure 6.5: Successful NestJS project run result

The next subsections will help us to understand how to prepare our environment and build our microservice easily.

Dockerizing your PostgreSQL instance

PostgreSQL is one of the best choices when it comes to storing data in the database. We will use Docker to containerize our database, isolating it from other environments.

Right-click on your root project folder (it is `transactionservice` for us) and add a `docker-compose.yml` file.

Open this empty file and add the following lines:

```
networks:
  my-app-network:  # Define the network name exactly as used later

services:
  postgres:
    image: postgres
    env_file:
      - .env
    environment:
      - POSTGRES_USER=${POSTGRES_USER}
      - POSTGRES_PASSWORD=${POSTGRES_PASSWORD}
      - POSTGRES_DB=${POSTGRES_DB}
    ports:
      - ${POSTGRES_PORT}:5432
    volumes:
      - postgres_data:/var/lib/postgresql/data
    networks:
      - my-app-network  # Add the service to the network

  pgadmin:
    image: dpage/pgadmin4
    env_file:
      - .env
    environment:
      - PGADMIN_DEFAULT_EMAIL=${PGADMIN_DEFAULT_EMAIL}
      - PGADMIN_DEFAULT_PASSWORD=${PGADMIN_DEFAULT_PASSWORD}
      - POSTGRES_HOST=postgreshost
      - POSTGRES_USER=${POSTGRES_USER}
      - POSTGRES_PASSWORD=${POSTGRES_PASSWORD}
      - POSTGRES_DB=${POSTGRES_DB}
      - PGADMIN_CONFIG_SERVER_MODE=False
```

```
      - PGADMIN_CONFIG_MASTER_PASSWORD_REQUIRED=False
    ports:
      - ${PGADMIN_PORT}:80
    depends_on:
      - postgres
    user: root
    volumes:
      - postgres_data:/var/lib/pgadmin/data
    networks:
      - my-app-network  # Add the service to the network

volumes:
  postgres_data:
```

We used `docker-compose.yml` in *Chapter 4* when we talked about installing Apache Kafka. We have a separate chapter about containerization, but let's explain the file itself here for more clarity.

A `docker-compose.yml` file is a YAML configuration file used to define and manage multi-container Docker applications. Docker Compose is a tool that allows you to define services, networks, and volumes required for your application in a single file, making it easier to manage complex setups.

Each service represents a containerized application component.

You can define custom networks for your services to communicate with each other. By default, Docker Compose creates a default network for your application, but you can define custom networks to control communication between specific services.

You can also define named volumes or mount host directories into containers to persist data or share files between containers.

Docker Compose allows you to start all your services together with a single command, instead of running services one by one, `docker-compose` helps you to spin up your entire infrastructure with a single command (`docker-compose up`) and manage it consistently across different environments.

This `docker-compose.yml` file defines a Docker Compose configuration for setting up two services: `postgres` and `pgadmin`. Let's break it down:

- `networks`: This section within your Docker Compose YAML file defines named networks that can be used by your application's services. These networks provide a way for containers to communicate with each other in a controlled and isolated manner.

- `services`: This section defines the services to be created.

  - `postgres`: This service uses the official PostgreSQL Docker image. It sets up a PostgreSQL database container.

  - `image: postgres`: Specifies the Docker image to be used for this service.

- env_file: Specifies a file from which to read environment variables.

- environment: Sets environment variables for the PostgreSQL container, including username, password, and database name.

- ports: Maps the container's PostgreSQL port to a port on the host machine, allowing external access.

- volumes: Mounts a volume to persist PostgreSQL data.

- pgadmin: This service uses the pgAdmin 4 Docker image to set up a web-based administration interface for PostgreSQL.

  - image: dpage/pgadmin4: Specifies the Docker image for pgAdmin 4.

  - env_file: Similar to the postgres service, this specifies a file from which to read environment variables.

  - environment: Sets environment variables for pgAdmin, including default email, password, and PostgreSQL connection details.

  - ports: Maps the container's port 80 to a port on the host machine.

  - depends_on: Specifies that this service depends on the postgres service, ensuring that the PostgreSQL database is available before starting pgAdmin.

  - user: root: Specifies that the container should run as the root user.

  - volumes: Mounts a volume to persist pgAdmin data.

- volumes: This section defines a named volume postgres_data, which is used by both services to persist data.

In the end, this Docker Compose configuration sets up a PostgreSQL database container and a pgAdmin container, providing a convenient way to manage and interact with the PostgreSQL database using a web-based interface. To run your docker-compose file, just navigate to the folder of it and type docker-compose up -d from the terminal.

Instead of directly adding credentials/values to the docker-compose file, we can specify it from a .env file (we have already talked about this file), and Docker can read the required data from environment variables. Just create a .env file inside your main folder (it is the transactionservice folder for us) and add the missing configuration for Docker to run successfully:

```
# PostgreSQL settings
POSTGRES_USER=postgres
POSTGRES_PASSWORD=postgres
POSTGRES_DB=tservice_db
POSTGRES_PORT=5438
```

```
# pgAdmin settings
PGADMIN_DEFAULT_EMAIL=admin@tservice.com
PGADMIN_DEFAULT_PASSWORD=tservice_password
PGADMIN_PORT=5050
```

We now have our PostgreSQL database up and running. In most cases, developers prefer not to directly interact with databases using SQL queries. Not all developers have a solid understanding of SQL, and even so, using pure SQL queries to manipulate to database in most cases is not a good choice nowadays. Instead, we have various packages available that abstract away the complexity of raw SQL, enabling us to create beautiful applications without needing deep expertise in SQL. One of these packages is Prisma. As we mentioned before, Prisma is an open source ORM that automates and abstracts most of the operations you need to do when you deal with a database.

To start work with Prisma, we need a *CLI*. Prisma CLI is a combination of tools that help us migrate, seed, and do additional database-oriented operations easily. You just need to run the `npm install prisma -D` command from the terminal. After executing the command, npm should successfully install Prisma CLI as a dev dependency. You can check `package.json`'s `devDependencies` section.

After Prisma CLI, it is time to install Prisma itself. The `npx prisma init` command handles the initialization of the Prisma package. It will create an additional folder called `prisma` with a `schema.prisma` file and a `.env` file. In our case, we already have a `.env` file, so running the preceding command will end up updating our existing `.env` file. Open your `.env` file, and at the end of the file, update the value of `DATABASE_URL`:

```
DATABASE_URL="postgres://postgres:postgres@localhost:5438/tservice_db"
```

At the heart of your Prisma setup lies the `schema.prisma` file. This file uses **Prisma Schema Language** (**PSL**), a declarative approach to defining your database structure. It acts as the central configuration for Prisma, specifying both your database connection and the generation of the Prisma Client API. The following code demonstrates how to define a simple schema file for Prisma:

```
generator client {
  provider = "prisma-client-js"
}
datasource db {
  provider = "postgresql"
  url      = env("DATABASE_URL")
}
```

The `schema.prisma` file, written in PSL, acts as your database blueprint with three key sections:

- `generator`: This section configures the Prisma Client generator. The Prisma Client, a powerful API, is then generated to help you access your database.

- `datasource`: Here, you define the database connection details. This includes the database provider and the connection string, often leveraging the `DATABASE_URL` environment variable for convenience.

- `Model`: This is where the heart of your database schema lies. You define the structure of your data by specifying tables and their corresponding fields.

The next section describes how to model your data inside the `schema.prisma` file.

Modeling the data

The `schema.prisma` file is the main place where we need to add our models. Modeling is a special language over SQL. It isolates you from the internals of SQL and provides data in a more human-readable language.

Open the `schema.prisma` file under the `prisma` folder and add the following model structure:

```
model Transaction {
  id           Int        @id @default(autoincrement())
  status       Status
  accountId    String     @default(uuid())
  description  String?
  createdAt    DateTime @default(now())
  updatedAt    DateTime @updatedAt
}
enum Status {
  CREATED
  SETTLED
  FAILED
}
```

The provided code defines a Prisma model named `Transaction` and an enum named `Status` within your NestJS application schema.

Here's a breakdown of each section:

- `id`: This field represents the unique identifier for each transaction. It's of type `Int` and is automatically marked as the primary key with the `@id` directive. Additionally, `@ default(autoincrement())` ensures a new, unique ID is generated for each transaction automatically.

- `status`: This field defines the current state of the transaction. It's of type `Status`, which will reference `Status Enumeration(enum Status)`.

- `accountId`: This field stores the identifier for the associated account involved in the transaction. It's of type `String` and uses `@default(uuid())` to generate a **universally unique identifier** (**UUID**) by default.

- `description`: This optional field allows for storing a brief description of the transaction. It's of type `String?`, indicating it can be `null`.

- `createdAt`: This field captures the timestamp of when the transaction was created. It's of type `DateTime` and uses `@default(now())` to automatically set the creation time to the current moment.

- `updatedAt`: This field is automatically updated whenever the transaction record is modified. It's of type `DateTime` and uses the `@updatedAt` directive to achieve this behavior.

OK – but how to generate SQL based on the model we defined in `schema.prisma`?

Run `npx prisma migrate dev --name init` from the command line (VS Code terminal) to start the migration journey. In the context of NestJS and Prisma, **migration** refers to a process that manages changes to your database schema over time.

Here is a breakdown of the command:

- `npx prisma migrate dev`: This command invokes the Prisma migration tool in development mode.

- `--name init`: This option specifies the name of the new migration. Here, it's set to `init`, likely signifying the initial setup of your database schema.

By running this command, you're essentially creating a starting point for managing your database schema changes using Prisma migrations. As you make modifications to your `schema.prisma` file, Prisma will automatically generate new migrations to reflect those changes.

The command will end up creating a `migrations` folder with a `migration.sql` file (*Figure 6.6*):

```
Applying migration `20240509180043_init`

The following migration(s) have been created and applied from new schema changes:

migrations/
  └ 20240509180043_init/
    └ migration.sql
```

Figure 6.6: Automatically generated migration structure

Check the generated `migration.sql` file:

```sql
-- CreateEnum
CREATE TYPE "Status" AS ENUM ('CREATED', 'SETTLED', 'FAILED');

-- CreateTable
CREATE TABLE "Transaction" (
    "id" SERIAL NOT NULL,
    "status" "Status" NOT NULL,
    "accountId" TEXT NOT NULL,
    "description" TEXT,
    "createdAt" TIMESTAMP(3) NOT NULL DEFAULT CURRENT_TIMESTAMP,
    "updatedAt" TIMESTAMP(3) NOT NULL,

    CONSTRAINT "Transaction_pkey" PRIMARY KEY ("id")
);
```

Now, you should have tables with the name `Transaction` and `_prisma_migrations` in your database. It may take a few seconds for Docker to set up the services, so a brief wait might be necessary. To check this, let's do the following operations:

1. Open Docker Desktop and ensure all services are running.
2. Click on the `postgres` container.
3. From the **Inspect** tab, find the IP address of the container (in our case, it is `172.26.0.2`):
4. Navigate to `http://localhost:5050/browser/` from your browser.
5. Right-click on **Servers**, then select **Register | Server** from the menu.
6. Under the **General** tab, type any name you want for **Name**. We have specified `localhost` for its value.
7. Go to the **Connection** tab and fill in the inputs (*Figure 6.7*):

    - **Host name/address**: The IP address you just took (it is `172.26.0.2` for us)
    - **Port**: `5432`
    - **Maintenance database**: `tservice_db`
    - **Username**: `postgres`
    - **Password**: `postgres`

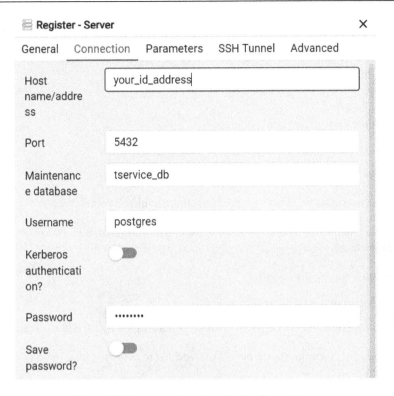

Figure 6.7: Server registration window for postgres

8. Click the **Save** button, and your server connection should be successful.

9. Now, expand `localhost` (or your name) | **Databases** | `tservice_db` | **Schemas** | **Public** | **Tables** (*Figure 6.8*):

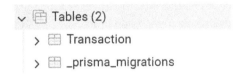

Figure 6.8: postgres tables after migration via Prisma

10. If you have locally installed `pgAdmin`, to connect to your Docker `postgres` instance, just enter the following to the server registration window for `postgres` (*Figure 6.7*):

- **Host name/address**: `localhost`

- **Port**: `5438`

- **Maintenance database**: `tservice_db`

- **Username**: `postgres`

- **Password**: `postgres`

11. Click the **Save** button, and your server connection should be successful.

The `_prisma_migrations` table you see when using NestJS and Prisma ORM plays a crucial role in managing database schema changes. It has the following responsibilities:

- Tracks applied database migrations

- Ensures migrations are applied only once

- Maintains consistency between your Prisma schema and the actual database structure

Each time you run a Prisma migration, a new entry is added to the `_prisma_migrations` table.

When Prisma needs to apply migrations, it checks the `_prisma_migrations` table to see which migrations have already been run based on the unique hash.

This prevents applying the same migration multiple times, potentially corrupting your data.

Modifying the `_prisma_migrations` table manually can lead to inconsistencies and errors. Don't edit, delete, or modify it. This table is essential for Prisma to manage migrations effectively.

Long story short, the `_prisma_migrations` table acts as a logbook for your database schema changes, ensuring a smooth and controlled migration process.

Seeding test data

Seeding data involves populating your database with an initial set of data. If you want your database to have initial data before running your application, you may apply seeding.

Add a seed.ts file under the prisma folder with the following content:

```
// prisma/seed.ts
import { PrismaClient } from '@prisma/client';

// initialize Prisma Client
const prismaClient = new PrismaClient();

async function seedData() {
  // create two dummy recipes
  const first_transaction = await
    prismaClient.transaction.upsert({
    where: { id:1 },
    update: {},
    create: {
      id:1,
      status: 'CREATED',
      accountId: '662c081370bd2ba6b5f04e94',
      description: 'simple transaction',
    }
  });
  console.log(first_transaction);
}

// execute the seed function
seedData()
  .catch(e => {
    console.error(e);
    process.exit(1);
  })
  .finally(async () => {
    // close Prisma Client at the end
    await prismaClient.$disconnect();
  });
```

Go to package.json and add the following after devDependencies:

```
"prisma": {
    "seed": "ts-node prisma/seed.ts"
  }
```

Now, open the terminal window and type the `npx prisma db seed` command. You should see a message that indicates a successful operation (*Figure 6.9*):

```
Environment variables loaded from .env
Running seed command `ts-node prisma/seed.ts` ...
{
  id: 1,
  status: 'CREATED',
  accountId: '662c081370bd2ba6b5f04e94',
  description: 'simple transaction',
  createdAt: 2024-05-10T08:43:41.389Z,
  updatedAt: 2024-05-10T08:43:41.389Z
}

The seed command has been executed.
```

Figure 6.9: Executing seed

Open the `Transaction` table using `PgAdmin`, and you'll see your first successfully inserted row (*Figure 6.10*):

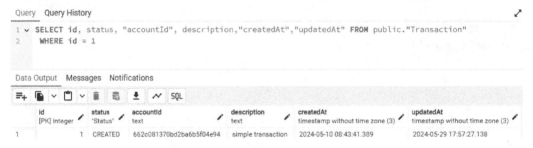

Figure 6.10: Transaction table after seed

It is time to explain what we have inserted into our `seed.ts` file:

- `PrismaClient from @prisma/client`: This line imports the necessary class to interact with our database schema using Prisma.

- `const prismaClient = new PrismaClient()`: Here, we create an instance of the `PrismaClient` class, which will be used to perform database operations.

- `async function seedData() { ... }`: This function is the heart of the script and is marked `async` because it includes asynchronous operations that involve interacting with the database.

- `const first_transaction = await prismaClient.transaction.upsert({ ... })`: This line performs the core seeding operation.

- `prismaClient.transaction`: This part accesses the transaction model of your Prisma schema through the initialized client.

- `.upsert({ ... })`: The upsert method is a convenient way to create or update a record in the database. It checks for existing data based on the provided `where` clause and performs the appropriate action.

- If a record with `id: 1` (assuming your schema has an ID field) already exists, the following happens:

  - The `update` object (empty here) would be used to update the existing record (but since it's empty, no update happens) if a record with `id: 1` exists.

  - The `create` object defines the data for the new transaction record if a record with an ID doesn't exist.

    - `create Object (Seed Data)`: This object defines the details of the dummy transaction to be created.

    - `id: 1`: Sets the ID of the transaction to 1 (replace with a unique value if needed).

    - `status: 'CREATED'`: Sets the initial status of the transaction to CREATED.

    - `accountId: '662c081370bd2ba6b5f04e94'`: Assigns an account ID to the transaction (you can use any ID).

    - `description: 'simple transaction'`: Provides a descriptive text for the transaction.

To apply business rules to our application, we need to add an extra layer over a database, and it is going to be our service layer. The next section will introduce a service layer for the transaction database.

Implementing the transaction service

We are done with the database. As a classical development style, it is time to create a service over our database. Creating a service layer is simple with NestJS, especially if you deal with Prisma ORM.

First, let's create our module using the `npx nest generate module prisma` command.

This Prisma CLI command should generate a new folder called `prisma` and should generate a `prisma.module.ts` file under this folder. This command also will affect your `app.module.js` file under the `src` folder.

We need one more command to run to generate our service files:

```
Npx nest generate service prisma
```

This command will create `prisma.service.ts, prisma.service.spec.ts` files under `src/prisma` and update the `prisma.module.ts` file.

For this chapter, you can remove all files that have `.spec.ts` extensions from the project. These files contain unit tests for the application's components, typically services and controllers. We have a separate chapter to work with unit tests; for the chapter's simplicity, we don't need them. For now, replace the content of `prisma.service.ts` with the following:

```
import { Injectable } from '@nestjs/common';
import { PrismaClient } from '@prisma/client';


@Injectable()
export class PrismaService extends PrismaClient {}
```

In this code, we have a straightforward implementation for the `prisma` service:

- `import { Injectable } from '@nestjs/common';`: This line imports the `Injectable` decorator from the `@nestjs/common` module. This decorator marks the class as a NestJS injectable service, making it available for **dependency injection (DI)** in other parts of your application.

- `import { PrismaClient } from '@prisma/client';`: This line imports the `PrismaClient` class from the `@prisma/client` package. This class provides an interface for interacting with your database using Prisma queries.

- `@Injectable()`: This decorator applied to the class declaration marks it as a NestJS injectable service. NestJS will manage the lifecycle of this service and provide it to other components that require database access.

- `export class PrismaService extends PrismaClient {}`: This line defines the `PrismaService` class. It inherits from the `PrismaClient` class, giving it access to all the database interaction methods provided by Prisma.

In essence, this code creates a service specifically for interacting with our database through Prisma. This service can then be injected into other parts of our application (such as controllers) to perform database operations.

The `prisma.service.ts` file acts as a wrapper over the Prisma client. It is an injectable element that we can use to inject it into modules.

Let's update our `prisma.module.ts` file to have the following content:

```
import { Module } from '@nestjs/common';
import { PrismaService } from './prisma.service';

@Module({
  providers: [PrismaService],
  exports: [PrismaService]
})
export class PrismaModule {}
```

To make the Prisma service accessible throughout your NestJS application, you'll need to create a dedicated module. This module will import the `PrismaService` class and provide it for injection into other modules or components. That is the reason why we have a `prisma.module.ts` file.

Nowadays, it is popular to use a UI for APIs, and it allows us to document and easily use endpoints. One of the packages that allows us to do it is Swagger. The next section explains how to integrate Swagger for our endpoints.

Configuring Swagger

To have visible documentation and visual usage for our APIs, we will configure Swagger UI.

Open the VS Code terminal and type the following:

```
npm install --save @nestjs/swagger swagger-ui-express
```

Open `src/main.ts` and update its content with the following to integrate Swagger:

```typescript
import { NestFactory } from '@nestjs/core';
import { AppModule } from './app.module';
import { SwaggerModule, DocumentBuilder } from '@nestjs/swagger';

// bootstrap function
async function bootstrap() {
  // Create a NestJS application instance
  const app = await NestFactory.create(AppModule);

  // new Swagger document configuration
  const config = new DocumentBuilder()
    .setTitle('Transaction API') // title of the API
    .setDescription('Transaction API description')
    // description of the API
    .setVersion('1.0') // version of the API
    .build(); // Build the document

  // Create a Swagger document
  const document = SwaggerModule.createDocument(app,
    config);

  // Setup Swagger module
  SwaggerModule.setup('api', app, document);
  // Start the application and listen for requests on port 3000
  await app.listen(3000);
}
```

```
// Call the bootstrap function to start the application
bootstrap();
```

Let's understand this code here:

- `NestFactory` from `@nestjs/core`: This import provides the core functionality for creating a NestJS application instance.

- `AppModule` from `./app.module`: This imports your main application module, where all the necessary components and services of your NestJS application are defined.

- `SwaggerModule` and `DocumentBuilder` from `@nestjs/swagger`: These imports are used for integrating Swagger documentation with your NestJS application.

- Bootstrap function (`async`):

  - This function is marked as `async` because it involves asynchronous operations such as creating an application instance and listening for incoming requests.

  - It serves as the entry point for your NestJS application and is typically called at the bottom of your `main.ts` file.

- `const app = await NestFactory.create(AppModule);`: This line creates a new NestJS application instance using the `AppModule` class. The `await` keyword signifies that the function will wait for the application creation to complete before proceeding.

- Swagger configuration:

  - `const config = new DocumentBuilder()...`: Here, you're configuring the Swagger documentation using the `DocumentBuilder` class.

  - `.setTitle('Transaction API')`: Sets the title of your API documentation to `Transaction API`.

  - `.setDescription('Transaction API description')`: Provides a brief description of your API.

  - `.setVersion('1.0')`: Sets the version of your API to `1.0`.

  - `.build()`: Builds the Swagger document based on the provided configuration options.

- `const document = SwaggerModule.createDocument(app, config);`: This line generates the actual Swagger document using the `SwaggerModule` class. It takes the NestJS application instance (`app`) and the built configuration (`config`) as arguments.

- `SwaggerModule.setup('api', app, document);`: This code integrates the Swagger documentation with your application. It sets the path prefix for the documentation to `api` (for example, `http://localhost:3000/api`) and associates the generated document (`document`) with the application (`app`). This allows developers to access the interactive Swagger documentation at the specified URL.

- `await app.listen(3000);`: This line starts the NestJS application and makes it listen for incoming requests on port `3000`. You can change this port number to your desired option.

Overall, this `main.ts` file performs two crucial tasks:

- **Boots up the NestJS application**: It establishes an instance using your `AppModule` class and starts the server listening for requests

- **Integrates Swagger documentation**: It configures and provides Swagger documentation for your API, allowing developers to explore your API endpoints, understand data models, and interact with your API using the interactive interface

Navigate to `localhost:3000/api`, and you should see the Swagger page (*Figure 6.11*):

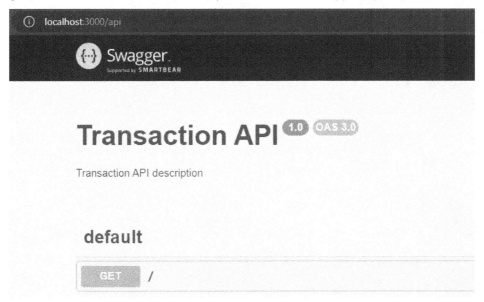

Figure 6.11: Swagger UI

As you'll realize, we don't have any endpoints yet; the next section talks about creating them.

Working on transaction implementation

To start to work with transactions, first, we need to generate resources. To implement **create, read, update, and delete** (**CRUD**) operations for transactions, we'll first generate REST resources, creating boilerplate code for the module, controller, service, and **Data Transfer Object** (**DTO**).

Run the `npx nest generate resource transaction` command to generate resources for a transaction:

```
? What transport layer do you use? (Use arrow keys)
> REST API
  GraphQL (code first)
  GraphQL (schema first)
  Microservice (non-HTTP)
  WebSockets
```

Figure 6.12: Selecting a transport layer

It will ask you which transport layer to choose (*Figure 6.12*). Select REST API and hit *Enter*. As the next question, you will be asked `Would you like to generate CRUD entry points?`. Select Y, and the following files should be generated (*Figure 6.13*):

```
? Would you like to generate CRUD entry points? Yes
CREATE src/transaction/transaction.controller.ts (1064 bytes)
CREATE src/transaction/transaction.controller.spec.ts (646 bytes)
CREATE src/transaction/transaction.module.ts (299 bytes)
CREATE src/transaction/transaction.service.ts (731 bytes)
CREATE src/transaction/transaction.service.spec.ts (513 bytes)
CREATE src/transaction/dto/create-transaction.dto.ts (38 bytes)
CREATE src/transaction/dto/update-transaction.dto.ts (196 bytes)
CREATE src/transaction/entities/transaction.entity.ts (29 bytes)
UPDATE src/app.module.ts (556 bytes)
```

Figure 6.13: CRUD generation for transaction

Run `npm run start:dev` and navigate to `localhost:3000/api`. You should get a page that stores transaction boilerplate endpoints (*Figure 6.14*):

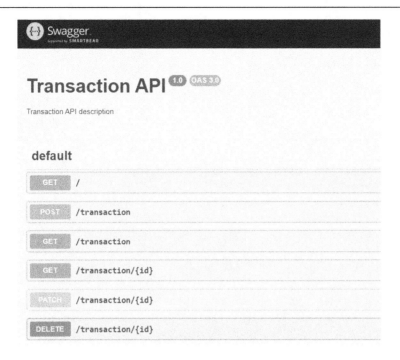

Figure 6.14: Swagger UI for transaction

Of course, we don't need to implement all these CRUD endpoints. We need the following functions:

- Get all transactions (`GET /transaction`)
- Get transaction by ID (`GET /transaction/{id}`)
- Create transaction (`POST /transaction`)

Let's remove the rest of the unused code blocks and files.

Remove the following files:

- `transaction/transaction.controller.spec.ts`
- `transaction/dto/update-transaction.dto.ts`
- `transaction/transaction.service.spec.ts`

Remove the following code blocks:

- `remove` and `update` functions from `transaction.service.ts`
- `remove` and `update` functions from `transaction.controller.ts`

If you haven't removed them yet, remove the following files too:

- `app.controller.ts`

- `app.module.ts`

- `app.service.ts`

Update `main.ts` to work with `TransactionModule`, not `AppModule`:

```
import { NestFactory } from '@nestjs/core';
import { TransactionModule } from
  './transaction/transaction.module';
import { SwaggerModule, DocumentBuilder } from
  '@nestjs/swagger';

// bootstrap function
async function bootstrap() {
  // Create a NestJS application instance
  const app = await NestFactory.create(TransactionModule);
.......
```

You'll end up with three endpoints (*Figure 6.15*):

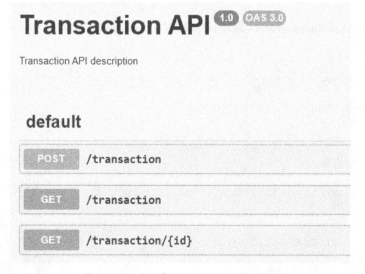

Figure 6.15: Final transaction endpoints

After having generated REST resources, we're ready to integrate our `PrismaClient` class. Having this client will help us to interact with the database easily. First, let's update our `transaction.module.ts` file to have `PrismaModule`:

```
import { Module } from '@nestjs/common';
import { TransactionService } from './transaction.service';
import { TransactionController } from
  './transaction.controller';
import { PrismaModule } from '../prisma/prisma.module';

@Module({
  imports: [PrismaModule],
  controllers: [TransactionController],
  providers: [TransactionService],
})
export class TransactionModule {}
```

Having `PrismaModule` in the `imports` array will make `PrismaService` available to `TransactionService`.

Now, open the `transaction.service.ts` file and make the following changes:

```
import { Injectable } from '@nestjs/common';
import { CreateTransactionDto } from
  './dto/create-transaction.dto';
import { PrismaService } from 'src/prisma/prisma.service';
@Injectable()
export class TransactionService {
  constructor(private readonly prisma: PrismaService) {}
.......
```

The transaction controller file (`transaction.controller.ts`) already has `transactionservice` as an injected service. It has all the required contracts to request the transaction service and retrieve data.

Open `transaction.controller.ts` and have a look at the `findAll()` method:

```
@Get()
  findAll() {
    return this.transactionService.findAll();
  }
```

The same applies to POST and the single GET request. The only thing we need to do is to call Prisma to provide all the data when we call transactionservice's findAll() method. For that reason, open transaction.service.ts and update the findAll() method content (*Figure 6.14*):

```
findAll() {
    return this.prisma.transaction.findMany();
}
```

Using findMany(), we're able to call all transaction data from the transaction table via Prisma. Let's run our application (run npm run start:dev) and run our endpoint from Swagger UI.

Open GET /transaction from Swagger UI, click the **Try it out** button, and click the **Execute** button. Now, you should see only the data we migrated to our database when we talked about seeding data (*Figure 6.16*):

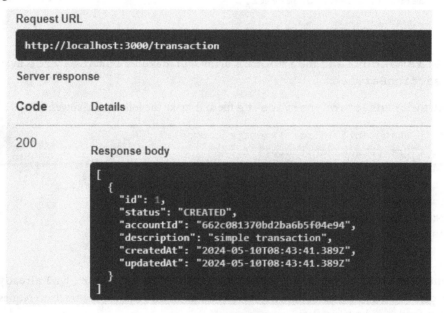

Figure 6.16: Response for "Get all transactions"

To modify your GET request by ID endpoint for it to work properly, open transaction.service.ts and replace the findOne() method with the following:

```
findOne(id: number) {
    return this.prisma.transaction.findUnique({
      where: { id },
    });
}
```

Everything is really simple when it comes to retrieving data, but how about creating it?

We have a POST endpoint in `transaction.controller.ts` that was automatically generated when we generated the file itself:

```
@Post()
  create(@Body() createTransactionDto:
    CreateTransactionDto) {
      return
      this.transactionService.create(createTransactionDto);
    }
```

When our resources were created, `CreateTransactionDTO` was also generated; you can find it inside the `src/transaction/dto` folder. Surprisingly, it has only one class declaration:

```
export class CreateTransactionDto {}
```

You should manually add the required properties into the class. Our DTOs just transfer data from the source to the destination. DTOs are used in various programming languages and frameworks, not specific to NestJS. They act as a way to efficiently transfer data between different layers of an application. We also have a validation possibility before getting data from the user and creating DTOs based on this data. That is why we will use the `class-validator` package to validate our data. To install it, run the following command from the terminal:

```
npm install class-validator
```

Open `create-transaction.dto.ts` and add the following content:

```
import { IsString, IsOptional, IsEnum, IsNotEmpty,IsUUID }
  from 'class-validator';

enum Status {
    CREATED = 'CREATED',
      SETTLED= 'SETTLED',
    FAILED = 'FAILED',
    }

export class CreateTransactionDto {
  @IsNotEmpty()
  @IsEnum(Status)
  status: Status;

  @IsUUID()
  @IsNotEmpty()
  accountID: string;
```

```
    @IsOptional()
    @IsString()
    description?: string;
}
```

Update your POST method (`transaction.controller.ts`) to accept `CreateTransactionDTO` and execute it:

```
@Post()
  create(@Body() createTransactionDto:
    CreateTransactionDto) {
      return
      this.transactionService.create(createTransactionDto);
    }
```

Now, let's run our application. From Swagger UI, open POST/ `transaction` and provide the following JSON payload:

```
{
  "status": "CREATED",
  "accountId": "662c081370bd2ba6b5f04e94",
  "description": "Optional transaction description"
}
```

Click the **Execute** button, and here we are (*Figure 6.17*):

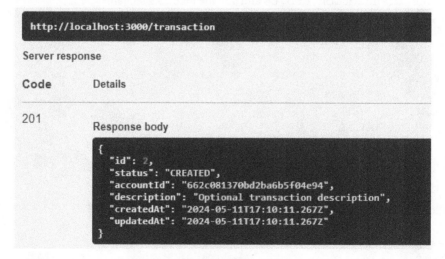

Figure 6.17: Successful transaction creation

Starting from the next section, we will explore how to establish communication between the transaction and account microservices.

Establishing synchronous communication with the account microservice

We're done with the transaction service, but the only thing missing is our account service. The transaction service allows us to specify an `accountId` value and status from the payload. We need to make the following changes:

- Verify if the provided `accountId` exists and is in a valid state (new or active)
- If `accountId` is valid, then create a transaction with the `Created` status
- If `accountId` is invalid, then create a transaction with the `Failed` status

The purpose here is not to fully implement the transaction domain. Of course, the current domain has more requirements than the previous one, but our focus is to practice and establish synchronous communication between the transaction and account services.

We have already talked about the pros and cons of synchronous communication between microservices. While asynchronous communication offers many benefits for microservices, there are situations where synchronous communication might be a better fit. If the interaction between microservices requires straightforward logic and an immediate response, synchronous communication can be easier to implement. Also, it is beneficial to use it for user interactions where you need to display information or confirm an action right away. It creates tight coupling, but in some cases, microservices might be tightly coupled and rely heavily on each other's results to complete a task. Synchronous communication allows for a more controlled flow, ensuring one service doesn't proceed until the other provides the necessary information. Synchronous communication can be easier to debug at times. Since the entire interaction happens in one go, tracing errors and understanding the flow of data is more straightforward. This can be helpful during development or troubleshooting specific issues.

To communicate with the account service, we need an HTTP client package. One of the most used packages is `axios`. Let's install it using npm:

```
npm i --save @nestjs/axios axios
```

Now, we need to import `HttpModule` from `axios` and import it from `transaction.module.ts`. Here is the final code in this file:

```
import { Module } from '@nestjs/common';
import { TransactionService } from './transaction.service';
import { TransactionController } from
  './transaction.controller';
import { PrismaModule } from '../prisma/prisma.module';
```

```
import { HttpModule } from '@nestjs/axios';

@Module({
  imports: [PrismaModule,HttpModule],
  controllers: [TransactionController],
  providers: [TransactionService],
})
export class TransactionModule {}
```

After importing `HttpModule` from `transaction.module.ts`, we're able to use `HttpService` from axios in `transaction.service.ts`. Let's import and inject it as a service for the transaction service. Open `transaction.service.ts` and change the code to have the following lines:

```
import { Injectable } from '@nestjs/common';
import { CreateTransactionDto } from
  './dto/create-transaction.dto';
import { PrismaService } from 'src/prisma/prisma.service';
import { HttpService } from '@nestjs/axios';
import { AccountApiResponse } from './dto/account.dto';

@Injectable()
export class TransactionService {
  constructor(
    private readonly prisma: PrismaService,
    private readonly httpService: HttpService) {}
//the rest of the code
```

As our business requires, we need to remove the status property from `createTransactionDto` because, depending on the account service, we should internally define the status of the transaction. That is why we're going to remove the status from `src/transaction/dto/create-transaction.dto`. The following is the final version of this file:

```
import { IsString, IsOptional, IsNotEmpty,IsUUID } from
  'class-validator';
export class CreateTransactionDto {
  @IsUUID()
  @IsNotEmpty()
  accountId: string;

  @IsOptional()
  @IsString()
  description?: string;
}
```

Great! Now, let's open our `transaction.service.ts` file again and change our *create* functionality. After injecting `httpService`, we should be able to make a request to any service and get a response back.

Here is what we plan to do:

- Make a request to the account service's `http://url/v1/accounts/{account_id}` endpoint and account information based on the provided ID from the endpoint
- If the given account by `accountId` doesn't exist, we throw an exception
- If the account exists, and its status is either `'new'` or `'active'`, then the transaction should be created with a `'CREATED'` status
- If the account exists, and its status is neither `'new'` nor `'active'`, we should create a transaction with a `'FAILED'` status

That is simply it. Open `transaction.service.ts` and update it with the following code lines:

```
import { Injectable } from '@nestjs/common';
import { CreateTransactionDto } from
  './dto/create-transaction.dto';
import { PrismaService } from 'src/prisma/prisma.service';
import { HttpService } from '@nestjs/axios';
import { AccountApiResponse } from './dto/account.dto';

@Injectable()
export class TransactionService {
  constructor(
    private readonly prisma: PrismaService,
    private readonly httpService: HttpService,
  ) {}

 async create(createTransactionDto: CreateTransactionDto) {
  const { accountId, description } = createTransactionDto;

  let accountApiResponse = await
    this.httpService.axiosRef.get<AccountApiResponse>(
      `http://localhost:3001/v1/accounts/${createTransactionDto.
accountId}`,
      );
    const {account} = accountApiResponse.data;
    if (!account) {
    throw new Error('Transaction creation failed: Account
      not found');
  }
    if(account.status == 'new' || account.status ==
```

```
        'active')
        {
          return this.prisma.transaction.create({
            data: { accountId, description, status:
              'CREATED' },
          });
        }
        else
        {
          return this.prisma.transaction.create({
            data: { accountId, description, status:
              'FAILED' },
          });
        }
    }
//rest of the functionalities
}
```

The last thing we need to do is to configure **cross-origin resource sharing (CORS)** in the account service. Follow the next steps:

1. Open your account service from VS Code.

2. From the menu, select **Terminal | New Terminal**.

3. Navigate to the src folder.

4. Execute npm install cors to install the cors package.

5. Open app.js and add the following code after the app object is created:

```
const corsOptions = {
    origin: 'http://localhost:3001', //(https://your-client-app.
com)
    optionsSuccessStatus: 200,
};
app.use(cors(corsOptions));
```

The final code in app.js should look like this:

```
const express = require('express');
const v1 = require('./routes/v1');
const cors = require('cors');

const app = express();

//added while implementing transaction service, for Ch06
```

```
const corsOptions = {
    origin: 'http://localhost:3001', //(https://your-client-app.com)
    optionsSuccessStatus: 200,
};

app.use(cors(corsOptions));
// service
app.use(express.json());

// V1 API
app.use('/v1', v1);

module.exports = app;
```

Before running our application, make sure of the following:

- Your account service lives in `localhost:3001`
- The account service has at least one piece of valid account information in your table
- Make sure that Docker is running and the `postgres` container is active

Go to our account service and run it (for more details, check *Chapter 5*). Run our newly created transaction service using `npm run start:dev`. Open your favorite browser, and navigate to `http://localhost:3000/api`. Open `POST /transaction` and add the following payload:

```
{
"accountId": "663fd142ecbdce73baf1ed1a",
 "description": "Optional transaction description"
}
```

The `accountId` value you provided from the payload should exist in the account service to have a successful operation. In the case of a successful request, you will get the following response:

```
{
  "id": {your_transaction_id},
  "status": "CREATED",
  "accountId": "663fd142ecbdce73baf1ed1a",
  "description": "Optional transaction description",
  "createdAt": "2024-05-12T17:21:38.727Z",
  "updatedAt": "2024-05-12T17:21:38.727Z"
}
```

If the service is not available and the account doesn't exist, you will get errors. We didn't cover exception handling in this chapter, but we'll learn about it in our upcoming chapters.

Summary

Another microservice journey ends here. The main points in this chapter were creating a second microservice and establishing synchronous communication between microservices. We started our chapter with business requirements. After getting a clear understanding of what we should do, we started to introduce main stack tools to develop our transaction microservice. We didn't use the tools we used before to develop our account service. JavaScript has really rich tools and frameworks to use when it comes to developing microservices. To demonstrate the beauty of having multiple tools, we used NestJS with some popular packages such as Prisma and Axios. In the end, we established communication with an already existing microservice (the account microservice) using a synchronous communication model. Of course, we still missed out a lot. We didn't cover exception handling, resiliency, and a lot of other interesting topics that we plan to introduce in our upcoming chapters.

Chapter 7 explores how to implement asynchronous communication in JavaScript microservices using Apache Kafka and NestJS, focusing on building scalable systems, configuring Kafka, and adapting services like transaction and account services for asynchronous messaging.

7

Asynchronous Microservices

Microservices are designed to be independent and self-contained. Clearly defined communication protocols and APIs ensure these services interact without relying on each other's internal workings. Defining proper communication between microservices is important for a well-functioning microservices architecture.

In this chapter, we plan to discuss and learn about another important communication mechanism: asynchronous communication between microservices.

This chapter covers the following topics:

- Understanding the requirements
- Exploring asynchronous communication
- Implementing an asynchronous transaction microservice
- Adapting an account service to new requirements
- Testing our microservices together

Let's get into it!

Technical requirements

To follow along with the chapter, you'll need an IDE (we prefer Visual Studio Code), Postman, Docker, and a browser of your choice.

It is preferable to download the repository from `https://github.com/PacktPublishing/Hands-on-Microservices-with-JavaScript` and open the `Ch07` folder to easily follow the code snippets.

Understanding the requirements

Up until now, we have developed two simple microservices and for the current chapter we plan to extend our transaction microservice to meet the following requirements:

- Every transaction should support the following statuses: CREATED, FAILED, APPROVED, DECLINED, and FRAUD.

- The transaction service should now have a new method that changes the status of the given transaction to FRAUD. It will update the status of the transaction to FRAUD and produce a message about the transaction.

- The account service will consume this message and after *three* fraudulent attempts, the account service should read and suspend/block the given account.

We plan to use asynchronous communication between microservices and any other microservice may use this message for internal purposes. You can check *Chapter 2* for more information about asynchronous communication between microservices.

Exploring asynchronous communication

You can implement asynchronous communication between microservices using various patterns and technologies, each suitable for different use cases and requirements. Here are some of the common ones:

- **Message brokers**: Message brokers facilitate asynchronous communication by allowing microservices to publish and subscribe to messages. Popular message brokers include **RabbitMQ**, which supports multiple messaging protocols and patterns such as pub/sub and routing, and **Apache Kafka**, designed for high-throughput and fault-tolerant event streaming – one of the best choices for real-time data processing. An example of a message broker would be a producer service sending a message to a queue or topic and the consumer service subscribing to the queue or topic and processing messages.

- **Event streaming platforms**: Event streaming platforms capture and process streams of events. These platforms are particularly useful for real-time analytics and data pipeline construction. Popular event streaming platforms include **Apache Kafka**, which is often used as both a message broker and an event streaming platform, and **Amazon Kinesis**, a managed service for real-time data processing at scale. Here is an example: a producer service emits events to a Kafka topic and consumer services consume events from the topic and react to them.

- **The Publish-Subscribe pattern**: In the pub/sub pattern, messages are published to a topic and multiple subscribers can consume these messages asynchronously. Popular services that use the pub/sub pattern include **Google Pub/Sub**, a fully managed real-time messaging service, and **AWS Simple Notification Service** (**SNS**), which allows publishing messages to multiple subscribers. For example, a publisher service publishes an event to a topic and the subscriber services receive notifications and process the event.

- **Task queues**: Task queues are used to distribute tasks to worker services asynchronously. This is useful for offloading heavy or time-consuming tasks from the main service. Some of the more popular task queues are **Celery**, an asynchronous task queue/job queue based on distributed message passing, and **Amazon Simple Queue Service (SQS)**, a fully managed message queue service. Here's how a task queue works: a producer service creates a task and places it in the queue and the worker service picks up the task from the queue and processes it.

- **Event-driven architecture**: In an event-driven architecture, services communicate through events. When something notable happens in one service, it emits an event that other services can listen to and act upon. In event-driven architecture an event source service publishes an event, and the event listener services react to the event and execute their logic.

- **WebSockets**: WebSockets allow for full-duplex communication channels over a single TCP connection, useful for real-time applications such as chat apps or live updates. Here's an example: the server pushes updates to clients via WebSockets and clients receive updates in real time and act upon them.

- **Server-Sent Events (SSE)**: SSE is a server push technology enabling servers to push real-time updates to the client once an initial client connection is established. Let's take an example: the server sends events to clients over an HTTP connection and clients listen to incoming messages and process them.

- **gRPC with streaming**: gRPC supports bidirectional streaming, allowing both client and server to send a sequence of messages using a single connection. gRPC works like this: the client and server can continuously exchange streams of messages as part of a single RPC call.

For this chapter, we will actively use Apache Kafka, an open source, high-performance event streaming platform. It is a popular choice for asynchronous communication between microservices due to its strengths in enabling a robust and scalable event-driven architecture. While we have already talked about how to run services via Docker, this chapter will focus on hosting Apache Kafka on Docker.

Let's take a quick look at the problems that Apache Kafka solves:

- **Communication complexity**: In a microservice environment, you have *multiple sources* (every API acts as a source) and *multiple targets* (every API can have multiple sources to write to). The fact that sources and targets are scaled is always accompanied by a communication problem. In this case, the problem is that we should solve the complexities created by the source and target rather than focus on business requirement implementations. Now you have multiple sources and targets, which can create the following issues:

  - Every target requires a different protocol to communicate.

  - Every target has its data format to work with.

  - Every different target requires maintenance and support.

In simple terms, say you have a microservice application, and every service has its own target. Besides that, every service can have multiple sources, and the services can use common sources. Apache Kafka helps you to avoid complex communication between microservices.

- **Communication complexity duplication**: Whenever similar systems are developed; we have to rewrite such communication processes again and again. Let's imagine that we are working on several different projects. Although the domain of these projects is different, and although they solve different problems at an abstract level, the common aspect of these projects is communication complexity. So, it means we're repeating ourselves and trying to resolve the same issue every time.

- **Fault tolerance**: The system should be able to continue functioning and provide reliable data processing and message delivery even in the presence of various types of failures, such as hardware failures, network issues, or software crashes.

- **High performance**: In most cases, such a communication problem (sources - targets) causes the application performance to drop. Regardless of dynamic changes in the number of targets and sources in the application, the program should always support the high-performance attribute.

- **Scalability**: The system should be possible to horizontally scale sources and targets. Horizontal scaling, also known as scaling out, is a technique in software design for increasing the capacity of a system by adding more machines (nodes) to distribute the workload.

- **Real-time communication**: One of the possible target and source communication attributes is real-time communication. Depending on the use cases, the system should allow real-time data exchange between the source and the target.

- **Log and data aggregation**: This is the ability to combine and process logs and data in certain aggregates. Log and data aggregation play a crucial role in modern software by centralizing and organizing information from various sources, making it easier to analyze, troubleshoot, and optimize applications.

- **Data transformation and processing**: The communication between the target and source is not only in the form of data exchange but also information should be based on the possibility of transformation.

Now let's talk about the infrastructure we need to use to implement our microservices.

Implementing an asynchronous transaction microservice

We will use the same transaction microservice we implemented in *Chapter 6* but with additional changes that will help us add asynchronous behavior to it. First, we should prepare our infrastructure. Here is what we will have in it:

- **Apache Kafka**: To create loose coupling between microservices.

- **Kafka UI**: This is a web application designed for managing Apache Kafka clusters. It provides a **graphical user interface** (**GUI**) instead of the traditional **command-line interface** (**CLI**) for Kafka, making it easier to interact with Kafka for many users.

- **Zookeeper**: This is open source software that acts as a central coordinator for large distributed systems. Think of it as a conductor for an orchestra, keeping everything in sync.

- **PostgreSQL**: To store data.

- **PgAdmin**: A graphical tool to visually see database elements.

We have our `docker-compose.yml` file in our root folder (`Ch07/transactionservice`).

This `docker-compose` file defines a multi-service setup for a PostgreSQL database, a PgAdmin instance for managing the database, and a Kafka messaging system with Zookeeper for coordination. The services are connected through a custom Docker network, `my-app-network`, which enables inter-container communication. For Kafka, ensure the correct network settings are configured to avoid connectivity issues, especially for multi-network setups where `advertised.listeners` may be needed for both internal and external addresses. The PostgreSQL service stores its data in a named volume, `postgres_data`, while PgAdmin depends on PostgreSQL to be up and running. The Kafka and Zookeeper services are set up for message brokering, with Kafka UI providing management and monitoring, relying on Zookeeper to maintain a distributed system configuration.

Navigate to the root folder and run the `docker-compose up -d` command to spin up the infrastructure.

Here is how it should look after a successful run (*Figure 7.1*).

	Name	Image
☐ ⌄	transactionservice	
☐	**kafka-ui-1** 74a8554e562d	provectuslabs/kafka-ui:latest
☐	**pgadmin-1** 0428919ca6e7	dpage/pgadmin4
☐	**kafka-1** 46cb35467bda	docker.io/bitnami/kafka:3.6
☐	**postgres-1** 9b68fa6856bf	postgres
☐	**zookeeper-1** e2b557b04c81	docker.io/bitnami/zookeeper:3.8

Figure 7.1: Docker infrastructure

After successfully running our docker infrastructure, we are ready to switch to our source code to implement our requirements.

First, we need to update our transaction service to support additional statuses. Open the `schema.prisma` file under the `prisma/migrations` folder and change `enum` to the following:

```
enum Status {
  CREATED
  FAILED
  APPROVED
  DECLINED
  FRAUD
}
```

As we already know, one of the responsibilities of Prisma is to isolate us from database internals and provide a unique, more understandable language over these internals. That is why we have the `.prisma` extension and to map it to real SQL, we need to run migration. We already know about the migration steps and their impact on your development (check *Chapter 6* for more detailed information), so in this chapter, we just provide the exact command without explanation:

```
npx prisma migrate dev --name transaction-status-updated
```

After running the command, you should end up with an additional folder that contains `migration.sql` and the folder name is a combination of the generation date and the name you provided from the command (*Figure 7.2*).

Figure 7.2: Newly generated migration context for statuses

The main functionality we plan to add to the transaction service is fraud functionality. This method should change the status of a transaction to FRAUD if it is not a failed transaction. After updating the status, it should publish a message to the broker (Apache Kafka in this case).

Getting started with Kafka for NestJS

As we learned in *Chapter 6*, NestJS has a lot of useful packages to work with different technologies. You don't need to write any of them to integrate them into your project. This applies to Apache Kafka also. We don't need to develop a separate package from scratch for it; just run the following command to install the required packages:

```
npm install @nestjs/microservices kafkajs
```

After successful installation, you will end up with additional changes in your package.json file. NestJS has a special pattern combination to configure services. That is why we first need to create our kafka module. As we already learned, there is no need to create this file manually. You just need to run the following command:

```
nest generate module kafka
```

It should generate a folder called kafka that contains the kafka.module.ts file. This module should have KafkaService as its provider element, but we don't have a Kafka service. Running the following command will generate kafka.service.ts and kafka.service.spec.ts files:

```
nest generate service kafka
```

We don't need to work on kafka.service.spec.ts and it is up to you to remove it. These files are automatically generated test files, and we won't run any tests for this chapter. To make things as simple as possible, we remove it. After running the last command, you should realize that kafka.module.ts was also automatically updated. Here is what it looks like:

```
import { Module } from '@nestjs/common';
import { KafkaService } from './kafka.service';
import { ConfigModule } from '@nestjs/config';
```

```
@Module({
  imports: [ConfigModule],
  providers: [KafkaService],
})
export class KafkaModule {}
```

The code in `kafka.module.ts` is straightforward and easy to understand due to its minimal lines.: A bit later we will talk about the `nestjs/config` package also. We will implement the main functionality inside `kafka.service.ts` file. Open your `kafka.service.ts` file and replace it with the following code lines:

```
import { Injectable, OnModuleInit, OnModuleDestroy } from
  '@nestjs/common';
import { ConfigService } from '@nestjs/config';
import { Kafka, Producer } from 'kafkajs';


@Injectable()
export class KafkaService implements OnModuleInit, OnModuleDestroy {
  private readonly producer: Producer;
  private readonly topic: string;

  constructor(private readonly configService: ConfigService) {
    const clientId = this.configService.get<
      string>('KAFKA_CLIENT_ID');
    const brokers = this.configService.get<string>('KAFKA_BROKERS')
      .split(',');
    this.topic = this.configService.get<string>('KAFKA_TOPIC');

    const kafka = new Kafka({ clientId, brokers });
    this.producer = kafka.producer({ retry: { retries: 3 }
      });
  }

  async onModuleInit(): Promise<void> {
    await this.producer.connect();
  }

  async onModuleDestroy(): Promise<void> {
    await this.producer.disconnect();
  }

  async send(value: any, key?: string): Promise<void> {
    const messages = [{ key, value: JSON.stringify(value)
      }];
```

```
    await this.producer.send({ topic: this.topic, messages
      });
  }
}
```

Now let's understand what we just did:

- `Injectable`: This indicates that the class is injectable into other services.

- `OnModuleInit` and `OnModuleDestroy`: These are lifecycle hooks for initialization and cleanup.

- `ConfigService`: This provides access to environment variables and configuration.

- `Kafka` and `Producer`: These are classes from the `kafkajs` library.

- `@Injectable()`: This makes the `KafkaService` injectable.

- `implements OnModuleInit` and `OnModuleDestroy`: This implements the lifecycle hooks.

- `producer`: The Kafka `producer` instance is used for sending messages.

- `topic`: This is the pre-configured Kafka topic for message delivery (fetched from environment variables).

- `configService`: This is the injected instance for accessing configuration.

- The constructor of the class fetches Kafka configuration values from environment variables:

  - `KAFKA_CLIENT_ID`: This is the client ID for your application.

  - `KAFKA_BROKERS`: This is a comma-separated list of Kafka broker addresses.

  - `KAFKA_TOPIC`: This is the Kafka topic for sending messages.

  - `const kafka = new Kafka({ clientId, brokers });`: This creates a Kafka client using the configuration.

  - `this.producer = kafka.producer({ retry: { retries: 3 } })`: This creates a producer instance with a retry configuration for message reliability (set to retry three times by default).

  - `onModuleInit`: This connects the Kafka producer when the NestJS module is initialized, ensuring the producer is ready to send messages.

  - `onModuleDestroy`: This disconnects the Kafka producer when the NestJS module is destroyed, releasing resources.

  - `send`: This takes a value (any) to be sent and an optional key (string) for message identification. It constructs a message object with a key and value (serialized as JSON) and sends the message to the pre-configured topic using the producer.

Sensitive information should not be stored directly in kafka.service.ts. For this chapter, store configuration settings in a .env file locally. However, avoid committing this file to version control. For production deployments, consider using a secure vault service, like AWS Secrets Manager or Azure Key Vault, to manage sensitive configurations securely. From the previous code, it is obvious that we store our three main Kafka configurations in a .env file. Open your .env file and add the following lines to the end of the file:

```
#KAFKA Configuration
KAFKA_CLIENT_ID=transaction-service
KAFKA_BROKERS=localhost:29092
KAFKA_TOPIC=transaction-service-topic
```

We have already used the .env file to configure postgresql (*Chapter 6*), but for this chapter, we need to specify a mechanism that can read .env files. Another NestJS package, called config, will help us to deal with this issue. Let's install it using the following command:

```
npm install @nestjs/config
```

That is all. We have imported the package to kafka.service.js to work with it. Now it is time to talk about Kafka's essentials. When we produce or consume messages, we need to interact with Apache Kafka, and you need to understand some basics of Kafka before using it.

Cluster and brokers in Kafka

In production, a Kafka cluster typically consists of multiple brokers, each of which stores and manages partitions for assigned topics. Kafka uses ZooKeeper (or KRaft in newer versions) to coordinate broker metadata and ensure consistent partition distribution across the cluster. A **broker** is synonymous with a **Kafka server**. Each broker is a server. The purpose of a broker is to serve data.

It doesn't matter whether it is physical or not; in the end, a broker should function as a server. While it is technically possible to have only one broker in a cluster, this is usually done only for testing or self-learning purposes.

The purposes of a cluster include the following:

- Handling multiple requests in parallel using multiple brokers
- Providing high throughput
- Ensuring scalability

Each broker within a Kafka cluster is also a bootstrap server, containing metadata about all other brokers, topics, and partitions. When consumers join a consumer group, Kafka's group coordinator uses assignment strategies like Range or RoundRobin to assign partitions, ensuring even distribution and balancing the load across consumers. This means that when you connect to one broker, you are automatically connected to the entire cluster. In most cases, a good starting point is to have three brokers.

Three brokers in Apache Kafka provide a balance between fault tolerance and efficiency. With three brokers, Kafka can replicate data across multiple nodes, ensuring high availability even if one broker fails. It also enables a replication factor of three, which allows the system to tolerate a broker failure without losing data, while avoiding the overhead of managing too many brokers. However, in high-load systems, you might end up with hundreds of brokers.

Depending on the topic's configuration, a broker, as a storage type, consists of multiple **partitions**. When we create a topic, we define the number of partitions under that topic. Kafka, as a distributed system, employs the best algorithm to distribute these partitions among brokers.

Let's consider a Kafka cluster with three brokers. When creating a topic named `tracking_accounts` with three partitions, Kafka will attempt to distribute the partitions among the three brokers. In the best scenario, this will result in one partition per broker. Of course, this depends on various factors, including load balancing. You don't need to intervene; Kafka, as a **distributed framework**, automatically manages all these internal operations.

If you have three partitions and four brokers, Kafka will attempt to distribute them, assigning one partition to each broker, leaving one broker without a partition. But why create more brokers than the partition count? The value becomes apparent when you encounter issues with a broker going down. As we know, one of the most important attributes of Kafka is its fault tolerance. When a broker fails, Kafka automatically recovers using other brokers. The other important question is how producers and consumers know which broker to communicate with for reading and writing data.

The answer is simple. Since Kafka brokers also act as **bootstrap servers**, they possess all the essential information about other servers.

For example, consider any producer. Before producing data, the producer sends a background request to any broker (it doesn't matter which one – even the nearest broker will do) to retrieve metadata information. This metadata contains all the relevant details about other brokers, their topics, partitions, and leader partitions (which we will cover in future discussions).

Using this metadata, the producer knows which broker to send data to. We call this process **Kafka broker discovery**.

Topic and partition concepts in Apache Kafka

The responsibility of the Kafka producer is to produce data. On the other hand, the Kafka consumer is a client for your message. The Kafka cluster acts as an isolator and *storage* for the producer and consumer. Before producing data, Kafka brokers need temporary storage to hold the data. These storage boxes are called **topics**.

A topic is a stream of data that acts as a logical isolator over partitions.

The topic is important from the user's point of view because when reading/writing the data, we're referring mostly to the topic rather than partitions. (Of course, when defining partitions in the producing/consuming process, it is mandatory to point to the topic name, but in general, it is possible to produce/consume data without directly indicating partitions.) The topic concept helps us mere mortals to interact with Kafka without worrying about the internal storage mechanism. Every topic should have a unique name because the identification process for topics is done through their names. You can create as many topics as you want/your business requires.

Topics are not a thing that can live in one broker in production systems. Instead, using partitions, topics spread out to brokers. This means that, using partitions, a topic lives in multiple brokers. It helps Kafka to make a fault-tolerant, scalable, and distributed system.

Topics are durable, meaning that the data in them is persisted on disk. This makes Kafka a good choice for applications that need to reliably store and process data streams.

But how about partitions? Under the hood, Kafka uses partitions to store data. Every topic in production consists of multiple partitions. Kafka uses the topic concept for mainly two purposes:

- To group partitions under one box for storing "one business point" data
- To help users interact with Kafka without worrying about the internal structure

Kafka uses partitions to achieve parallelism and scalability. This means that multiple producers and consumers can work on the same topic at the same time, and the data is evenly distributed across the brokers in the cluster.

So, why do we need the concept of partitions if we have topics? Well, using partitions, Kafka achieves distributive data storage and the **in-sync replica** (**ISR**) concept. Partitions help us to distribute topics and achieve fault-tolerant systems.

Every partition is identified by its ID. Every topic can have as many partitions as you want/your business requires. In production, it is very important to define the partition count when creating a topic – otherwise, the system will use the default configuration for the partition count. This means that, without defining the partition count, the system will automatically create the number of partitions per topic every time. The partition count should align with business requirements; for example, one topic might need forty partitions, while another may need two-hundred.

You can think about partitions as a collection with a stack algorithm. Every partition is an array, and their indexes are called **offsets.** A partition has a dynamic offset count and there is no fixed size for it. Partitions are dynamically extendable, and their sizes can vary within the same topic. Every unit of information in a partition is called a message. Consumers can read data in a stacked manner.

Kafka partitions are split into Kafka brokers using a round-robin algorithm. This means that each broker in the cluster is assigned an equal number of partitions, as much as possible.

But the process of splitting partitions across Kafka brokers also depends on the following factors:

- **Number of partitions**: When you create a Kafka topic, you should specify the number of partitions it can have. This number determines how many parallel consumers or producers can work with the topic. The number of partitions should be chosen based on the expected workload and the level of parallelism required.

- **Broker assignment**: The assignment is typically done in a balanced manner to ensure an even distribution of partitions across brokers, but it can be influenced by partition assignment strategies.

- **Partition assignment strategies**: Kafka provides different strategies for partition assignment, mainly controlled by the consumer group coordinator.

- **Replication factor**: Kafka ensures fault tolerance through data replication across multiple brokers. Each partition has a specified replication factor, which determines how many copies of the data are maintained.

In short, we need partitions in Kafka because they are a core unit of parallelism and distribution and help Kafka to horizontally scale and distribute data. They also enable high throughput and fault tolerance and act as an internal storage mechanism.

It makes sense to note that once a topic is created with a certain number of partitions, it's not proper to change the number of partitions for that topic. Instead, you need to create a new topic with the required number of partitions and migrate data if needed. Apache Kafka is a huge concept by its nature and if you want to learn more, you can check my *Apache Kafka for Distributed Systems* course on Udemy (`https://www.udemy.com/course/apache-kafka-for-distributed-systems/`).

Configuring Apache Kafka

We talked about theoretical aspects of Apache Kafka and now it is time to implement it in practice. You can use the Kafka CLI to interact with Kafka, but we have already installed Kafka UI to make our lives easy and not deal with the complexities of command lines.

Our `.env` file defines a topic named `transaction-topic`, and to create it, let's take the following steps:

1. Open Docker Desktop. Make sure that all the services are running for this chapter.

2. Open your favorite browser and navigate to `http://localhost:9100/`.

3. From the dashboard on the left, select **Topics**.

4.   Click the **Add a Topic** button at the top right and fill in the inputs (*Figure 7.3*).

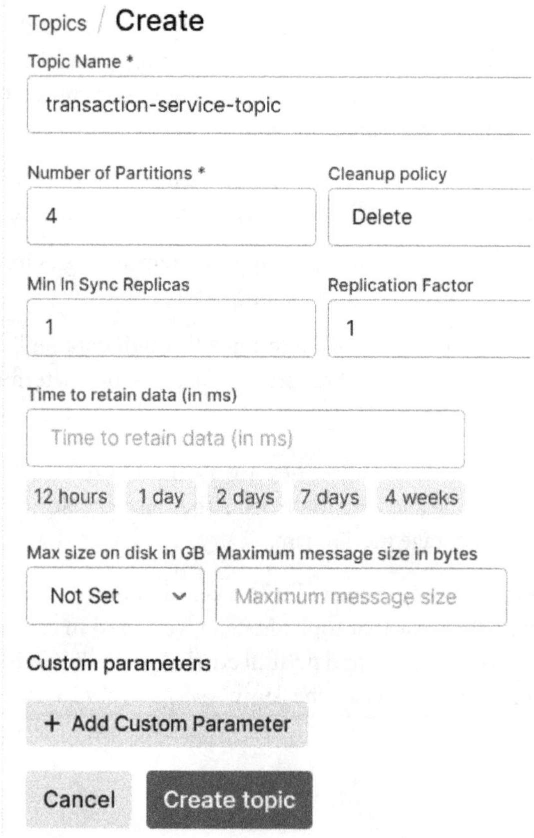

Figure 7.3: Creating a topic for the broker in Apache Kafka

After successfully creation, you will see your topic in the **Topics** list.

So far, we configured Apache Kafka's topic and created `kafka.service.ts` with `kafka.module.ts`. We plan to have fraud functionality in transactions and that is why we need to change three more files (`transaction.controller.ts`, `transaction.module.ts`, and `transaction.service.ts`) to integrate our new fraud functionality.

Adding an asynchronous nature to a transaction microservice

What we need to do is integrate configuration reading and Kafka functionalities into the transaction service. The final version of `transaction.module.ts` will look like this:

```
import { Module } from '@nestjs/common';
import { TransactionService } from './transaction.service';
```

```
import { TransactionController } from './transaction.controller';
import { PrismaModule } from '../prisma/prisma.module';
import { HttpModule } from '@nestjs/axios';
import { KafkaService } from 'src/kafka/kafka.service';
import { ConfigService } from '@nestjs/config';

@Module({
  imports: [PrismaModule,HttpModule],
  controllers: [TransactionController],
  providers:
    [TransactionService,KafkaService,ConfigService],
})
export class TransactionModule {}
```

We just added KafkaService and ConfigService. We plan to inject KafkaService into the transaction.service.ts file and it has a dependency on ConfigService. That is why we need to add both KafkaService and ConfigService to the providers list.

Let's switch to the transaction.service.ts file itself. The modified version of the file is shown here:

```
import { Injectable } from "@nestjs/common";
import { CreateTransactionDto } from "./dto/create-transaction.dto";
import { PrismaService } from "src/prisma/prisma.service";
import { HttpService } from "@nestjs/axios";
import { AccountApiResponse } from "./dto/account.dto";
import { KafkaService } from "src/kafka/kafka.service";
@Injectable()
export class TransactionService {
  constructor(
    private readonly prisma: PrismaService,
    private readonly httpService: HttpService,
    private readonly kafkaService: KafkaService
  ) {}

  async create(createTransactionDto: CreateTransactionDto)
  {
    //same as Chapter 6
  }

  findAll() {
    //same as Chapter 6
  }
```

```
  findOne(id: number) {
    //same as Chapter 6
  }
//newly added functionality
  async fraud(id: number) {
  const transaction = await this.findOne(id);

  if (transaction.status !== "FRAUD" &&
    transaction.status !== "FAILED") {
      const newTransaction =
        this.prisma.transaction.update({
          where: { id },
          data: { status: "FRAUD" },
        });

      this.kafkaService.send(transaction, null);

      return newTransaction;
    } else throw new Error("Transaction is not in a valid
status");
  }
```

As you might have already noticed, we injected `KafkaService` and the transaction has one more function, called `fraud`.

This asynchronous function, named `fraud`, is designed to handle marking a transaction as fraudulent. It fetches the transaction details, verifies its current status, updates it to FRAUD if valid, potentially sends a notification, and returns the updated transaction object. The function takes `id: number` as input, representing the unique identifier of the transaction to be flagged as fraudulent. The function begins by using `await this.findOne(id)` to retrieve the transaction data asynchronously from a database. It then checks that the transaction's current status is neither FRAUD nor FAILED using the strict inequality operator (`!==`). This ensures the function doesn't attempt to mark an already fraudulent or failed transaction again. If the status doesn't meet the criteria, an error is thrown with the message `Transaction is not in a valid status` to prevent unexpected behavior. Assuming the status check passes (i.e., the transaction isn't already fraudulent or failed), the code proceeds to update the transaction data. It utilizes the Prisma library (`this.prisma.transaction.update`) to modify the transaction record. The `where` property specifies that the update should target the specific transaction with the provided ID.

The `data` property defines the changes to be made. In this case, it sets the `status` property of the transaction to FRAUD.

The function includes the line `this.kafkaService.send(transaction, null)`. This suggests the use of a Kafka message broker to broadcast a notification about the fraudulent transaction. The second argument is a key. A message key is an optional element you can include with a message in Apache Kafka. It plays an important role in how messages are routed and processed within the system. Message keys are primarily used for partitioning messages within a topic. Kafka topics are further divided into partitions, serving as storage units for distributed data. By including a key, you can influence which partition a message gets sent to.

Finally, if the status check is passed and the update is successful, the function returns the `newTransaction` object. This object contains the updated transaction details, including the newly set FRAUD status.

In essence, this function provides a mechanism to flag a transaction as fraudulent, considering the current status and sending a notification through Kafka.

The final element is the controller. In the transaction controller, we have a new endpoint with the following behavior:

```
@Post(':id')
  fraud(@Param(<id>) id: string) {
    return this.transactionService.fraud(+id);
  }
```

To test everything together, you should do the following:

1. Run `npm run start:dev` from the root (the `Ch07/transactionservice` folder).

2. Navigate to `localhost:3000/api`.

We already have default migrated transactions. You can use their IDs to test our newly created API or you can create a transaction from scratch and test it. Let's test one of our seed transactions. I'll use the `id = 1` transaction (*Figure 7.4*).

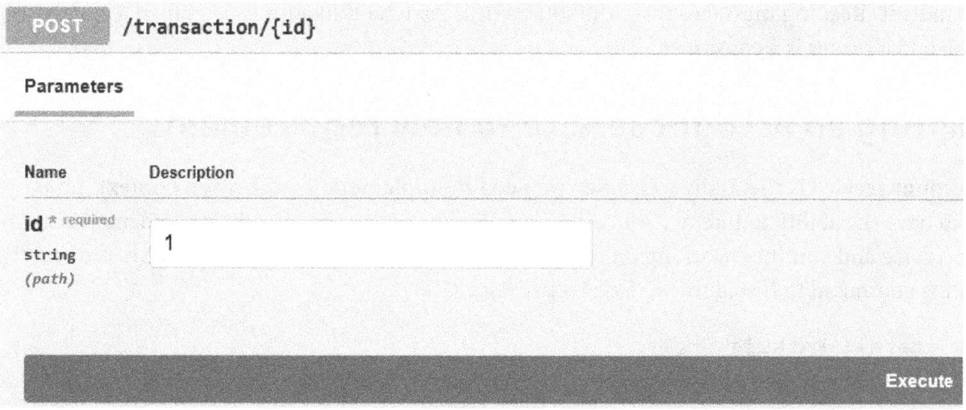

POST	/transaction/{id}

Parameters

Name	Description
id * required string *(path)*	1

Execute

Figure 7.4: Executing the fraud endpoint

After successfully executing the fraud endpoint, we will end up with the following response:

```json
{
  "id": 1,
  "status": "FRAUD",
  "accountId": "662c081370bd2ba6b5f04e94",
  "description": "simple transaction",
  "createdAt": "2024-05-10T08:43:41.389Z",
  "updatedAt": "2024-05-29T17:47:07.233Z"
}
```

Now let's open Apache Kafka and check our message. Open `localhost:9100` from your favorite browser and go to **Topics**. Click on `transaction-service-topic` and select the **Value** section from the **Messages** tab (*Figure 7.5*):

Figure 7.5: Success message in Apache Kafka

Great! We're able to send a message to Apache Kafka and now we need to somehow take this message and handle it. Reading messages from the source (it is Apache Kafka for us) is called a consuming process and a reader is a consumer.

Adapting an account service to new requirements

An account service is the main consumer we need to implement for the given context. First, we need to have the ability to interact with Apache Kafka. Just copy the already implemented account microservice and continue working on that. Navigate to `Ch07/accountService` and run the following command to install the `kafkajs` package:

```
npm install kafkajs
```

Now we need to develop a separate module to work with Apache Kafka. Apache Kafka has its variables (brokers, topics, etc.) and that is why we use a .env file as we did for the transaction service. Under the accountService folder, we have configs/.env, and we added the following config items:

```
#KAFKA Configuration
KAFKA_CLIENT_ID=account-service
KAFKA_BROKERS=localhost:29092
KAFKA_TOPIC=transaction-service-topic
KAFKA_GROUP_ID=account-group
```

To read the .env file, we use a special configuration that lives under src/config and is called config.js. But we need to add the required changes to that file to support new key-value pairs. Here is the final version of config.js:

```
const dotenv = require('dotenv');
const Joi = require('joi');

const envVarsSchema = Joi.object()
    .keys({
        PORT: Joi.number().default(3000),
        MONGODB_URL:
          Joi.string().required().description('Mongo DB url'),
        KAFKA_CLIENT_ID: Joi.string().required(),
        KAFKA_BROKERS: Joi.string().required(),
        KAFKA_TOPIC: Joi.string().required(),
        KAFKA_GROUP_ID: Joi.string().required()
    })
    .unknown();

function createConfig(configPath) {
    dotenv.config({ path: configPath });

    const { value: envVars, error } = envVarsSchema
        .prefs({ errors: { label: <key> } })
        .validate(process.env);

    if (error) {
        throw new Error(`Config validation error:
          ${error.message}`);
    }

    return {
        port: envVars.PORT,
        mongo: {
```

```
                url: envVars.MONGODB_URL,
            },
            kafka: {
                clientID: envVars.KAFKA_CLIENT_ID,
                brokers: envVars.KAFKA_BROKERS,
                topic: envVars.KAFKA_TOPIC,
                groupId: envVars.KAFKA_GROUP_ID,
            }
        };
    }
module.exports = {
    createConfig,
};
```

We just added additional lines to support config elements newly added to the .env file.

So far, we added a configuration reading mechanism and a Kafka package. Now it is time to develop a Kafka module to interact with Apache Kafka.

Inside the src folder, create a new folder called modules and add a new file called kafkamodule.js. Thisto new requirements" module should have the following implementation:

```
const { Kafka } = require('kafkajs');
const Account = require('../models/account');
const path = require('path');
const { createConfig } = require('../config/config')

const configPath = path.join(__dirname, '../../configs/.env');
const appConfig = createConfig(configPath);
const kafka = new Kafka({
    clientId: appConfig.kafka.clientId,
    brokers: [appConfig.kafka.brokers],
});

const consumer = kafka.consumer({ groupId:
  appConfig.kafka.groupId });

const consumerModule = async () => {
    await consumer.connect();
    await consumer.subscribe({ topic: appConfig.kafka.topic });

    await consumer.run({
      eachMessage: async ({ topic, partition, message }) =>
      {
        const transaction =
```

```
        JSON.parse(message.value.toString());
    const accountId = transaction.accountId;
    try {
        const blockedAccount =
          await Account.findOne({ accountId, status:
          { $ne: 'blocked' } });
        if (!blockedAccount) {
          const updatedAccount =
            await Account.findOneAndUpdate(
                { _id: accountId },
                { $inc: { count: 1 } },
                { new: true }
            );
          if (updatedAccount.count === 3)
            await Account.findOneAndUpdate(
                { _id: accountId },
                { status: 'blocked' },
                { new: true }
            );
        }
        else
            console.log(`not a valid accountId ${accountId}`);
      }
      catch (error) {
          console.log(error);
      }
    },
  });
};

module.exports = consumerModule;
```

We need the following elements to adapt the account microservice to communicate with the transaction service:

- Kafka: To consume the message from Kafka
- Account: To interact with the database
- path: To specify the path to read config files
- createConfig: To retrieve the Kafka configuration

Let's go through the code step by step to understand what it does:

- `const configPath = path.join(__dirname, '../../configs/.env');`: This line constructs a path to the `.env` configuration file, which is located two directories up from the current directory, and then in the `configs` directory.

- `const appConfig = createConfig(configPath);`: This line calls the `createConfig` function with `configPath` as an argument. The `createConfig` function reads the configuration file and returns the configuration settings as an object (`appConfig`).

- The following lines create an instance of the Kafka client using the `KafkaJS` library. It configures the client with a `clientId` and a list of brokers, both of which are obtained from the `appConfig` object.

```
const kafka = new Kafka({
    clientId: appConfig.kafka.clientId,
    brokers: [appConfig.kafka.brokers],
});
```

- `const consumer = kafka.consumer({ groupId: appConfig.kafka.groupId })`;: This line creates a new Kafka consumer instance, specifying a `groupId` obtained from the `appConfig` object. The `groupId` is used to manage consumer group coordination in Kafka.

- We have implemented the main functionality of our module inside the `consumerModule` function. This function connects to Kafka and subscribers to the given topic.

- `await consumer.connect()`;: This line connects the Kafka consumer to the Kafka broker.

- `await consumer.subscribe({ topic: appConfig.kafka.topic })`;: This line subscribes the consumer to the specified Kafka topic, which is obtained from the `appConfig` object.

- `Consumer.run` starts the consumer to listen for messages from the subscribed Kafka topic. It defines an asynchronous handler function for each message that processes each consumed message. The function takes an object with `topic`, `partition`, and `message` properties. For each message, it parses the retrieved message and extracts the account ID. The real business rules start here. First, we check whether the given account ID exists in our database and that it is not blocked. If the account ID exists, then we should update this account, incrementing its count. If the increment count is 3, then the status will be updated to `blocked`.

The rest of the code lines are straightforward.

To use the `kafkamodule.js` file capabilities, we need to import it into `app.js` and call it. Here is what `app.js` looks like:

```
const express = require('express');
const v1 = require('./routes/v1');
const consumerModule = require('./modules/kafkamodule');
const app = express();

consumerModule();
// service
app.use(express.json());

// V1 API
app.use('/v1', v1);

module.exports = app;
```

Well, as you might guess, we missed one important piece of information. Yes – it is a newly created `count`. To track fraud operations, we need to add a new item called `count` to the *account schema*. Open `models/account.js` and add the following lines to your schema:

```
count: {
          type: Number,
          default: 0, // Optional:(defaults to 0)
       },
```

We don't need to change the account service and account controller to use our new `count` : `{ }`. It is an implementation detail and a user should not be able to interact with this column directly. Everything is ready and we can test our service.

Previously, we ran the account microservice without Docker Compose, but now we've added a `docker-compose.yml` file for it (`Ch07/accountservice/docker-compose.yml`). The transaction service already has its own `docker-compose.yml` file that hosts Kafka. To test both services together, we must run the `docker-compose.yml` files from the `accountservice` and `transactionservice` directories.

Testing our microservices together

We should run transaction and account microservices together to test producing and consuming processes. First, let's start with the account microservice. As mentioned before, don't forget to run the `docker-compose.yml` files for both services.

To test the newly updated account, follow these steps:

1. Navigate to Ch07/accountservice/src from the terminal.

2. Run the account service from the command line using the node index.js command.

3. Open Postman and, from the new tab, paste the service URL (it is http://localhost:3001/ v1/accounts for us), and for the HTTP method, select POST. Select **Body** | **raw**, change **Text** to **JSON**, and paste the following:

```
{
    "name":"AccName1",
    "number":"Ac12345",
    "type":"root",
    "status":"new"
}
```

You should get the following response:

```
{
    "success": true,
    "Account": {
        "id":{your_account_id}, //for the given request, it
is  "6658ae5284432e40604018d5" for us
        "name": "AccName1",
        "number": "Ac12345",
        "type": "root",
        "status": "new"
    }
}
```

Here is what it looks like in our database:

```
{
  "_id": {
    "$oid": "6658ae5284432e40604018d5"
  },
  "name": "AccName1",
  "number": "Ac12345",
  "type": "root",
  "status": "new",
  ..................
}
```

Everything is okay for now based on what we have in the account microservice. Our main trigger, the producer, is the transaction microservice. Let's produce a message and see whether the account microservice can consume this message or not. We still need the account service to run in parallel with transaction microservice, and that is why we need to open a new terminal to run the transaction microservice:

1. Open a new terminal and navigate to `Ch07/transactionservice`.

2. Run `npm run start:dev` to start the transaction microservice.

3. Navigate to `http://localhost:3000/api/` and select `POST /transaction/`.

4. Paste the following JSON to create a new transaction:

    ```
    {
        "accountId": "6658ae5284432e40604018d5",
        "description": "Optional transaction description"
    }
    ```

    You should use the account ID created by the account microservice. You will get the following response:

    ```
    {
        "id": {your_id},//it is '37' for us but in your case, it may
    have a different value
        "status": "CREATED",
        "accountId": "6658ae5284432e40604018d5",
        "description": "Optional transaction description",
        ...............
    }
    ```

5. Now let's provide this ID (it is 37 for us) to the `POST /transaction/Id` API. It is a fraud endpoint. The response will be like the following:

    ```
    {
        "id": 37,
        "status": "FRAUD",
        "accountId": "6658ae5284432e40604018d5",
        "description": "Optional transaction description",
        ........
    }
    ```

    Before executing the fraud endpoint, make sure that the Docker infrastructure is running. After running a fraud request, the account microservice should read and update the data. Running the same account ID in a fraud context three times should block the account itself in the account microservice:

    ```
    {
        ....
        "type": "root",
    ```

```
    "status": "blocked",
    "count": 3,
    .........
}
```

With an understanding of the asynchronous communication technique, you can easily apply it to your projects with confidence.

Summary

In this chapter, we started our journey by learning the importance of defining proper communication between microservices. We mostly use two main communication forms: async and sync. Choosing one over another is always a context-dependent choice – context is king. Then, we talked about the advantages of asynchronous communication. There are multiple ways of implementing asynchronous communication and we talked about most of the popular choices. Everything has a price and integrated microservices architecture is not an exception. It brings a lot of additional complexity we need to take into account and one of them is asynchronous communication.

We talked about Apache Kafka, which helps us to overcome the problem we have. We learned about essential concepts such as clusters, brokers, topics, messages, and partitions. Our practical examples covered two main microservices. The transaction service was our producer, which produces a message, and the account microservice was a consumer that consumers that message. Of course, there are a lot of subtopics, such as refactoring, exception handling, testing, and deploying, that we haven't covered yet, and the following chapters will cover these in detail.

8

Real-Time Data Streaming Using Microservices

Certain microservice applications, such as financial trading platforms and ride-hailing services, demand events to be produced and consumed with minimal latency. Real-time data streaming has become increasingly crucial in modern software development due to its ability to provide immediate, continuous insights and responses based on the most current data. This type of real-time data usage is particularly important in industries such as finance, healthcare, and logistics, where delays in data processing can lead to significant losses or even life-threatening situations.

Applications that rely on real-time data can offer a more responsive and interactive user experience. For example, social media platforms, online gaming, and live sports streaming rely on real-time data to keep users engaged and provide a seamless experience.

This chapter is all about real-time streaming with microservices. Our purpose is to understand when and how to establish such a type of communication when dealing with microservices.

This chapter covers the following:

- What is real-time streaming?
- Getting started with the earthquake streaming API
- Implementing the earthquake stream consumer

Technical requirements

To follow along with the chapter, you will need an IDE (we prefer Visual Studio Code), Postman, Docker, and a browser of your choice.

It is preferable to download our repository from `https://github.com/PacktPublishing/Hands-on-Microservices-with-JavaScript` and open the Ch08 folder to easily follow along with the code snippets.

What is real-time streaming?

Real-time streaming is a data-processing paradigm where data is continuously generated, transmitted, and processed as it is created, with minimal delay. Unlike batch processing, which collects and processes data in large groups or batches at regular intervals, real-time streaming focuses on the immediate and continuous flow of data, enabling instant analysis and response. It's like watching a live stream instead of waiting for a video to download entirely.

Before we continue any further, let us look at some of the key characteristics of real-time streaming:

- **Continuous data flow**: Real-time streaming is like a never-ending flow of information coming in all at once from different places. This information can be from sensors, people using things online, money being bought and sold, such as Bitcoin, and so on.

- **Low latency**: The main goal of real-time streaming is to make the delay between information being created and it being used as short as possible.

- **Event-driven processing**: Real-time streaming works by following events as they happen, such as things being created or changing. Each event is dealt with on its own or in small batches, so the system can react right away to new situations.

- **Scalability**: Real-time streaming systems can handle different amounts and speeds of information, growing bigger or smaller depending on how much information is coming in

- **Fault tolerance**: To ensure continuous operation, real-time streaming systems incorporate fault tolerance mechanisms, such as data replication and automatic recovery from failures. As we mentioned in previous chapters, this is one of the important attributes of Apache Kafka, which we plan to also use for this chapter.

- **Data consistency**: Maintaining data consistency is important in real-time streaming, especially when processing brings multiple distributed components into the table. Techniques such as **exactly-once processing** and **idempotency** are employed to ensure accuracy. Exactly-once processing ensures that each message is processed only once, even in the case of failures or retries, preventing duplicates. As we use Apache Kafka for most chapters, you can easily configure idempotency and exactly-once behavior in it.

The importance of real-time data in modern applications cannot be overstated. In today's data-driven world, the ability to process and act on data as it is generated provides a significant competitive edge.

Why real-time data is essential

Here are some key reasons why real-time data is a must-have for most modern applications:

- **Enhanced decision-making**: Real-time data can enhance an application's decision-making abilities because of the following:

  - **Immediate insights**: Real-time data provides immediate insights, allowing businesses to make informed decisions quickly. This is important in dynamic environments such as stock trading, where market conditions can change rapidly.

  - **Proactive problem-solving**: By continuously monitoring data, organizations can identify and address issues before they escalate, reducing downtime and enhancing operational efficiency.

- **Improved user experience**: Real-time data empowers applications to provide a more dynamic and personalized user experience by enhancing interactivity and responsiveness while tailoring content to individual preferences.

- **Operational efficiency**: Organizations can significantly boost their efficiency by using real-time data, which enables both real-time monitoring and automation of processes, helping to streamline operations and reduce costs.

- **Competitive advantage**: Leveraging real-time data gives businesses a distinct edge by enhancing their agility and fostering innovation, allowing them to swiftly respond to market changes and create cutting-edge products and services.

- **Increased revenue**: Utilizing real-time data enables businesses to enhance their revenue streams through optimized marketing strategies and dynamic fraud detection, ensuring more effective customer engagement and financial security.

- **Enhanced security**: Real-time data strengthens security by enabling continuous monitoring and anomaly detection, allowing organizations to quickly identify and respond to potential threats and system irregularities.

- **Scalability and flexibility**: Real-time data systems provide the ability to efficiently handle large volumes of data while maintaining adaptability, ensuring optimal performance even as data loads and requirements fluctuate.

- **Customer satisfaction**: Real-time data enhances customer satisfaction by enabling instant support and immediate feedback, allowing businesses to quickly address concerns and continuously improve their products and services.

Real-time streaming allows data to be processed as it's generated, offering immediate insights and responses. This continuous flow of data, coupled with low latency and event-driven processing, is crucial in industries such as finance, healthcare, and logistics. The ability to make real-time decisions, enhance user experiences, and improve operational efficiency provides businesses with a competitive edge, fostering innovation and increasing revenue while ensuring system scalability, fault tolerance, and enhanced security.

Understanding use cases

At the beginning of the chapter, I briefly mentioned that the use of real-time data can have incredible impacts on some industries. Therefore, it is crucial to understand the use cases of real-time data when you design your microservices. Let's look at these use cases here:

- **Financial services**: Real-time data plays a pivotal role in this industry, enabling algorithmic stock trading with split-second decisions and supporting continuous risk management to ensure compliance and mitigate potential financial threats.

- **Healthcare**: Real-time data is transforming healthcare by enabling continuous patient monitoring for timely interventions and enhancing telemedicine through real-time video consultations and data sharing, improving patient care and accessibility.

- **Retail and e-commerce**: Real-time data enhances retail and e-commerce operations by optimizing inventory management to prevent shortages and enabling dynamic pricing strategies that adjust to demand and competitor activity.

- **Transportation and logistics**: Real-time data optimizes fleet management by improving route planning and delivery times, while real-time traffic data enhances traffic management, reducing congestion and improving overall mobility.

- **Telecommunications**: Real-time data enhances network management by ensuring continuous performance monitoring for optimal service quality, while also improving customer experience through the rapid resolution of network issues

In the end, what we can say for sure is that real-time data is a cornerstone of modern applications, driving enhanced decision-making, improved user experiences, operational efficiency, and competitive advantage. By leveraging real-time data, organizations can innovate, adapt, and thrive in a rapidly changing digital landscape.

Relationship between real-time streaming and microservices

Now that we have understood what real-time data is and exactly why it's necessary, it's time we understood the relationship between real-time streaming and microservices. The union of real-time streaming with microservices is a symbiotic one, which extends the power, productivity, and scalability of modern software architectures. Systems now, as a service, are more reactive, more adaptable, and faster as a result of this integration. Let's try to understand how real-time streaming and microservices play well with each other:

- **Decoupling and scalability**: Real-time streaming complements microservices by promoting loose coupling and independent scaling, allowing services to communicate asynchronously and scale efficiently based on demand.

- **Flexibility and agility**: The combination of real-time streaming with microservices enhances flexibility and agility, enabling continuous service evolution and real-time data processing for applications requiring immediate insights and rapid iteration.

- **Resilience and fault tolerance**: Integrating real-time streaming with microservices enhances resilience and fault tolerance by isolating failures to individual services and ensuring data durability, allowing for seamless recovery and continuous operation even in the event of service disruptions.

- **Real-time communication**: Real-time streaming enhances communication within microservices by enabling event-driven architecture and immediate data propagation, allowing services to interact asynchronously and respond quickly to events, leading to more responsive and synchronized systems.

- **Operational efficiency**: Combining real-time streaming with microservices enhances operational efficiency by optimizing resource utilization and simplifying data pipelines, allowing continuous data flow and reducing the complexity of traditional batch-processing methods.

- **Enhanced monitoring and analytics**: Integrating real-time streaming with microservices enables real-time monitoring and analytics, offering immediate visibility into service performance and providing actionable insights that allow for the proactive management and dynamic optimization of services.

The synergy between real-time streaming and microservices offers a robust framework for building responsive, scalable, and efficient systems. By leveraging the strengths of both paradigms, organizations can create applications that are capable of handling dynamic workloads, providing real-time insights, and delivering superior user experiences. This combination is particularly powerful in environments where rapid data processing and immediate reactions are critical to success.

Microservices we will develop

To make our learning process more interactive and more understandable, we will develop two simple microservices. The first microservice will act as a producer of stream and the domain of this microservices will be an earthquake. An API that streams real-time information about earthquakes can be valuable for several reasons:

- **Emergency response**: Real-time data can be crucial for emergency responders who need to assess damage and deploy resources quickly after an earthquake. The API will provide information on the location, magnitude, and depth of the earthquake, which can help responders prioritize areas that may be most affected.

- **Public awareness**: The API could be used for public awareness to create applications that send alerts to people in affected areas. This could help people take shelter or evacuate if necessary.

- **Research:** Researchers can use the API to track earthquake activity and improve their understanding of earthquake patterns. This data can be used to develop better earthquake prediction models and improve building codes.

- **News and media:** News organizations can use the API to get real-time updates on earthquake activity, which can help them report on the latest developments.

In addition to these, there are commercial applications for such an API as well. For instance, insurance companies could use it to assess potential risks and losses, or engineering firms could use it to design earthquake-resistant structures.

Of course, when building such type of APIs for production, we will need to choose a reliable source of earthquake data; but to demonstrate the purpose and implementation of real-time data streaming, our API will act as a source of truth.

From a data format perspective, we should select a format for the data that is easy to use and integrate with other applications. Common formats include JSON and XML. Our choice is JSON.

By providing valuable and timely data, your earthquake API can be a useful tool for a variety of users.

The second microservice is going to be a consumer of the data. Throughout our learning process, we have implemented our microservices using different packages and frameworks with nearly full skeletons. For the current chapter, our focus is streaming rather than building an application skeleton from scratch. Our focus is not on implementing any architecture. You can refer to previous chapters if you want to add additional functionalities and make it a fully self-contained architectural application.

Getting started with an earthquake streaming API

In our GitHub repository, in the Ch08 folder, we have two subfolders: earthquakeService, the earthquake streaming API, and earthquakeConsumer, the consumer API. As we mentioned before, our main focus is on implementing streaming. To make this chapter more focused on the topic, we haven't implemented a proper detailed design for this API. This is also the case with the consumer API.

It is best to follow along by creating everything with us from scratch.

earthquakeService has the following dependencies:

```
"dependencies": {
    "dotenv": "^16.4.5",
    "express": "^4.19.2",
    "joi": "^17.13.1",
    "node-rdkafka": "^3.0.1"
}
```

First, you need to generate a `package.json` file that contains all dependencies. To create the file, run `npm init` and follow the prompts from the terminal. After `package.json` is created, run the `npm install 'your_required_package_names'` template command to install packages one by one. For example, to install the `express` package, just run `npm install express`, and hit *Enter*. We have already talked about `package.json` and the package installation process. You can check the previous chapters for more information. While we have reused some of the microservices from our previous chapter in our current chapter, we're also going to use `node-rdkafka` package which is new for us.

`node-rdkafka` is a Node.js library that provides a wrapper around the native librdkafka library, enabling efficient communication with Apache Kafka for high-performance data streaming. It leverages the power of `librdkafka` for efficient communication with Kafka and handles complexities such as balancing writes and managing brokers, making Kafka interaction easier for developers.

You can install `node-rdkafka` using npm:

```
npm install node-rdkafka
```

It is not the only package to use for streaming, and depending on your personal preference, you can select any other one. The `node-rdkafka` package supports a really easy stream writing and reading process, which is why we prefer to use it in this chapter for learning purposes.

> **Note**
>
> You should always try to use official packages for production apps. Using official packages helps keep your app safe because trusted developers manage them, and they are checked often. They are also more reliable, as they are tested, updated, and have good support, which is important for apps in production.

We use Apache Kafka as a streaming platform. So, you need Apache Kafka to be running. As before, we plan to use the `docker-compose.yml` file, which should be up and running with Apache Kafka. Our `docker-compose.yml` file for this example will only contain the services needed for Kafka, excluding unnecessary components like PostgreSQL to reduce resource usage. Of course, you can run the `docker-compose.yml` file from the previous chapters that use Apache Kafka, but having additional services will use up more resources on your PC.

Here is our `docker-compose.yml` file:

```
services:
  zookeeper:
    image: bitnami/zookeeper:3.8
    ports:
      - "2181:2181"
    volumes:
      - zookeeper_data:/bitnami
```

```
    environment:
      ALLOW_ANONYMOUS_LOGIN: "yes"


  kafka1:
    image: bitnami/kafka:3.6
    volumes:
      - kafka_data1:/bitnami
    environment:
      KAFKA_CFG_ZOOKEEPER_CONNECT: zookeeper:2181
      KAFKA_CFG_LISTENERS: INTERNAL://:9092,EXTERNAL://0.0.0.0:29092
      KAFKA_CFG_ADVERTISED_LISTENERS: INTERNAL://
kafka1:9092,EXTERNAL://localhost:29092
      KAFKA_CFG_LISTENER_SECURITY_PROTOCOL_MAP:
INTERNAL:PLAINTEXT,EXTERNAL:PLAINTEXT
      KAFKA_CFG_INTER_BROKER_LISTENER_NAME: INTERNAL
      KAFKA_CFG_AUTO_CREATE_TOPICS_ENABLE: 'true'
      ALLOW_PLAINTEXT_LISTENER: 'yes'
    ports:
      - "9092:9092"
      - "29092:29092"
    depends_on:
      - zookeeper


  kafka-ui:
    image: provectuslabs/kafka-ui:latest
    ports:
      - 9100:8080
    environment:
      KAFKA_CLUSTERS_0_NAME: local
      KAFKA_CLUSTERS_0_BOOTSTRAPSERVERS: kafka1:9092
      KAFKA_CLUSTERS_0_ZOOKEEPER: zookeeper:2181
    depends_on:
      - kafka1

volumes:
  zookeeper_data:
    driver: local
  kafka_data1:
    driver: local
```

In this configuration, we define INTERNAL and EXTERNAL listeners to differentiate between connections within the Docker network (INTERNAL://kafka1:9092) and connections from outside the Docker network, such as your local machine (EXTERNAL://localhost:29092).

This separation ensures that services within the Docker network can use the internal address, while external clients (like a Node.js app running on your host) can connect using the external port. By doing so, Kafka can properly advertise the correct addresses to different clients, avoiding connection issues caused by mismatched listener configurations.

This file contains Apache Kafka, the Kafka UI, and ZooKeeper. Just check our root folder (Ch08/ earthquakeService) to find and run it. To run the docker-compose.yml file, first launch Docker Desktop, ensure it's running, and then follow these steps:

1. Pull and open Ch08 from the repository.

2. Open the project from Visual Studio Code (or any text editor you prefer) and navigate to Ch08.

3. If you use Visual Studio Code, then go to **Terminal | New Terminal** from the **Menu**; otherwise, use the command line to navigate to the root folder.

4. Run the docker-compose up -d command from the terminal (*Figure 8.1*).

Name	Container ID	Image	Port(s)
● earthquakeservice	-	-	-
● kafka1-1	5eda68a2a3ba	bitnami/kafka:3.6	9092:9092 ⟐
● zookeeper-1	c080e5c410a3	bitnami/zookeeper:3.8	2181:2181 ⟐
● kafka-ui-1	5d7966226417	provectuslabs/kafka-ui:latest	9100:8080 ⟐

Figure 8.1: Docker Desktop after running the docker-compose.yml file

To connect to Apache Kafka, we need to store the required configuration in a separate file. That is why we use the dotenv package to read configuration information. Create a configs folder under the root folder (Ch08/earthquake) and add a .env file.

> **Note**
>
> The config and configs folders are separate and serve different purposes. Be sure to use the correct folder to avoid confusion. We store the .env file under the configs folder. On the other hand, we store the config.js file under the config folder, which loads environment variables using the dotenv package, validates them with Joi, and returns a configuration object for a Kafka-based microservice, throwing an error if validation fails.

Here is what the configs/.env file should look like:

```
PORT=3001
#KAFKA Configuration
KAFKA_CLIENT_ID=earthquake-service
KAFKA_BROKERS=localhost:29092
KAFKA_TOPIC=earthquake-service-topic
```

We have Kafka configuration such as client ID, brokers, and topic name with port information. As we learned before, all application source code lives under the `src` folder. Create the `src` folder on the same level as your `configs` folder (*Figure 8.2*).

Figure 8.2: General structure of earthquakeService

We store configuration information in the `.env` file, but we need to add a reading and validating mechanism over our `config`. To implement proper reading and validating, we need to create a `configs.js` file under the `src/configc` folder. Here is what it looks like:

```
const dotenv = require('dotenv');
const Joi = require('joi');

const envVarsSchema = Joi.object()
    .keys({
        PORT: Joi.number().default(3000),
        KAFKA_CLIENT_ID: Joi.string().required(),
        KAFKA_BROKERS: Joi.string().required(),
        KAFKA_TOPIC: Joi.string().required()
    })
    .unknown();

function createConfig(configPath) {
    dotenv.config({ path: configPath });

    const { value: envVars, error } = envVarsSchema
        .prefs({ errors: { label: 'key' } })
        .validate(process.env);
```

```
    if (error) {
        throw new Error(`Config validation error:
          ${error.message}`);
    }

    return {
        port: envVars.PORT,
        kafka: {
            clientID: envVars.KAFKA_CLIENT_ID,
            brokers: envVars.KAFKA_BROKERS,
            topic: envVars.KAFKA_TOPIC
        }
    };
}

module.exports = {
    createConfig,
};
```

We are using the same `config` read and validation mechanism as the account microservice. We have already explained this file in the *Chapter 7*.

Our `services` folder is responsible for storing service files. To implement real-time streaming functionality, we need to create a new file called `earthquake.js` under the `services` folder. Here is what it looks like:

```
const Kafka = require('node-rdkafka');
const { createConfig } = require('../config/config');
const path = require('path');

class EarthquakeEventProducer {

constructor() {
        this.intervalId = null;
    }

    #generateEarthquakeEvent() {
        return {
            id: Math.random().toString(36).substring(2,
              15),
            magnitude: Math.random() * 9, // Random magnitude between
0 and 9
            location: {
                latitude: Math.random() * 180 - 90, // Random latitude
between -90 and 90
```

```
              longitude: Math.random() * 360 - 180, // Random
longitude between -180 and 180
            },
            timestamp: Date.now(),
        };
    }
........
```

This code defines a class called `EarthquakeEventProducer` that simulates generating and publishing earthquake event data to a Kafka topic. Let's walk through the code's elements here:

- `require('node-rdkafka')`: Imports the `node-rdkafka` library for interacting with a Kafka cluster.

- `require('../config/config')`: Imports a function (likely from `../config/config.js`) that reads configuration settings from a file.

- `require('path')`: Imports the `path` module for file path manipulation.

- The `EarthquakeEventProducer class`: This class handles earthquake event generation and publishing.

- `#generateEarthquakeEvent()`: This private method generates a simulated earthquake event object with the following properties:

  - `id`: A random unique identifier string.

  - `magnitude`: A random floating-point number between 0 and 9 representing the earthquake's magnitude

  - `location`: An object containing the following:

  - `latitude`: A random floating-point number between -90 and 90 representing the latitude.

  - `longitude`: A random floating-point number between -180 and 180 representing the longitude.

  - `timestamp`: The current timestamp in milliseconds.

Here is how we specify our main method called `runEarthquake`:

```
async runEarthquake() {
    const configPath = path.join(__dirname,
      '../../configs/.env');
    const appConfig = createConfig(configPath);

    // Returns a new writable stream
    const stream = Kafka.Producer.createWriteStream({
        'metadata.broker.list':
```

```
            appConfig.kafka.brokers,
         'client.id': appConfig.kafka.clientID
     }, {}, {
         topic: appConfig.kafka.topic
     });

     // To make our stream durable we listen to this event
     stream.on('error', (err) => {
         console.error('Error in our kafka stream');
         console.error(err);
     });

   this.intervalId  = setInterval(async () => {
         const event =
           await this.#generateEarthquakeEvent();
         // Writes a message to the stream
         const queuedSuccess = stream.write(Buffer.from(
           JSON.stringify(event)));

         if (queuedSuccess) {
             console.log('The message has been queued!');
         } else {
             // If the stream's queue is full
             console.log('Too many messages in queue already');
         }
     }, 100);
   }
```

Let's break this code down here:

- `runEarthquake()`: This async method is responsible for setting up the Kafka producer and publishing earthquake events.

- `configPath`: This constructs the path to the configuration file using `path.join`.

- `appConfig`: This reads configuration from the file using the imported `createConfig` function.

- `stream`: This creates a Kafka producer write stream using `Kafka.Producer.createWriteStream`. The configuration includes the following:

  - `'metadata.broker.list'`: A comma-separated list of Kafka broker addresses from the configuration

  - `'client.id'`: A unique identifier for this producer client from the configuration

  - `Topic`: The exact topic that should get the streamed data

- `stream.on('error')`: This attaches an event listener for errors in the Kafka stream. It logs the error message to the console.

- `setInterval`: This sets up an interval timer to generate and publish events every 100 milliseconds (adjustable). Inside the interval callback is the following:

  - event: Generates a new earthquake event object using #generateEarthquakeEvent

  - `stream.write`: Attempts to write the event data (converted to a buffer using `JSON.stringify`) to the Kafka stream

  - queuedSuccess: Checks the return value from `stream.write`:

    - `true`: Indicates successful queuing of the message. A success message is logged to the console.

    - `false`: Indicates the stream's queue is full. A message about exceeding the queue capacity is logged to the console.

In order to stop our earthquake service, we need to clear the interval:

```
stopEarthquake() {
      if (this.intervalId) {
          clearInterval(this.intervalId);
          this.intervalId = null;
          console.log('Earthquake event stream stopped.');
      } else {
          console.log('No running earthquake event stream to
stop.');
      }
   }
module.exports = EarthquakeEventProducer;
```

The `stopEarthquake()` method stops the ongoing earthquake event stream by checking whether there is an active interval running, indicated by the presence of `this.intervalId`. If the interval exists, it uses `clearInterval()` to stop the event generation and resets `this.intervalId` to `null` to indicate that the stream has stopped. A success message is logged when the stream is stopped. If no interval is running (i.e., `this.intervalId` is null), it logs a message saying there's no active stream to stop. This ensures that the function can only stop an existing stream and won't attempt to stop a non-existent one.

In the end, this code simulates earthquake event generation and publishes these events to a Kafka topic at regular intervals, demonstrating basic Kafka producer usage with error handling and logging.

We plan to launch streaming using an API, but to make things as simple as possible, we use a minimal API approach that doesn't require us to create controllers. This behavior is implemented in the app. js file. Here is the file:

```
const express = require('express');
const EarthquakeEventProducer = require('./services/earthquake');

const app = express();
const earthquakeProducer = new EarthquakeEventProducer();

// Function to run streaming
app.post('/earthquake-events/start', async (req, res) => {
    earthquakeProducer.runEarthquake();
    res.status(200).send('Earthquake event stream started');
});

// Stop the earthquake event stream
app.post('/earthquake-events/stop', (req, res) => {
    earthquakeProducer.stopEarthquake();
    res.status(200).send('Earthquake event stream stopped');
});

module.exports = app;
```

The code defines two API endpoints using Express.js to start and stop an earthquake event stream. The /earthquake-events/start endpoint triggers the runEarthquake() function from the EarthquakeEventProducer class, starting the event stream, and responds with a success message. The /earthquake-events/stop endpoint calls the stopEarthquake() function to stop the event stream and also responds with a success message. The earthquakeProducer object is an instance of the EarthquakeEventProducer class, which manages the event stream operations. Finally, the Express app is exported to be used in other parts of the application. This setup allows external clients, such as Postman, to control the Kafka event stream through API calls.

In an Express.js application, the index.js file in the root directory typically serves as the entry point for your server. It acts as the central hub where you configure and launch your Express app. Here is our index.js file:

```
const path = require('path');
const app = require('./app');
const { createConfig } = require('./config/config');

async function execute() {
    const configPath = path.join(__dirname, '../configs/.env');
    const appConfig = createConfig(configPath);
```

```
    const server = app.listen(appConfig.port, () => {
        console.log('earthquake service started',
          { port: appConfig.port });
    });

    const closeServer = () => {
        if (server) {
            server.close(() => {
                console.log('server closed');
                process.exit(1);
            });
        } else {
            process.exit(1);
        }
    };
    const unexpectedError = (error) => {
        console.log('unhandled error', { error });
        closeServer();
    };

    process.on('uncaughtException', unexpectedError);
    process.on('unhandledRejection', unexpectedError);
}
execute();
```

We have the following functionalities in the index.js file:

- Imports the Express app (app.js) and configuration function (config.js).
- Reads configuration from a file using createConfig.
- Starts the server using app.listen on the configured port and logs a message.
- Defines functions to gracefully close the server and handle unexpected errors.
- Attaches event listeners for uncaught exceptions and unhandled promise rejections, calling the error-handler function.
- Finally, calls the execute function to start everything.

We have implemented our `earthquakeService`; now it is time to test it. Here's how you can do that:

1. Open **Terminal | New Terminal** from the menu if you're using Visual Studio Code.

2. Navigate to the `src` folder.

3. Run the `node index.js` command:

```
PS C:\packtGit\Hands-on-Microservices-with-JavaScript\Ch08\
earthquakeService\src> node index.js
Debugger listening on ws://127.0.0.1:61042/876d7d9e-3292-482a-
b011-e6c2d66e7615
For help, see: https://nodejs.org/en/docs/inspector
Debugger attached.
earthquake service started { port: 3001 }
```

4. Open Postman and send a POST request to `http://localhost:3001/earthquake-events/start`.

5. To stop streaming, open Postman and send a POST request to `http://localhost:3001/earthquake-events/stop` (*Figure 8.3*).

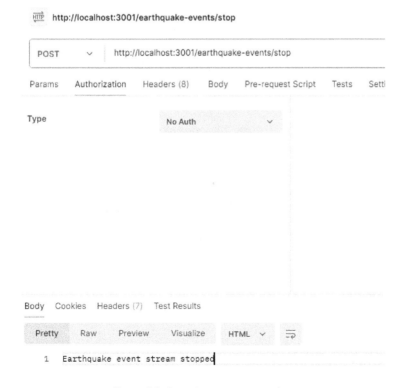

Figure 8.3: Stopping event streaming

The topic should automatically be created with some events (*Figure 8.4*).

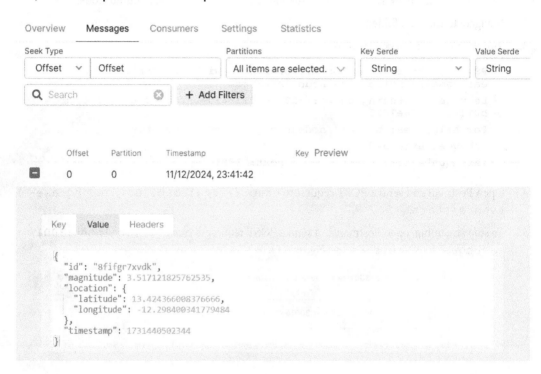

Figure 8.4: Apache Kafka event after streaming

We have implemented the streaming API. Now it is time to consume data.

Implementing the earthquake stream consumer

Producing is not very valuable if you don't have a consumer to consume data. Our second microservice, called earthquakeConsumer, is going to consume data from Apache Kafka. It has a similar code structure to our streaming API (*Figure 8.5*).

Figure 8.5: Earthquake consumer API structure

Let's start from the `configs` folder. As in our first microservice in *Chapter 5*, we have a `.env` file inside the folder. The responsibility of this folder is to store relevant configurations. Here is what it looks like:

```
PORT=3002
#KAFKA Configuration
KAFKA_CLIENT_ID=earthquake-consumer-service
KAFKA_BROKERS=localhost:29092
KAFKA_TOPIC=earthquake-service-topic
KAFKA_GROUP_ID=earthquake-consumer-group
```

We introduced an additional configuration, `KAFKA_GROUP_ID`, which identifies the consumer group, allowing Kafka to balance partition assignments among consumers. It is a string property used to identify a collection of consumer instances and acts as the glue that binds consumers together for collaborative consumption.

Kafka automatically distributes topic partitions among consumers in the same group, allowing parallel processing while ensuring that each partition is consumed by only one consumer at a time within the group. If a consumer in the group fails, Kafka reassigns its partitions to remaining active consumers, ensuring uninterrupted message processing. With proper configuration, consumer groups can achieve exactly-once delivery semantics, guaranteeing each message is processed by only one consumer exactly once. When working with Kafka consumer groups, it's essential to understand how they manage message consumption and workload distribution across multiple consumers. The following are key points to keep in mind when configuring and utilizing consumer groups for efficient message processing:

- Only one consumer can process a partition at a time within a group.

- Consumers with different group IDs treat topics as independent streams and don't share the workload.

- Always consider using a meaningful group ID to improve cluster management and monitoring.

To read and validate this config, we use the same mechanism as we did for the streaming API. We have `src/config/config.js`. It reads and validates our configuration with the additional `KAFKA_GROUP_ID`.

The main functionality has been implemented inside the `src/service/earthquake.js` file. Here is our stream-consuming process:

```javascript
const Kafka = require('node-rdkafka');
const { createConfig } = require('../config/config');
const path = require('path');

class EarthquakeEventConsumer {
    constructor() {
        const configPath = path.join(__dirname,
          '../../configs/.env');
        this.appConfig = createConfig(configPath);

        // Create the Kafka consumer stream here (once)
        this.stream =
          Kafka.KafkaConsumer.createReadStream({
            'metadata.broker.list':
              this.appConfig.kafka.brokers,
            'group.id': this.appConfig.kafka.groupID,
            'socket.keepalive.enable': true,
            'enable.auto.commit': false
        }, {}, {
            topics: this.appConfig.kafka.topic,
            waitInterval: 0,
            objectMode: false
        });
    }

    async consumeData() {
        // Now use the pre-created stream for data consumption
        this.stream.on('data', (message) => {
            console.log('Got message');
            console.log(JSON.parse(message));
        });
    }
}
module.exports = EarthquakeEventConsumer;
```

This code defines a class named `EarthquakeEventConsumer`, which acts as a consumer for messages from a Kafka topic containing earthquake event data. Here's a breakdown of the code:

- `Kafka` from `node-rdkafka`: This library provides functionalities to interact with Kafka as a consumer or producer.

- `createConfig` from `../config/config`: This imports a function from another file (`config/config.js`) that reads configuration details.

- `path`: This is a built-in Node.js module for manipulating file paths.

- `EarthquakeEventConsumer`: This class is responsible for consuming earthquake event data.

- `constructor()`: This special method is called when you create a new instance of `EarthquakeEventConsumer`.

- `configPath`: This constructs the path to a configuration file (such as a `.env` file) containing Kafka connection details such as brokers and group ID.

- `appConfig`: This calls the `createConfig` function (imported from another file) to read the configuration details from the `.env` file and stores it in `this.appConfig`. This makes the configuration accessible throughout the object's lifetime.

- `this.stream`: This line is the key part. It uses `Kafka.KafkaConsumer.createReadStream` to create a stream for reading messages from Kafka. Here's what the options passed to `createReadStream` do:

  - `'metadata.broker.list'`: This specifies the list of Kafka brokers to connect to, obtained from the configuration stored in `this.appConfig`.

  - `'group.id'`: This sets the consumer group ID, also obtained from the configuration. Consumers in the same group will share the messages from a topic among themselves.

  - `'socket.keepalive.enable'`: This enables a mechanism to keep the connection alive with the broker.

  - `'enable.auto.commit'`: This is set to `true` to enable the automatic committing of offsets.

  - `topics`: This specifies the Kafka topic name to consume from, obtained from the configuration (likely `librdtesting-01` in this case).

  - `waitInterval`: This is set to 0, indicating no waiting between attempts to receive messages if none are available.

  - `objectMode`: This is set to `false`, meaning the messages received from the stream will be raw buffers, not JavaScript objects.

Crucially, this stream creation happens only once in the constructor, ensuring efficiency.

- `async consumeData()`: This is an asynchronous method that initiates the data consumption process.

- `.on('data', ...)`: This sets up a listener for the data event emitted by the pre-created stream (`this.stream`). The callback function executes each time a new message arrives, logging that a message was received and parsing the JSON-encoded data for further handling. The callback function logs a message indicating a new message was received. It then parses the raw message buffer (assuming it's JSON-encoded data) using `JSON.parse` and logs the parsed data.

- `module.exports = EarthquakeEventConsumer`: This line exports the `EarthquakeEventConsumer` class so it can be used in other parts of your application.

To summarize, the code defines a consumer that connects to Kafka, subscribes to a specific topic, and listens for incoming earthquake event data. It then parses the JSON-encoded messages and logs them to the console. The key improvement here is creating the Kafka consumer stream only once in the constructor, making the code more efficient.

To run the service, we have `app.js` and `index.js`, which follow the same structure as our streaming API.

We have now implemented our `earthquakeConsumer` and it is time to test it:

1. Open **Terminal | New Terminal** from the menu if you use Visual Studio Code.

2. Navigate to the `src` folder (`Ch08/earthquakeConsumer/src`).

3. Run the `node index.js` command.

> **Note**
>
> You don't need to manually navigate to the `src` folder and run `node index.js` every time you want to start the application. Instead, you can streamline this process by configuring a script in your `package.json` file. Simply add the following to the `scripts` section of `package.json`:
>
> ```
> {
>   "scripts": {
>   "start": "node src/index.js"
>   }
> }
> ```

4. Once this is set up, you can start your application from the root of your project by simply running the following:

```
npm start
```

This will automatically launch the application, saving you time and effort each time you run the code. When running the earthquake consumer service using Node.js, the following output confirms that the service has started successfully and is ready for operation:

```
PS C:\packtGit\Hands-on-Microservices-with-JavaScript\Ch08\
earthquakeConsumer> npm start
Debugger listening on ws://127.0.0.1:62120/3f477ceb-6d5a-4d84-
a98a-8f6185f8f11d
For help, see: https://nodejs.org/en/docs/inspector
Debugger attached.
> earthquakeconsumer@1.0.0 start
> node src/index.js
Debugger listening on ws://127.0.0.1:62125/d84e3d2b-6be1-4a3f-
8ba3-2bca4d1fe710
For help, see: https://nodejs.org/en/docs/inspector
Debugger attached.
earthquake Consumer started { port: 3002 }
```

5. Run the `earthquakeService` streaming API to start the streaming process.

6. Go to Postman and hit **Send**.

7. While the `earthquakeService` streaming API prints **The message has been queued!**, our consumer API will print consumed data such as that shown here:

```
Got message
{
  id: 's0iwb737f2',
  magnitude: 6.473388041641288,
  location: { latitude: -26.569165455403734, longitude:
-167.263244317978 },
  timestamp: 1725611270994
}
Got message
{
  id: 'agmk58tick6',
  magnitude: 1.9469044303512526,
  location: { latitude: -19.102647524780792, longitude:
58.15282259841075 },
  timestamp: 1725611271106
}
```

You can add some more logic to these services, but this should be enough to demonstrate streaming as simply as possible.

Summary

This chapter explored the concept of real-time data streaming in microservices architecture. We used the example of an earthquake data-streaming service to illustrate how microservices can efficiently handle continuous flows of information.

Rather than storing data in bulk, the producer service publishes data as a continuous stream, allowing immediate processing and analysis as each new data point arrives. This approach is beneficial for real-time scenarios where immediate processing and analysis are crucial.

Another microservice acts as the consumer in this scenario. It subscribes to the earthquake data stream produced by the first service. As new data arrives, the consumer microservice receives and processes it in real time.

The consumer microservice can perform various actions based on the earthquake data. It might trigger alerts, update dashboards, or integrate with other services for further analysis and response.

Real-time data streaming with microservices offers a powerful approach to handling continuous information flows. In *Chapter 9*, you'll learn how to secure microservices through authentication, authorization, and API protection, while also implementing logging and monitoring tools to proactively detect and address potential issues.

Part 3:
Securing, Testing, and Deploying Microservices

In this final part, we will focus on the crucial aspects of securing, testing, and deploying microservices. We'll learn about implementing authentication, authorization, and monitoring tools to ensure that your microservices are secure and reliable. This section also covers the process of building a CI/CD pipeline, which is vital for automating the deployment of your microservices, and concludes with strategies to deploy our microservices to production.

This part contains the following chapters:

- *Chapter 9, Securing Microservices*
- *Chapter 10, Monitoring Microservices*
- *Chapter 11, Microservices Architecture*
- *Chapter 12, Testing Microservices*
- *Chapter 13, A CI/CD Pipeline for Your Microservices*

9

Securing Microservices

In today's digital world, many applications are built from smaller, independent services working together. These *microservices* offer flexibility and scalability, but keeping them secure is crucial. Imagine a microservice as a small shop on a busy street. You want to ensure that only authorized customers can enter (authentication) and only those with permission can access specific areas (authorization). Likewise, you'd encrypt sensitive information such as credit card details (data encryption). By constantly monitoring for suspicious activity and keeping the shops updated (patching), you can maintain a safe and secure shopping experience. This chapter will guide you through securing your microservices using similar practical strategies and more!

This chapter covers the following topics:

- Security, authentication, and authorization in microservices
- Getting started with JSON Web Tokens
- Implementing an Authentication Microservice

Technical requirements

To follow along in the chapter, you need to have installed an IDE (we prefer Visual Studio Code), Postman, Docker, and a browser of your choice.

It is preferable to download our repository from `https://github.com/PacktPublishing/Hands-on-Microservices-with-JavaScript/tree/main/Ch09` to easily follow our code snippets.

Security, authentication, and authorization in microservices

In a microservices architecture, ensuring robust security, authentication, and authorization is crucial due to the distributed nature of the system. Implementing these mechanisms properly protects microservices from unauthorized access, ensuring data integrity and confidentiality across the system.

Understanding security

In microservices, **security** refers to the measures and practices used to protect the system's components, data, and communication channels from unauthorized access, breaches, and attacks. It involves securing each service individually, as well as the interactions between services, ensuring data is safe both in transit and at rest. Security in microservices typically includes mechanisms such as encryption, authentication, authorization, and monitoring to safeguard the system against vulnerabilities.

Microservices, while offering advantages in flexibility and scalability, introduce unique security challenges. Unlike monolithic applications with a single attack surface, microservices create a distributed system with many potential entry points for attackers. That is why security becomes even more important compared to monolithic applications. A security breach in one microservice can quickly compromise the entire system. Before deploying our services, we should provide a properly tested and fully functional security layer over our microservices.

Exploring authentication

Authentication is a process of verifying a user's or service's identity, and it plays a critical role in securing microservice applications. In a world of distributed systems with numerous access points, authentication ensures that only authorized users and services can interact with your microservices.

But why is authentication valuable in microservices? Let's answer this question here:

- **Enhanced security**: Microservices create a distributed attack surface. Robust authentication acts as a gatekeeper, preventing unauthorized access and potential breaches.

- **Granular control**: Authentication allows you to define access levels for different users and services. This ensures that only authorized entities can perform specific actions within each microservice.

- **Improved trust**: By implementing strong authentication, you build trust with users and external systems relying on your microservices. They can be confident their data is secure.

- **Microservice communication security**: Authentication secures communication between microservices themselves. This prevents unauthorized services from impersonating legitimate ones and gaining access to sensitive data.

Applying authentication is not hard thanks to the packages of Node.js but there are some microservice and authentication challenges you should consider before starting to apply it. We will discuss two of them in this section.

The first challenge is choosing either a **centralized** or **decentralized** authentication service. Deciding on a centralized authentication service or embedding it within each microservice can be a challenge. There's a trade-off between simplicity and potential bottlenecks. Let's look at both of these types of services here:

- A centralized authentication service, also known as an **Identity Provider** (**IdP**), is a trusted third-party system that manages the authentication process for users across multiple applications or microservices. Instead of each microservice handling authentication independently, the IdP takes on this responsibility, offering a consistent, secure, and streamlined authentication mechanism.

- A decentralized authentication service involves each microservice independently managing its own authentication process. Unlike a centralized system where a single IdP handles authentication, decentralized services allow each microservice to have its own embedded authentication logic, providing greater autonomy and flexibility to each service but introducing complexity in maintaining consistency.

When choosing between centralized and decentralized authentication, consider factors such as application complexity, scalability needs, security tolerance, and development resources, as a centralized IdP simplifies security enforcement but adds complexity, while decentralized options require more development effort per microservice.

If you cannot pick one or the other, a *hybrid* approach might be more suited for your case. A hybrid approach can be a good option in some cases. A central IdP can handle user authentication and issue tokens, while individual microservices validate those tokens independently. This offers a balance between security, flexibility, and resilience. As we mentioned before, there's no one-size-fits-all solution. Evaluate your specific requirements and choose the approach that best aligns with your security goals and development needs.

The second challenge can be session management. Traditional session management techniques might not be ideal for the stateless nature of microservices. Alternatives such as **JSON Web Tokens** (**JWTs**) are often preferred. We will talk about JWTs in more detail later in this chapter.

Defining authorization

Authorization in microservices is critical for several reasons, primarily focusing on security, resource management, and compliance. It ensures that only users or services with the appropriate permissions can access or perform actions on specific resources or data. This prevents unauthorized access and potential misuse. By *enforcing* strict access controls, the potential attack surface is minimized. Unauthorized users are restricted from accessing sensitive parts of the system, reducing the risk of data breaches and other malicious activities.

Microservices often deal with a wide range of functionalities and data. Authorization allows for granular control over who can access which service and what operations they can perform, ensuring resources are used appropriately. By *defining* clear access controls, resources are allocated and utilized more efficiently, preventing unauthorized consumption of resources that could degrade system performance.

In a microservice architecture, each microservice is designed to perform a specific function. Authorization ensures that each service has access only to the data and operations it requires, promoting the principle of least privilege. This minimizes potential security risks and helps to maintain a secure, efficient system.

Centralized authorization management can further streamline this process by defining and enforcing access policies uniformly across all services. This approach simplifies the maintenance and updating of access controls, making it easier to ensure consistency across the microservices ecosystem.

There are various ways to implement authorization, such as **Role-Based Access Control** (RBAC), **Attribute-Based Access Control** (ABAC), and **Policy-Based Access Control** (PBAC). While these are out of the scope of this book, by adopting the appropriate method, you can ensure that your system's security policies are both robust and adaptable to your specific requirements.

Best practices for authorization

Best practices are essential to ensure robust security, consistency, and efficiency in managing access controls and authorization across microservices. Let's look at some of these best practices here:

- **Least privilege principle**: Give only the permissions that users or services need to do their jobs, which helps reduce the chance of unauthorized access.

- **Centralized authorization management**: Use a single system to manage who can access what across all microservices, making it easier to maintain and ensure security.

- **Regular audits and reviews**: Check and review who has access to what regularly to make sure everything is safe and up to date.

- **Reserve access**: Set permissions based on roles so users and services only have access to what matches their responsibilities.

- **Token expiration and revocation**: Use tokens that expire quickly and have a way to cancel them if needed, to lower the risk if a token is compromised.

We delved into the critical importance of authorization in microservices and its role in maintaining security, resource management, and compliance. Now, let's differentiate between authorization and authentication.

Difference between authentication and authorization

In microservices architectures, authorization plays a critical role in securing access to resources and data. Before diving into details, we need to understand and differentiate between the terms **authentication** and **authorization**. Authentication verifies the identity of a user or service trying to access the system. It typically involves checking credentials such as usernames and passwords, API keys, or tokens issued by an authorization server. It is similar to checking your ID at the entrance of a building.

On the other hand, authorization determines what actions a verified user or service can perform within the system. It Involves enforcing predefined rules based on user roles, permissions, or attributes associated with the request. It is similar to how, once you're verified to enter the building (authentication), your access card determines which floors or areas you can enter (authorization).

Here are the key differences between authentication and authorization:

- **Objective**: Authentication answers *Who are you?*, while authorization answers *What can you do?*.

- **Timing**: Authentication typically happens first, followed by authorization checks on specific actions.

- **Focus**: Authentication deals with identity verification, while authorization focuses on access control.

Microservices and authorization:

In monolithic systems, authorization is often centralized. But microservices, with their distributed nature, require a more distributed approach to authorization. Here are some common strategies:

- **Per-service authorization**: Each microservice manages authorization for its resources and data.

- **API gateway**: A central API gateway can handle authorization checks before routing requests to individual services

- **Dedicated authorization service**: A separate service manages authorization policies and enforces them across all microservices

---

Which one to select? Well, choosing the right approach depends on factors such as the complexity of your system, security requirements, and scalability needs. As we mentioned before, let's learn about the JWT together. A JWT is widely used for authentication and authorization purposes in distributed systems such as microservices because it is stateless, meaning the server does not need to store session data.

Getting started with JWTs

The real world is constantly changing, and programs need to be adaptable to handle different situations. The elements of programs are also evaluated. The technique you used 10 years ago may not be valid nowadays.

Years ago, we used to use **session-based authorization**, which was simple, popular, easy to grasp, and easy to adapt. It is still a topic for discussion but we mostly prefer to use different types of authentication techniques that are more secure. Before switching to JWT, it is helpful to talk about session-based authentication.

In this type of authentication, you enter your username and password. The server checks whether your credentials are valid. If valid, the server creates a session with a unique identifier (session ID). This session ID might be stored in a cookie on your browser. With each request to the website during that session, your browser sends the session ID back to the server. The server checks the session ID and grants access if it's valid, allowing you to stay logged in. The session expires after a period of inactivity (e.g., 30 minutes) or when you log out. This invalidates the session ID.

On the other hand, **token-based authentication** offers several advantages over session-based authentication. Your sessions rely on the server storing information about each active user. This can become burdensome for applications with a large user base. Tokens, stored on the client side, alleviate this pressure on the server.

The second important difference is that session-based authentication requires the server to maintain session data for each user. Token-based authentication is stateless, meaning the server only verifies the token itself, not referencing any stored user data. This simplifies server architecture and potentially improves performance.

From the security perspective, tokens can be self-contained, including information such as expiry time and user roles. This reduces reliance on cookies, which can be vulnerable to theft. Additionally, tokens can be configured for short lifespans, minimizing the window of opportunity if compromised.

Another important feature of tokens is flexibility. Tokens, such as JWTs, can embed additional data beyond just user identity. This allows for more granular control over access and simplifies authorization processes. Tokens can also be used for API calls between different services, whereas sessions are typically tied to a specific web application. JWTs are a compact, URL-safe means of representing claims to be transferred between two parties. It is commonly used for authorization purposes. A JWT is composed of three parts: header, payload, and signature. These parts are separated by dots (.) and encoded in Base64 URL format.

The **header** typically consists of two parts: the type of token (JWT) and the signing algorithm being used, such as *HMAC-SHA256* or *RSA*. Here is an example of a header:

```
{
  "alg": "HS256",
  "typ": "JWT"
}
```

The **payload** contains the claims. **Claims** are statements about an entity (typically, the user) and additional data. There are three types of claims:

- **Registered claims**: Predefined claims that are not mandatory but recommended, such as `iss` (issuer), `exp` (expiration time), `sub` (subject), and `aud` (audience).

- **Public claims**: Custom claims that can be defined by users. They should be collision-resistant names, such as using a URI or a namespace to avoid conflicts.

- **Private claims**: Custom claims are created to share information between parties that agree to use them.

Here is an example of a payload:

```
{
  "sub": "1234567890",
  "name": "David West",
  "admin": true,
  "iat": 1516239022
}
```

The last element is the **signature**. To create the signature part, you have to take the encoded header, the encoded payload, a secret, and the algorithm specified in the header. The signature is used to verify that the sender of the JWT is who it says it is and to ensure that the message wasn't changed along the way.

For example, if you use the *HMAC-SHA256* algorithm, the signature will be created as follows:

```
HMACSHA256(
  base64UrlEncode(header) + "." +
  base64UrlEncode(payload),
  secret)
```

The output of the algorithm is three Base64-URL strings joined by dots that can be easily passed in HTML and HTTP environments.

Here is an example of *HMAC-SHA256* output:

```
eyJhbGciOiJIUzI1NiIsInR5cCI6IkpXVCJ9.eyJzdWIiOiIxMjM0NTY3ODkwIiwibm
FtZSI6IkpvaG4gRG9lIiwiYWRtaW4iOnRydWUsImlhdCI6MTUxNjIzOTAyMn0.SflKxw
RJSMeKKF2QT4fwpMeJf36POk6yJV_adQssw5c
```

Now that we have understood the various components of a JWT, let's look at how it works in authentication with the help of the preceding example. A user logs in using their credentials. The server verifies the credentials and issues a JWT signed with a secret key. The client (usually a browser) stores the JWT (typically in local storage or a cookie).

The client sends the JWT in the `Authorization` header of each subsequent request to access protected resources:

```
Authorization: Bearer <token>
```

Then, it does token verification where the server verifies the token's signature and checks its validity (expiration, issuer, etc.). If the token is valid, the server processes the request. Before moving on, it's important to note that JWTs are stateless, compact, and self-contained, making them efficient for securely transmitting user information without server-side session storage. When using JWTs, ensure the secret key is secure, always transmit tokens over HTTPS, and use short-lived tokens with periodic refreshes to mitigate security risks. Now we know that JWTs are a powerful and flexible way to handle authentication and authorization in modern web applications, providing both security and convenience.

Now that we've covered the theory, let's move on to the practical part and implement the authentication microservice together.

Implementing an Authentication microservice

In microservices development, it's a common practice to develop a separate microservice for authentication and authorization (often referred to as an Auth service). Here's why it's valuable:

- **Centralized security management**: Having a dedicated Auth service allows us to manage authentication and authorization logic in one place. This simplifies updates and security audits and ensures consistent rules across all microservices.

- **Scalability**: The Auth service can be scaled independently based on its load, separate from other microservices with different resource requirements.

- **Reusability**: The Auth service can be reused by all your other microservices, reducing code duplication and promoting consistency.

- **Improved maintainability**: Isolating authentication logic makes it easier to maintain and update the security aspects of your system.

- **Separation of concerns**: Decoupling authentication and authorization from other microservices keeps their responsibilities focused, promoting cleaner code and better maintainability.

- **Flexibility**: A dedicated Auth service can be designed to support different authentication flows (e.g., OAuth, JWT) and authorization strategies (e.g., RBAC), providing a flexible foundation for your microservices architecture.

Let's implement our Auth microservice together. We will use a classical approach to develop our new microservice via ExpressJS as we did before. Most of the things are the same. You should open/create a new folder anywhere you want on your computer and type `npm init -y` to initialize start our project. Throughout our development process, we will use the following libraries: `bcryptjs`, `dotenv`, `express`, `joi`, `jsonwebtoken`, and `mongoose`.

> **Note**
>
> The npm init -y command does not automatically generate the scripts section in package.
> json. You'll need to add it manually to simplify running the application.

Let's walk through our package.json file:

- bcryptjs: This library provides secure password hashing and comparison functionalities. It allows you to store passwords securely in your database and verify user login attempts against the hashed passwords.

- dotenv: This library helps you load environment variables from a .env file. This is a secure way to store sensitive information such as API keys, database credentials, and your JWT secret key, keeping them out of your code.

- express: This is a popular Node.js web framework that helps you build web applications and APIs. It provides a structured approach for handling requests, routing, middleware, and responses.

- joi: This library offers schema validation for data coming into your application. You can define validation rules for request bodies and ensure that the data received adheres to your expected format and structure, improving data integrity and preventing potential errors.

- jsonwebtoken (JWT): This library helps you work with JWTs. It allows you to generate tokens for authentication purposes, containing user information in a secure and verifiable format. You can use JWTs to authorize users for access to protected resources in your microservices.

- mongoose: This is an **Object Data Modeling** (**ODM**) library for MongoDB in Node.js. It provides a convenient way to interact with your MongoDB database by mapping your application data models to MongoDB documents. It simplifies data manipulation and retrieval.

We need a secure way to store user information, and a database is commonly used for this purpose. The mongoose package will help us to work with the database. To connect and disconnect from the database, create a new file called index.js under the src/db folder with the same content as we have in *Chapter 5*.

Under the src/models folder, create a new file called user.js with the following code block:

```
const mongoose = require('mongoose');
const bcrypt = require('bcryptjs');

const userSchema = new mongoose.Schema({
    email: {
        type: String,
        required: true,
        unique: true
    },
    password: {
```

```
        type: String,
        required: true
    }
});

// Hash password before saving
userSchema.pre('save', async function (next) {
    if (this.isModified('password')) {
        const salt = await bcrypt.genSalt(10);
        this.password = await bcrypt.hash(this.password, salt);
    }
    next();
});

module.exports = mongoose.model('User', userSchema);
```

You can extend this schema with additional information but to demo authentication and authorization, we need only these fields.

We have already talked about mongoose in our previous chapters and that is why we will bypass already known details. The only new logic here is working with a hash password. When we create a user via API, we will provide an email and password. For security reasons, we need to hash passwords before storing them in our database.

The code that starts with userSchema.pre("...") is a mongoose middleware function that is executed before a user document is saved to the database. This middleware ensures that passwords are never stored in plain text in our database. It securely hashes passwords before saving them, making it computationally infeasible to recover the original password from the stored hash.

Now, we need to provide a service layer that interacts with the database. For simplicity, you can bypass this layer, but to provide a full picture, we will have it. Under the src/services folder, create a new file called user.js with the following code block:

```
const User = require('../models/user');

const createUser = async (userData) => {
    const user = new User(userData);
    await user.save();
    return user;
};

const getUserById = async (userId) => {
    return await User.findById(userId);
};
```

```
const getUserByEmail = async (email) => {
    return await User.findOne({ email: email });
};
// ... Add methods for other user operations (e.g., update, delete)
module.exports = { createUser, getUserById, getUserByEmail };
```

To make things simple, we haven't implemented full CRUD operations. To demo our functionality, we only need a few of them such as create and get user.

Now, let's switch to our controller and see how we create a user. Under the src/controllers folder, create a new file called user.js with the following code block:

```
const userService = require('../services/user');
const bcrypt = require('bcryptjs');
const jwt = require('jsonwebtoken');
const path = require('path');
const { createConfig } = require('../config/config');
// Register a new user
const createUser = async (req, res) => {
    try {
        const { email, password } = req.body;
        const existingUser = await userService.getUserByEmail(email);
        if (existingUser) {
            return res.status(400).json({ message: 'Email already
              exists' });
        }
        const user = await userService.createUser({ email, password
          });
        res.status(201).json({ message: 'User created successfully',
          user: user });
    } catch (error) {
        console.error(error);
        res.status(500).json({ message: 'Server error' });
    }
};
```

This code snippet defines an asynchronous function named createUser that handles user registration in your Node.js application. Here are the details:

- const createUser = async (req, res) => { ... }: This defines an asynchronous function named createUser that takes two arguments, req (request object) and res (response object).

- `const { email, password } = req.body;`: This extracts the `email` and `password` properties from the request body (`req.body`). These are assumed to be sent by the client in the registration request.

- `const existingUser = await userService.getUserByEmail(email);`: This calls a function from `userService` (to check whether a user with the provided email already exists. It awaits the result (`existingUser`).

- `if (existingUser) { ... }`: If `existingUser` is not `null` (meaning a user with the email exists), it returns a `400 Bad Request` response with a message indicating the email conflict.

- `const user = await userService.createUser({ email, password });`: If the email is unique, it calls another function from `userService` (likely for user creation) with an object containing the extracted email and password. It awaits the result (`user`), which is the newly created user document.

- `.status(201).json({ message: 'User created successfully', user: user });`: If user creation is successful, it sends a `201 Created` response with a message and the newly created user object (`user`) in the response body.

- A `try...catch` block: This wraps the core logic in a `try-catch` block to handle any potential errors during the registration process.

- `res.status(500).json({ message: 'Server error' });`: This sends a generic `500 Internal Server Error` response in case of any errors.

- `createUser`: This function provides a basic structure for user registration in our application. It checks for email conflicts, delegates user creation logic to a separate service, and handles successful and error scenarios with appropriate responses.

But creating a user is not enough. We need to implement sign-in/log-in functionality. In the same file, we have the following code to log in:

```
const loginUser = async (req, res) => {
    try {
        const { email, password } = req.body;

        // Fetch user by email
        const user = await userService.getUserByEmail(email);
        if (!user) {
            return res.status(401).json({ message: 'Invalid email or
                password' }); // Use 401 for unauthorized
        }

        // Compare password hashes securely using bcrypt
        const isMatch = await bcrypt.compare(password, user.password);
```

```
        if (!isMatch) {
            return res.status(401).json({ message: 'Invalid email or
              password' });
        }

        const configPath = path.join(__dirname, '../../configs/.env');
        const appConfig = createConfig(configPath);

        const payload = { userId: user._id }; // Include only
essential user data
        const jwtSecret = appConfig.jwt.access_token; // Replace with
your secret from an environment variable
        const accessToken = await jwt.sign(payload, jwtSecret, {
          expiresIn: '1h' }); // Set appropriate expiration time
        // Send successful login response
        res.status(200).json({ accessToken: accessToken });
    } catch (error) {
        console.error(error);
        res.status(500).json({ message: 'Server error' });
    }
};
```

The code defines an asynchronous function named `loginUser` that handles user login in your Express.js application. Here's a breakdown of what it does:

- `const loginUser = async (req, res) => { ... }`: This defines an asynchronous function named `loginUser` that takes two arguments, `req` (request object) and `res` (response object).

- `const { email, password } = req.body;`: This extracts the `email` and `password` properties from the request body (`req.body`). These are assumed to be sent by the client in the login request.

- `const user = await userService.getUserByEmail(email);`: This calls a function from `userService` (likely another module) to fetch a user with the provided email. It awaits the result (`user`).

- `if (!user) { ... }`: If `user` is `null` (meaning no user found with the email), it returns a `401 Unauthorized` response with a message indicating invalid credentials.

- `const isMatch = await bcrypt.compare(password, user.password);`: This uses `bcrypt.compare` to compare the provided password with the hashed password stored in the fetched user document (`user.password`). It awaits the result (`isMatch`), which is a boolean indicating whether the passwords match.

- `if (!isMatch) { ... }`: If `isMatch` is `false` (meaning passwords don't match), it returns a `401 Unauthorized` response with a message indicating invalid credentials.
- `const configPath = path.join(__dirname, '../../configs/.env');`: This constructs the path to the environment variable file (assuming it's located four folders above the current file).
- `const appConfig = createConfig(configPath);`: This calls a function to read and parse the environment variables from the `.env` file.
- `const payload = { userId: user._id };`: This creates a payload object for the JWT containing the user's ID. Include only essential user data here.
- `const jwtSecret = appConfig.jwt.access_token;`: This retrieves the JWT access token secret from the parsed environment configuration.
- `const accessToken = await jwt.sign(payload, jwtSecret, { expiresIn: '1h' });`: This uses `jsonwebtoken` to sign the JWT with the payload, secret, and an expiration time of one hour (`expiresIn: '1h'`). It awaits the generated token (`accessToken`).
- `res.status(200).json({ accessToken: accessToken });`: If login is successful, it sends a `200 OK` response with the generated `accessToken` in the response body.

Overall, the login function provides a secure login flow using JWT authentication. It fetches the user, validates credentials, generates a JWT with a secret key, and sends it back to the client for subsequent authorized access.

In order to have a fully functional login functionality, we need to provide the secret access token. In JWT, the secret access token plays a vital role in ensuring the integrity and authenticity of the token. When a JWT is created, a cryptographic hash algorithm (e.g., HMAC-SHA256) signs the header and payload (containing user information) using a secret access token. This secret key is like a password known only to the server that issued the JWT and the party verifying it. When a client sends a JWT in an authorization header to access a protected resource, the server receives the token.

The server uses the same secret access token to verify the signature of the received JWT. This verification process ensures the following:

- The token has not been tampered with in transit.
- The token was indeed issued by a trusted source (the server that knows the secret).

If the secret access token is compromised (e.g., leaked or stolen), anyone with the secret can forge valid-looking JWTs, potentially impersonating legitimate users and gaining unauthorized access to resources. Therefore, the secret access token is critical for maintaining the security of JWT-based authentication. Never store the secret access token in your code or within the application itself. Use environment variables or a dedicated secret management service to keep it confidential. Choose a cryptographically strong random string (ideally, at least 256 bits) for your secret access token to make it difficult to guess or crack. Consider rotating your secret access token periodically to mitigate the impact of a potential compromise. By following these practices, you can leverage the benefits of JWTs for secure authentication in your application while minimizing the risks associated with secret access tokens.

When implementing access tokens, be careful to not to generate long-lived access tokens. Long-lived access tokens pose security risks because, if stolen, they allow attackers prolonged access, and revoking them is difficult. In contrast, refresh tokens offer better security by allowing short-lived access tokens to be issued, limiting potential damage. They also enable more granular control, as compromised tokens can be individually blacklisted without affecting other tokens, reducing the need for frequent authentication and lowering server load.

Refresh tokens provide a good balance between user convenience (avoiding frequent logins) and security. Even though they have longer expirations compared to access tokens, their use is limited to obtaining new, short-lived access tokens.

Before implementing our refresh token, consider providing limited time for access tokens as short-lived access tokens reduce the risk of misuse if they are compromised, minimizing the window of opportunity for attackers. In this example, we set it to 5 minutes. After five minutes, the given access token will expire and we should send our refresh token to a new endpoint to obtain a new short-lived access token. First of all, let's modify our login endpoint to return a refresh token:

```
const jwtRefreshTokenSecret = appConfig.jwt.refresh_token;
        const accessToken = await jwt.sign(payload, jwtSecret, {
expiresIn: '5m' }); // Set appropriate expiration time
        const refreshToken = await jwt.sign(payload,
jwtRefreshTokenSecret, { expiresIn: '7d' });

        // Send successful login response
        res.status(200).json({ accessToken: accessToken, refreshToken:
refreshToken });
```

We use the same method to get both tokens. For refresh tokens, we set a bit longer period such as such as seven days. We will create a new endpoint to return new access tokens and that is why we need a new functionality in our controller:

```
const getAccessTokenbyRefreshToken = async (req, res) => {
    try {
        const refreshToken = req.body.refreshToken;

        if (!refreshToken) {
            return res.status(400).json({ message: 'Missing refresh
            token' });
        }

        const configPath = path.join(__dirname, '../../configs/.env');
        const appConfig = createConfig(configPath);
        const refreshTokenSecret = appConfig.jwt.refresh_token;

        // Verify the refresh token
```

```
        jwt.verify(refreshToken, refreshTokenSecret, (err, decoded) =>
          {
            if (err) {
                return res.status(401).json({ message: 'Invalid
                  refresh token' });
            }

            const userId = decoded.userId;

            // Generate a new access token
            const newAccessTokenPayload = { userId };
            const newAccessToken = jwt.sign(newAccessTokenPayload,
              appConfig.jwt.access_token,
              { expiresIn: '5m' });

            res.status(200).json({ accessToken: newAccessToken });
          });
      } catch (error) {
        console.error(error);
        res.status(500).json({ message: 'Server error' });
      }
};
```

This function lets users get a new access token (key to access resources) by providing a refresh token (like a spare key). It checks whether the refresh token is valid using a secret key. If valid, it can generate a new, short-lived access token (with a 5-minute expiration by default) for the user. This way, users don't need to log in frequently but still maintain security with short-lived access tokens.

The best practice for storing refresh tokens involves a balance between security and user convenience. Here is what you need to know:

- Refresh tokens should not be stored in browser cookies due to their accessibility to JavaScript and potential theft through XSS attacks.

- If using cookies, opt for HttpOnly cookies with the Secure flag set. This prevents JavaScript access and mitigates XSS attacks. However, this approach has limitations (e.g., not supported by all browsers in cross-site context).

- On the other hand, local storage is a viable option, but implement security measures such as encryption at rest and in transit to protect the token if compromised. Evaluate libraries or frameworks that provide secure local storage mechanisms.

- In some scenarios, you might consider storing refresh tokens on the server side (e.g., database) for added security or centralized management. However, this is not always necessary and adds complexity.

- While refresh tokens have longer expirations than access tokens (e.g., days or weeks), avoid excessively long durations to minimize potential damage if compromised.

- Implement a mechanism to blacklist refresh tokens after a period of inactivity (e.g., a week) or upon user logout. This prevents attackers from using stolen tokens indefinitely.

- Consider refresh token rotation. When a new access token is issued using a refresh token, generate a new refresh token and store it. This reduces the risk of a single refresh token being compromised for an extended period.

- If performance and fast access are top priorities, consider using Redis for its speed and automatic handling of expiration times. However, address potential persistence concerns if necessary.

- If data durability and integration with your existing database are crucial, storing refresh tokens in a database can be an option. However, evaluate potential performance impacts compared to Redis.

To access our new controller functionality, let provide a route for it. Open the `routes/v1/users/index.js` file and add the following line:

```
router.post('/token', validate(loginSchema),userController.
getAccessTokenbyRefreshToken);
```

That is all. Now we have endpoints to register, log in, and retrieve a new access token.

We store secret tokens and refresh tokens in an `.env` file. Create a `configs` folder on the same level as the `src` folder and add an `.env` file with the following content:

```
PORT=3006
MONGODB_URL=mongodb://localhost:27017/auth-microservice #provide your
MONGO_URL
SECRET_ACCESS_TOKEN={YOUR_SECRET_KEY}
SECRET_REFRESH_TOKEN={YOUR_REFRESH_TOKEN}
```

In order to generate refresh and secret tokens, do the following operations:

1. Open the terminal and type `node`.

2. In the given input window, type `require('crypto').randomBytes(64).toString('hex')`.

The following figure show how easily you can do it:

```
PS C:\packtGit\Hands-on-Microservices-with-JavaScript\Cp9\authMicroservice\src> node
Debugger listening on ws://127.0.0.1:60233/30a041dc-66f0-479d-8784-da7bdf159fda
For help, see: https://nodejs.org/en/docs/inspector
Debugger attached.
Welcome to Node.js v20.12.1.
Type ".help" for more information.
> require('crypto').randomBytes(64).toString('hex')
'75bd90e66fe2dcb5a21f25ae349eaf058b81584346c3402f266d5cbe4ea83b0c1d5fa0c1749cbd78d7a4d48dc3a31e70a44e27544afb05f7
5f91ed8229411cb1'
>
```

Figure 9.1: Generating secret tokens

You will get a different generated result every time you call the last command. Just copy the value and paste it to the .env file to be paired with SECRET_ACCESS_TOKEN. Try the same comment a second time to get a completely different value and paste it for SECRET_REFRESH_TOKEN. The refresh token and secret token must have different values.

As you already know, we have the src/config folder with config.js that can read .env files programmatically. We add token reading functionality to it.

Here is what it looks like:

```
const dotenv = require('dotenv');
const Joi = require('joi');

const envVarsSchema = Joi.object()
    .keys({
        PORT: Joi.number().default(3006),
        MONGODB_URL: Joi.string().required().description('Mongo DB
url'),
        SECRET_ACCESS_TOKEN: Joi.string().hex().required(),
        SECRET_REFRESH_TOKEN: Joi.string().hex().required(),
    })
    .unknown();

function createConfig(configPath) {
    dotenv.config({ path: configPath });

    const { value: envVars, error } = envVarsSchema
        .prefs({ errors: { label: 'key' } })
        .validate(process.env);

    if (error) {
        throw new Error(`Config validation error: ${error.message}`);
    }
    return {
```

```
        port: envVars.PORT,
        mongo: {
            url: envVars.MONGODB_URL,
        },
        jwt: {
            access_token: envVars.SECRET_ACCESS_TOKEN,
            refresh_token: envVars.SECRET_REFRESH_TOKEN
        }
    };
}
module.exports = {
    createConfig,
};
```

This code provides an object called jwt to access refresh and secret tokens.

As you might guess, we haven't validated user-provided data directly. We need to validate the data, and that is why we plan to use the same structure that we used for the account microservice. Under the src/middlewares folder, we have the same validate.js file to validate our schema. That is the main reason why we haven't implemented validation per endpoint. It is time to provide rules for email and password validation. Create user.js under the src/validation folder with the following code block:

```
const Joi = require('joi');

const loginSchema = Joi.object({
    body: Joi.object().keys({
        email: Joi.string()
            .required()
            .error(errors => {
                if (errors[0].code === 'any.required') {
                    return new Error('Email is required');
                }
                if (errors[0].code === 'string.email') {
                    return new Error('Invalid email format');
                }
                return errors;
            }),
        password: Joi.string()
            .min(6) // Minimum password length
            .required()
            .error(errors => {
                if (errors[0].code === 'any.required') {
                    return new Error('Password is required');
```

```
                }
                if (errors[0].code === 'string.min') {
                    return new Error('Password must be at least 6
characters long');
                }
                return errors;
            })
        })
});

module.exports = { loginSchema };
```

This code snippet uses Joi to define a validation schema specifically for login requests in your application. It focuses on the request body, ensuring it contains a valid email address and password that meets the minimum length requirement (defined as six characters in this example). The schema also provides informative custom error messages for missing or invalid email and password, improving the user experience by guiding them toward proper credential format. By implementing this validation, you can prevent malformed login requests from reaching your backend logic and enhance the overall security of your application.

We can directly provide routing in our controllers but we will follow the same convention we did before when we implemented the account microservice. So, under the routes/v1/users folder, create an index.js file with the following content:

```
const { Router } = require('express');
const userController = require('../../../controllers/user');
const { loginSchema } = require('../../../validation/user');
const validate = require('../../../middlewares/validate');

const router = Router();

router.post('/register', validate(loginSchema), userController.
createUser);
router.post('/login', validate(loginSchema), userController.
loginUser);
module.exports = router;
```

The code defines two endpoints. One for registration (/register) and the other for the login (/login) functionality. The routes/v1 folder also contains the index.js file with the following content:

```
const { Router } = require('express');
const userRouter = require('./users');

const router = Router();
```

```
router.use('/users', userRouter);

module.exports = router;
```

As you can see, we use the same code we used in our account microservice. We just changed the route to `users`. Now, users can access our endpoints using `v1/user/{endpoint_name}`. The last elements in our microservice are `app.js` and the root `index.js` file, which are the same as our already implemented account microservice.

Let's test our Auth microservice's endpoints. Run `npm start` from the terminal and let's prepare our POST request to create a user:

1. Open the Postman application.

2. Create a new Postman request window.

3. Change **GET** to **POST**.

4. Provide the endpoint URL (it is `http://localhost:3006/v1/users/register` for us).

5. Go to **Body**, select **raw**, and select **JSON**.

6. Provide a payload and click **Send** (*Figure 9.2*).

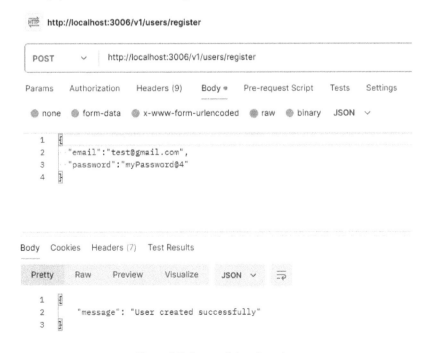

Figure 9.2: Successful registration

The user is ready. Now, we can get a JWT. Here are the steps to get a JWT:

1. Create a new Postman request window.

2. Change **GET** to **POST**.

3. Provide the endpoint URL (it is `http://localhost:3006/v1/users/login` for us).

4. Go to **Body**, select **raw**, and select **JSON**.

5. Provide a payload and click **Send** (*Figure 9.3*).

Figure 9.3: Successful login

The generated access token will expire in a given time slot (*Figure 9.4*). After expiration, we do not need to provide an email and password to get a new access token. We can simply use a refresh token to refresh and to get a new access token.

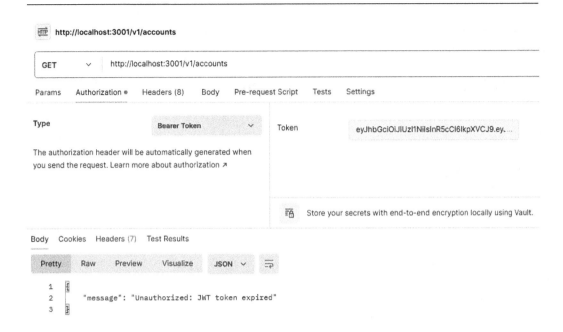

Figure 9.4: Message about expired token

But what if you want a new access token based on a refresh token? That is easy. Here's how:

1. Open a new window on Postman and set the request type to **POST** for the v1/users/ token endpoint.

2. Open the **Body** section and provide a refresh token. Click the **Send** button (*Figure 9.5*).

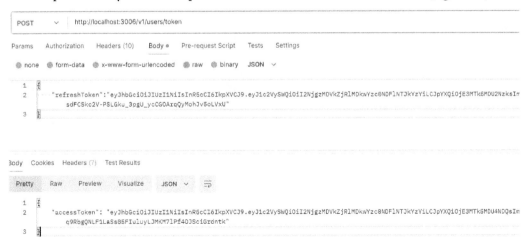

Figure 9.5: Getting a new access token based on the refresh token

Now you can use this access token to access our account microservice resources. Well, that is simply it. It is time to test the JWT in our account microservice.

Integrating token-based authentication for the account microservice

The microservices we implemented so far don't have authentication and authorization functionalities. As homework, you can start to integrate these into them, and for learning purposes, we will implement JWT for the account microservice. Open the account microservice we developed so far. To use the same access token from the Auth microservice, the account microservice should use the same secret token. Open the `configs/.env` file and add the following line:

```
SECRET_ACCESS_TOKEN={USE_THE_SAME_TOKEN_YOU_USED_IN_AUTH_MICROSERVICE}
```

Open the `config/config.js` file and make the following changes in order to read the secret token configuration field:

```
const dotenv = require('dotenv');
const Joi = require('joi');

const envVarsSchema = Joi.object()
    .keys({
        ....
        SECRET_ACCESS_TOKEN: Joi.string().hex().required(),
        .....
    })
    .unknown();

function createConfig(configPath) {
    .............
    return {
        ...............
        jwt: {
            access_token: envVars.SECRET_ACCESS_TOKEN
        }
    };
}

module.exports = {
    createConfig,
};
```

The only real functionality we need to add to the account microservice is a middleware to verify our token.

Under the `src/middlewares` folder, create a file called `verify.js` with the following content:

```javascript
const jwt = require('jsonwebtoken');
const path = require('path');
const { createConfig } = require('../config/config');

const verifyJWT = (req, res, next) => {
    const authHeader = req.headers.authorization;

    // Check for presence and format of Authorization header
    if (!authHeader || !authHeader.startsWith('Bearer ')) {
      return res.status(401).json({
        message: 'Unauthorized: Missing JWT token',});
    }

    const token = authHeader.split(' ')[1];
    const configPath = path.join(__dirname, '../../configs/.env');
    const appConfig = createConfig(configPath);

    // Verify the JWT token
    jwt.verify(token, appConfig.jwt.access_token, (err, decoded) => {
      if (err) {
        // Handle JWT verification errors
        if (err.name === 'JsonWebTokenError') {
          return res.status(401).json({
            message: 'Unauthorized: Invalid JWT token format',
          });
        } else if (err.name === 'TokenExpiredError') {
          return res.status(401).json({
            message: 'Unauthorized: JWT token expired',
          });
        } else {
          // Handle other errors (e.g., signature verification
  failure)
          console.error('JWT verification error:', err);
          return res.status(500).json({
            message: 'Internal Server Error',});
        }
      }
      // Attach decoded user information to the request object
      req.user = decoded;
```

```
        next(); // Allow the request to proceed
    });
};

module.exports = verifyJWT;
```

This code defines a middleware function named `verifyJWT` for Express.js applications. It handles JWT verification for incoming requests. It checks if the authorization header exists in the request and starts with `Bearer`. If not, it returns a `401 Unauthorized` response indicating a missing JWT.

If the header is present and formatted correctly, it extracts the JWT itself from the authorization header. Our middleware constructs the path to the environment variable file containing the JWT secret key. It calls a function (likely from a separate `config` module) to read and parse the configuration.

Then, we use `jsonwebtoken.verify()` to verify the extracted token against the secret key retrieved from the configuration. If verification fails (`err`), it checks the error type:

- `JsonWebTokenError`: Indicates invalid token format, returning `401` with a specific message
- `TokenExpiredError`: Indicates an expired token, returning `401` with a specific message
- Other errors (e.g., signature verification failure) are logged and a generic `500 Internal Server Error` response is sent for security reasons

If verification is successful (`!err`), it attaches the decoded user information from the JWT to the `req.user` object for further access within your application logic.

Finally, it calls `next()` to allow the request to proceed to the intended route handler.

Overall, this middleware acts as a gatekeeper, ensuring that only requests with valid JWTs can access protected resources in your application.

In order to use our middleware, we import it in our `app.js` file and use it:

```
const express = require('express');
const v1 = require('./routes/v1');
const consumerModule = require('./modules/kafkamodule');
const morganMiddleware = require('./middlewares/morganmiddleware');
const jwtVerifyMiddleware = require('./middlewares/verify');
const app = express();

app.use(jwtVerifyMiddleware);
app.use(morganMiddleware);

consumerModule();

app.use(express.json());
```

```
// V1 API
app.use('/v1', v1);

module.exports = app;
```

The code imports our middleware and uses it. Now, let's run the account microservice and try to get all account information. Do the following operations:

1. Navigate to the Ch09/accountservice folder.

2. To run the account microservice properly, you also need to run the docker-compose file from the root folder using the docker-compose up -d command.

3. After executing both docker-compose setups, start the account microservice by running the npm start command.

4. Open Postman and send a GET request to v1/accounts (in our case, it is http://localhost:3001/v1/accounts).

5. You will get a message about an unauthorized request (*Figure 9.6*).

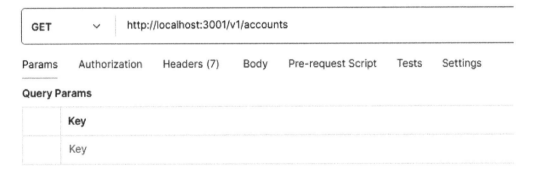

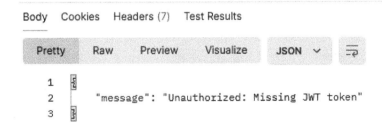

Figure 9.6: Unauthorized access

6. Now, run our Authentication microservice and do the steps we mentioned in the Auth microservice to get an access token (*Figure 9.3*). For the same query for the account microservice, just open the **Authorization** section from Postman, change the type of authorization to **Bearer Token**, and paste the token you get from the Authentication service into the input (*Figure 9.7*).

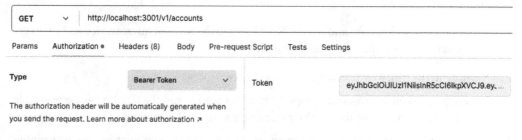

Figure 9.7: Accessing the account microservice

7. Press the **Send** button and here we are:

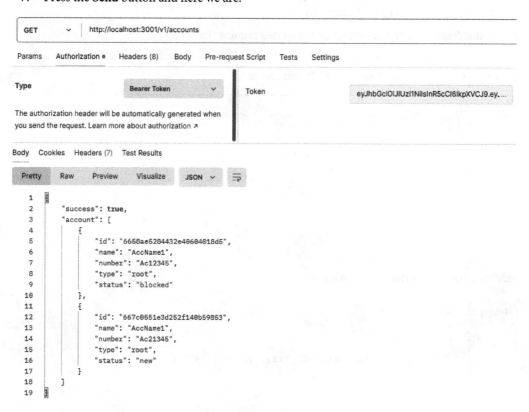

Figure 9.8: Getting account microservice resources

If you've followed the steps correctly, you should now be able to retrieve account data. In the next chapter, we'll dive into observability and explore how to implement it using the ELK stack.

Summary

This chapter explored the fundamental security concepts of authentication, authorization, and their role in securing microservices. We clarified the importance of verifying user identities (authentication) and determining access permissions (authorization) for robust system protection.

To achieve this, we implemented a dedicated microservice for issuing access tokens (JWTs) and refresh tokens. JWTs grant temporary access, while refresh tokens allow users to obtain new access tokens without re-entering credentials. A practical demonstration showcased how this microservice interacts with another microservice, the account microservice.

In our next chapter, we will explore the monitoring of microservices and its significance in microservice architectures. We will implement logging functionality within the account microservice and integrate it with the **Elasticsearch, Logstash, and Kibana (ELK)** stack. This will establish a centralized logging system, enabling efficient log collection, analysis, and visualization.

10

Monitoring Microservices

Microservices have become a core architectural approach for building scalable and flexible applications, but ensuring their health and performance is just as important as their functionality. Without proper visibility, identifying issues in such a distributed system can be like trying to find a needle in a haystack. Think of monitoring and logging as placing cameras and sensors in different parts of a bustling city, where each microservice is a shop. These tools help you observe how the system is functioning, capture key events, and detect any unusual behavior. By establishing robust logging and monitoring practices, you can quickly pinpoint problems and keep your microservices running smoothly.

This chapter covers the following topics:

- Importance of observability
- Introduction to logging
- Centralized logging with the **Elasticsearch, Logstash, and Kibana (ELK)** stack

Technical requirements

To follow along with this chapter, we need to have an IDE installed (we prefer Visual Studio Code), Postman, Docker, and a browser of your choice.

It is preferable to download our repository from `https://github.com/PacktPublishing/Hands-on-Microservices-with-JavaScript/tree/main/Ch10` to easily follow our code snippets.

Importance of observability

In the world of software, particularly microservices, **observability** is crucial. It allows us to gain deep insights into how our system functions by analyzing its outputs. Observability is an important concept in monitoring and understanding systems. It refers to the ability to gain insight into the internal workings of a system by examining its outputs. Let's try to understand the building blocks of it:

- **Logs**: Logs are detailed records of events that happen within a system. They provide a history of what has occurred, including errors, warnings, and informational messages. Logs can help in identifying and diagnosing issues by showing a step-by-step account of system activities.

- **Metrics**: Metrics are numerical values that represent the performance and behavior of a system. They can include data such as CPU usage, memory consumption, request rates, and error rates. Metrics provide a quantitative measure of the system's health and performance.

- **Alerts**: Alerts are notifications that are triggered when metrics reach certain thresholds. They are used to inform administrators or operators about potential problems or abnormal behavior in real time, allowing for quick responses to issues.

- **Traces**: Traces provide a detailed view of the flow of requests through a system. They show how requests move from one component to another, highlighting the interactions and dependencies between different parts of the system. Traces help in understanding the path of a request and identifying bottlenecks or points of failure.

Observability helps in understanding what is happening inside a system by using logs, metrics, alerts, and traces. Logs give detailed records of events, metrics provide numerical data on performance, alerts notify of potential problems, and traces show the flow of requests. Together, these outputs offer a comprehensive view of a system's state, aiding in monitoring, troubleshooting, and optimizing performance.

Now that we've covered the concept, let's dive into the world of logging in microservices.

Introduction to logging

Have you ever driven a car with a broken dashboard? The speedometer might be stuck, the fuel gauge unreliable, and warning lights might flicker mysteriously. Without clear information about how the engine is running, it's difficult to diagnose problems or ensure a safe journey.

In the world of software, particularly complex systems built with microservices, logging plays a similar role. **Logs** are detailed records of events and activities within a system.

When building your microservices, just thinking about business implementations is not enough. Microservices are, by nature, complex, with many independent services interacting. Logging helps understand individual service behavior and pinpoint issues within a specific service. When things go wrong, logs provide the audit trail to diagnose and fix problems. They help identify errors, dropped requests, or performance bottlenecks. Every microservice application should have a proper logging mechanism.

Logging microservices is essential for diagnostics, but it comes with challenges such as handling high volumes of distributed logs across different machines and languages, making it harder to aggregate and interpret them. Additionally, missing key details and ensuring sensitive information in logs is securely stored add complexity to managing logs effectively.

By understanding these challenges, we can implement effective logging strategies to keep our microservices teams talking and our systems running smoothly.

Logging levels and node libraries

Before practical examples, we need to understand some basics related to logging and one of them is **log levels**. Different log levels are used to categorize the severity or importance of log messages.

Error logs capture critical issues that need immediate attention, such as crashes or system failures, while **warning logs** highlight potential problems that may need investigation. **Info logs** track general system operations, **debug logs** provide detailed diagnostic information, and **trace logs** offer the most granular level of logging for tracking execution flow.

Of course, you don't need to implement logging algorithms from scratch. One of the beauties of Node. Js is it provides a cool collection of libraries for us to use. We have different popular log libraries to integrate and use when we build our microservices. You can use `winston`, `pino`, `morgan` (log middleware for Express.js), `bunyan`, `log4js`, and so on when logging your microservices. We will integrate `winston` and `morgan` as a logging library for the current chapter but it is up to you to select one of them.

Log formats

In Node.js microservices, logging formats can be categorized into unstructured logging, structured logging, and semi-structured logging. Here is an explanation of each:

- **Unstructured logging**: Unstructured logging involves writing plain text log messages. This format is straightforward but can be harder to parse and analyze programmatically. Here is an example showing unstructured logging:

```
const logger = console;
logger.log('Server started on port 3000');
logger.error('Database connection failed: connection
  timeout');
logger.info('User login successful: userId=12345');
```

- **Structured logging**: Structured logging involves writing logs in a consistent, machine-readable format, such as JSON. You can use `.csv`, `.xml`, or other formats as well, but the most used format is JSON. This approach makes it easier to search, filter, and analyze logs programmatically. Here is an example showing structured logging:

```
{
  "level": "error",
  "time": "2024-06-26T12:34:57.890Z",
  "service": "my-microservice",
  "buildInfo": {
    "nodeVersion": "v16.13.0",
    "commitHash": "abc123def456"
  },
  "msg": "Failed to connect to database",
  "eventId": "evt-2000",
  "correlationId": "corr-67890",
  "stack": "Error: Connection timeout\n    at Object.<anonymous>
(/path/to/your/file.js:15:19)\n    at Module._compile (internal/
modules/cjs/loader.js:999:30)\n    at Module.load (internal/
modules/cjs/loader.js:985:32)\n    at Function.Module._load
(internal/modules/cjs/loader.js:878:14)\n    at Function.
executeUserEntryPoint [as runMain] (internal/modules/run_main.
js:71:12)\n    at internal/main/run_main_module.js:17:47",
  "source": {
    "file": "/path/to/your/file.js",
    "line": 15,
    "function": "logError"
  }
}
```

- **Semi-structured logging**: It combines elements of both unstructured and structured logging. It often involves a consistent pattern or delimiter within plain text logs, making them somewhat easier to parse than completely unstructured logs but not as robust as fully structured logs.

We explored the importance of logging in microservices, and its challenges, and discussed the different log levels, popular Node.js logging libraries, and how to choose the right logging format for your microservices. Now, let's cover best practices for logging.

Best practices for logging

Effective logging can help you understand system behavior, diagnose issues, and monitor performance. Here are some essential best practices for logging in Node.js microservices:

- **Use a structured logging format**: Ensure logs are structured (e.g., JSON), making them easily parsed and searchable by log management tools. This facilitates more efficient log analysis and filtering.

- **Include contextual information**: Enrich logs with context such as timestamps, service names, correlation IDs, and user information, enabling better tracing and correlation across microservices.

- **Log at appropriate levels**: Apply suitable log levels (error, warn, info, debug, trace) to categorize log messages based on severity, which helps in filtering logs for relevance and troubleshooting.

- **Avoid logging sensitive information**: Ensure sensitive, data such as passwords and personal details, are redacted or masked before logging to maintain security and compliance.

- **Centralize logs**: Aggregate logs from all microservices in a centralized location using tools such as the ELK stack or cloud-based logging services for streamlined monitoring, analysis, and alerting.

These practices will help you ensure that your logging is efficient, secure, and scalable, making it easier to monitor system behavior, diagnose issues, and maintain overall performance.

Implementing logging in your microservices

It is really simple to implement logging thanks to the packages of Node.js. In this section, we will use winston and morgan to demonstrate the usage of logging in microservices. Let's integrate log support into the Account microservice we developed before. To follow this chapter, go to our GitHub repository and download the source code and Ch10 using your favorite IDE. We plan to integrate monitoring functionality into our microservice, which we implemented in *Chapter 9*. You can just copy the Ch09 folder and start to work on it.

To install the winston and morgan libraries on the account microservice, run the following command from the accountservice folder:

```
npm install -E winston morgan
```

Now, our package.json file should contain appropriate versions to use the libraries. Let's first try to use winston for logging. Create a file called logger.js under the src/log folder with the following content:

```
const winston = require('winston');
const logger = winston.createLogger({
    level: process.env.LOG_LEVEL || 'info',
    defaultMeta: {
        service: "account-microservice",
        buildInfo: {
            version: '1.0.0',
            nodeVersion: process.version
        }
    },
    transports:
        [new winston.transports.Console({
```

```
                    format: winston.format.combine(
                        winston.format.colorize(),
                        winston.format.simple()
                    )
                }),
            new winston.transports.File({
                format: winston.format.combine(
                    winston.format.json(),
                    winston.format.timestamp()
                ),
                filename: 'combined.log'
            }),
            new winston.transports.File({
                format: winston.format.combine(
                    winston.format.json(),
                    winston.format.timestamp()
                ),
                filename: 'error.log',
                level: 'error'
            })
            ]
});

module.exports = {
    logger
};
```

This code defines a `winston` logger in Node.js for an application named `account-microservice`. Let's break down the code step by step:

- `const winston = require('winston');`: This line imports the `winston` library, which is a popular logging framework for Node.js.

- `const logger = winston.createLogger({...});`: This line creates a new `winston` logger instance and stores it in the logger constant. The curly braces (`{}`) contain configuration options for the logger.

- `level: process.env.LOG_LEVEL || 'info'`: This sets the minimum severity level of logs that will be captured. It checks the `LOG_LEVEL` environment variable first. If that's not set, it defaults to the `'info'` level. Levels such as `'error'`, `'warn'`, `'info'`, `'debug'`, and so on exist, with `'error'` being the most severe.

- `defaultMeta`: This defines additional information that will be attached to every log message. Here, it includes the service name (`account-microservice`) and build information (version and `nodeVersion`).

- `transports`: This configures where the log messages will be sent. Here, it's an array defining three transports:

  - `winston.transports.Console`: This sends logs to the console (usually your terminal)

- `format: winston.format.combine(...)`: This defines how the log message will be formatted when sent to the console. It combines two formatters:

  - `winston.format.colorize()`: This adds color to the console output for better readability.

  - `winston.format.simple()`: This formats the message in a simple text format.

- `winston.transports.File({ filename: 'combined.log' })`: This sends all logs (based on the level setting) to a file named `combined.log`.

- `format: winston.format.combine(...)`: Similar to the console, it combines formatters:

  - `winston.format.json()`: This formats the message as a JSON object for easier parsing by machines.

  - `winston.format.timestamp()`: This adds a timestamp to each log message.

- `winston.transports.File({ filename: 'error.log', level: 'error' })`: This sends only error-level logs to a separate file named `error.log`. It uses the same formatters (`json` and `timestamp`).

- `module.exports = [];`: This line makes the created logger (`logger`) available for import and use in other parts of your application.

In summary, this code sets up a comprehensive logging system for our application. It logs messages to both the console and files, with different formatting and filtering based on severity level. This allows us to easily monitor application behavior, debug issues, and analyze logs for further insights.

Let's integrate logging into `accountController` and see the result. Here is a simplified version:

```
const accountService = require('../services/account');
const { logger } = require('../log/logger');

const getAccountById = async (req, res) => {
    logger.info('getAccountById method called', { accountId: req.
params.id });
    ....
```

When you call the endpoint that is responsible for delivering the `getAccountById` method, you will get a log message in your terminal and a `combined.log` file. We also integrated logging in `index.js` of our application to see whether everything is OK with the application running:

```
{
  "buildInfo": {
    "nodeVersion": "v20.12.1",
    "version": "1.0.0"
  },
  "level": "info",
  "message": "account service started",
  "port": 3001,
  "service": "account-microservice"
}


{
  "accountId": "6658ae5284432e40604018d5",
  "buildInfo": {
    "nodeVersion": "v20.12.1",
    "version": "1.0.0"
  },
  "level": "info",
  "message": "getAccountById method called",
  "service": "account-microservice"
}
```

If you have any errors, you'll get the error message in your terminal and it will automatically be added to the `error.log` file.

In Node.js, particularly when using Express.js for building web applications, the `morgan` package is a popular tool for streamlining HTTP request logging. It automates the process of capturing and recording information about incoming requests to your application.

Here's why you may use it:

- **Simplified logging**: Manually logging request details can be cumbersome. `morgan` eliminates this by automatically capturing data such as the request method, URL, status code, response time, and more. This saves development time and ensures consistent logging.

- **Debugging and analysis**: The logged information from `morgan` provides valuable insights into how your application handles requests. This can be crucial for debugging purposes, helping you identify potential issues or performance bottlenecks within your application's request processing.

- **Monitoring application traffic**: By reviewing the logs, you can gain a better understanding of your application's traffic patterns. This can be useful for monitoring overall application health, identifying usage trends, and making informed decisions about scaling or resource allocation.

- **Customizable logging**: Morgan offers various predefined logging formats (such as `combined`, `common`, and `dev`) that cater to different levels of detail. You can also create custom formats to capture specific data points relevant to your application's needs.

We've already installed the `morgan` package and it is time to use it. We usually use it as middleware and here is how to implement your own `morgan` middleware. Create a new file called `morganmiddleware.js` under the `src/middlewares` folder. Copy and paste the following inside it:

```
const fs = require('fs');
const path = require('path');
const morgan = require('morgan');
const { logger } = require('../log/logger-logstash');

const morganFormat = JSON.stringify({
    method: ':method',
    url: ':url',
    status: ':status',
    responseTime: ':response-time ms',});

// Path to the combined.log file
const logFilePath = path.join(__dirname,
  '../../combined.log');

// Create a write stream for the log file
const logFileStream = fs.createWriteStream(logFilePath,
  { flags: 'a' });

// Custom message handler function for logging
function messageHandler(message) {
    const parsedMessage = JSON.parse(message.trim());

    // Write log to logstash
    logger.info('Request received for logging',
      parsedMessage);

    // Also write the log to combined.log file
    logFileStream.write(`${message}\n`);
}

// Create morgan middleware with custom format and stream
const morganMiddleware = morgan(morganFormat, {
    stream: {
        write: messageHandler,
    },
```

```
    });
    module.exports = morganMiddleware;
```

This code defines a custom middleware function for logging HTTP requests in JSON format using the `morgan` library. The code defines a logging mechanism that uses the `morgan` middleware to log HTTP requests in a Node.js application. It integrates logging with both a `combined.log` file and a Logstash server for external log management.

`morganFormat` is a custom format that logs details such as the HTTP method, URL, status code, and response time for each request. These logs are then handled by a custom `messageHandler` function.

In the `messageHandler`, the incoming log message is parsed from a JSON string into an object. The parsed log is then sent to Logstash using the `logger.info` function, which is imported from the `logger-logstash` module. At the same time, the original log message is also written to a local file named `combined.log`. This is done by creating a write stream to the file using Node.js's `fs` module, which appends each new log to the file.

Finally, the custom `morganMiddleware` is created using the `morgan` function, with the logging stream directed to `messageHandler`. This middleware is then exported to be used in other parts of the application for logging purposes.

This setup ensures that HTTP request logs are recorded both locally in a file and sent to an external Logstash service for further processing.

We're done with middleware functionality and now it is time to apply it. Open `app.js`, which is where we have configured our middleware flow and make the following changes:

```
    const morganMiddleware = require('./morganmiddleware');

    const app = express();

    app.use(morganMiddleware);
```

Before everything else in the middleware flow, we need to use `morganMiddleware` and now you can just remove the previous logging functions we did via `winston`. Run the application and call any endpoint you want. Before running the account microservice, make sure that Docker is running with the appropriate `docker-compose` file. Don't forget to run both `docker-compose` files (`accountservice/docker-compose.yml` and `accountservice/elk-stack/docker-compose.yml`).

Here is the terminal output for logging:

```
info: Request received for logging {"buildInfo":{"nodeVersion":"v20.12.1","version":"1.0.0"},"
method":"GET","responseTime":"60.806 ms","service":"account-microservice","status":"200","url"
:"/v1/accounts"}
```

Figure 10.1: Terminal output for logging

Check the `combined.log` file and terminal window to see the logs.

In the next section, we will cover centralized logging.

Centralized logging with Elasticsearch, Logstash, and Kibana (ELK) stack

In a microservices architecture, where applications are broken down into independent, loosely coupled services, **centralized logging** becomes crucial for effective monitoring and troubleshooting. We have a lot of reasons to use it:

- **Spread out logs**: Normally, logs would be all over the place, on each individual mini-app. Imagine hunting for a problem that jumps between them – like looking for a lost sock in a messy house!

- **See everything at once**: Centralized logging brings all the logs together in one spot, like putting all your socks in a basket. This way, you can easily see how everything is working and if any parts are causing trouble.

- **Fixing problems faster**: With all the logs in one place, it's like having a super magnifying glass to find issues. You can search through the logs quickly to see what went wrong, saving you time and frustration.

- **Keeping an eye on things**: Centralized logging often works with monitoring tools, like having a dashboard for your socks. This lets you see how well everything is performing and identify any slow spots.

- **Log care made easy**: Having everything in one place makes taking care of the logs much simpler. It's like having a dedicated sock drawer! Tools can be used to keep things organized, get rid of old logs, and follow any rules you need to follow.

By using centralized logging, you get a powerful tool to watch over your microservices, fix problems faster, and keep everything running smoothly.

We have many different options to implement centralized logging when building microservices and one of them is the ELK stack.

The **ELK stack** is a powerful suite of tools used for centralized logging, real-time search, and data analysis. Here's a brief overview of each component:

- **Elasticsearch**: This is a distributed search and analytics engine. We use it to store, search, and analyze large volumes of data quickly and in near real time. Elasticsearch is built on Apache Lucene and provides a RESTful interface for interacting with your data.

- **Logstash**: This is a server-side data processing pipeline that ingests data from multiple sources simultaneously, transforms it, and then sends it to your chosen *stash*, such as Elasticsearch. It can handle a variety of data formats and provides a rich set of plugins to perform different transformations and enrichments.

- **Kibana**: This is a data visualization and exploration tool used for analyzing and visualizing the data stored in Elasticsearch. It provides a user-friendly interface for creating dashboards and performing advanced data analysis.

But how do they work together? Well, Logstash collects and processes the log data from various sources (e.g., server logs, application logs, network logs) and forwards it to Elasticsearch. Elasticsearch indexes and stores the data, making it searchable in near real time. Kibana connects to Elasticsearch and provides the tools necessary to query, visualize, and analyze the data, allowing users to create custom dashboards and reports.

There are multiple benefits of using the ELK stack:

- **Scalability**: The ELK stack can scale horizontally, allowing you to handle large volumes of log data.
- **Real-time insights**: Elasticsearch's real-time search capabilities provide instant insights into your data.
- **Flexibility**: Logstash's ability to ingest data from various sources and formats makes it highly flexible.
- **Visualization**: Kibana's rich visualization options enable you to create interactive dashboards for monitoring and analysis.
- **Open source**: The ELK stack is open source, with a large community and a wealth of plugins and extensions.

As always, we prefer to install tools via Docker and it applies to the ELK stack also. Go to the `Ch10/accountservice/elk-stack` folder and run the `docker-compose.yml` file using the `docker-compose up -d` command. We will not dive into the details of `docker-compose` because we did it in our previous chapters. Simply, we install Elasticsearch, Logstash, and Kibana in the given `docker-compose.yml` file.

A brief introduction to Logstash

We can collect and transform logs using Logstash. We are able to get input from multiple different sources such as logs generated by other applications, plain text, or networks. For log ingestion, we have different approaches that we can follow:

- **Direct transport**: We can configure our application to directly send data to Elasticsearch. Yes, that is an option but not a preferable way of ingesting logs.
- **Write logs to the file**: As we implement in our microservices, it is preferable to implement such types of logging because other applications, such as Logstash, as a separate process, will be able to read, parse, and forward the data to Elasticsearch. It requires more configuration but it is the more robust and preferable way of doing logging for production.

Logstash configuration is typically written in a configuration file (e.g., `logstash.conf`). This file consists of three main sections: `input`, `filter`, and `output`. Each section defines different aspects of the data processing pipeline. Here's a breakdown of each section and an example configuration:

- The `input` section defines where Logstash should collect data from. This could be from files, syslog, **Transmission Control Protocol (TCP)**/ **User Datagram Protocol (UDP)** ports, or various other sources.

- The `filter` section is used to process and transform the data. Filters can parse, enrich, and modify the log data. Common filters include `grok` for pattern matching, `mutate` for modifying fields, and `date` for parsing date/time information.

- The `output` section specifies where the processed data should be sent. This could be Elasticsearch, a file, a message queue, or another destination.

To see the detailed explanation in action, simply open the `logstash.conf` file:

```
input {
  tcp {
    port => 5000
  }
}

filter {
  json {
    source => "message"
  }
}

output {
  elasticsearch {
    hosts => ["elasticsearch:9200"]
    index => "app-%{+YYYY.MM.dd}"
  }
  stdout { }
}
```

Let's dive into the details of the given configuration:

- **Inputs**:

  - `tcp { port => 5000 }`: This section defines an `input` plugin that listens for data coming in over a TCP socket on port `5000`. Any logs or events sent to this port will be ingested by Logstash.

- **Filters**:

  - `json { source => "message" }`: This `filter` plugin parses the incoming data, assuming it's in JSON format, and extracts the value from the field named `message`. This field is likely where the actual log content resides. By parsing it as JSON, Logstash can understand the structure of the data and make it easier to work with in subsequent processing steps.

- **Outputs**:

  - `elasticsearch { hosts => ["elasticsearch:9200"], index => "app-%{+YYYY.MM.dd}" }`: This output plugin sends the processed data to Elasticsearch, a search and analytics engine optimized for handling large volumes of log data. The host's option specifies the location of the Elasticsearch instance (presumably running on a machine named `elasticsearch` with the default port `9200`).

- The `index` option defines a dynamic index naming pattern. Each day's logs will be stored in a separate index named `app-YYYY.MM.dd` (where `YYYY` represents the year, `MM` the month, and `dd` the day). This pattern helps in efficient log management and allows you to easily search for logs from specific dates.

- `stdout { }`: This output plugin simply prints the processed data to the console (standard output) for debugging or monitoring purposes. The empty curly braces (`{ }`) indicate the default configuration for the standard output.

This Logstash configuration ingests data from TCP source, parses JSON-formatted logs, and then sends them to Elasticsearch for storage and analysis. Daily indexes are created for organized log management. The `stdout` plugin provides a way to view the processed data during development or troubleshooting.

Let's integrate logging into our account microservice. Create a new file called `logger-logstash.js` under the `accountmicroservice/src/log` folder with the following content:

```
const winston = require('winston');
const LogstashTransport = require('winston-logstash
  /lib/winston-logstash-latest.js');

const serviceName = 'account-microservice'

const logstashTransport = new LogstashTransport({
    host: 'localhost',
    port: 5000
```

```
})

const logger = winston.createLogger({
    level: 'info',
    format: winston.format.combine(winston
      .format.timestamp(), winston.format.json()),
    defaultMeta: {
        service: serviceName,
        buildInfo: {
            nodeVersion: process.version
        }
    },
    transports: [
        new winston.transports.Console({
            format: winston.format.combine(
                winston.format.colorize(),
                winston.format.simple()
            )
        }),
        logstashTransport
    ]
})

module.exports = {
    logger
};
```

We have already talked about winston configuration and the only new thing here is logstashTransport. We added two transports channel: one for the terminal's console and the other one for sending logs to logstash. To use the given file with morgan, just change morganmiddleware.js's logger to the following:

```
const { logger } = require('./log/logger-logstash');
```

Now, run our application and go to http://localhost:5601; this is our Kibana. From the left menu, find **Management | Dev tools**. Click on the **Execute** button and you will see the total value with your logs (*Figure 10.2*)

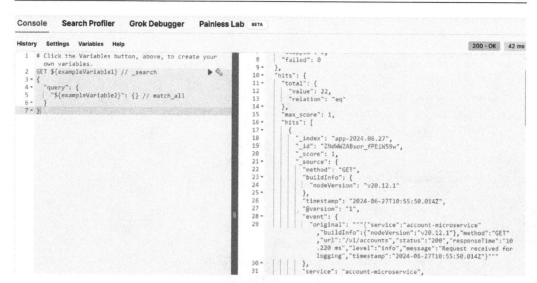

Figure 10.2: Getting logs from Kibana

Now, our logs are flowing to the ELK stack. You can think of Elasticsearch as a search and analytics engine with a data warehouse capability.

A brief introduction to Elasticsearch

Elasticsearch is a powerhouse search engine built for speed and scalability. At its core, it's a distributed system designed to store, search, and analyze large volumes of data in near real time. It is document-oriented and uses JSON.

Let's dive deeper into the key attributes of Elasticsearch:

- **Distributed**: Elasticsearch can store data across multiple nodes (servers) in a cluster. This distribution allows for the following:

  - **Fault tolerance**: If one node fails, other nodes can handle the requests, keeping your search service operational.

  - **Horizontal scaling**: You can easily add more nodes to the cluster as your data volume or search traffic grows.

- **Scalable**: As mentioned previously, Elasticsearch excels at horizontal scaling. You can add more nodes to the cluster to handle increasing data and search demands. This scalability makes it suitable for large datasets and high search volumes.

- **Search and analytics**: Elasticsearch specializes in full-text search, which analyzes the entire text content of your documents. This allows you to search for keywords, phrases, and even concepts within your data. It also provides powerful analytics capabilities. You can aggregate data, identify trends, and gain insights from your search results.

- **Flexible search**: Elasticsearch offers a wide range of query options. You can search for specific terms, filter results based on various criteria, and perform complex aggregations. This flexibility allows you to tailor your searches to your specific needs and uncover valuable information from your data.

- **Search speed**: Due to its distributed architecture and efficient indexing techniques, Elasticsearch delivers fast search results. This is crucial for applications where users expect an immediate response to their queries.

In this section, we provided a brief overview of Elasticsearch, focusing on the core attributes that make it a powerful tool for search and data analysis.

A brief introduction to Kibana

Kibana is the last item in our ELK stack. It is the visualization layer that complements the data storage and search muscle of Elasticsearch. It's an open source platform that acts as a window into your Elasticsearch data, allowing you to explore, analyze, and understand it with clear visualizations.

Kibana has the following interesting possibilities:

- **Visualization powerhouse**: Kibana lets you create interactive dashboards with various charts, graphs, and maps. This visual representation transforms raw data into easily digestible insights.

- **Data exploration**: Kibana provides tools to explore, search, and filter your data within Elasticsearch. You can drill down into specific details and uncover hidden patterns.

- **Sharing insights**: Created dashboards can be shared with others, fostering collaboration and promoting data-driven decision-making.

There are several compelling reasons to choose Kibana for microservices:

- **Effortless integration**: As part of the ELK Stack (Elasticsearch, Logstash, and Kibana), Kibana integrates seamlessly with Elasticsearch. This tight integration streamlines the process of visualizing data stored within Elasticsearch.

- **Real-time insights**: Kibana allows you to visualize data in near real-time, providing valuable insights as your data streams in. This is crucial for applications requiring immediate response to changes.

- **Customization options**: Kibana offers a wide range of visualizations and customization options. You can tailor dashboards to fit your specific needs and effectively communicate insights to your audience.

- **Open source and free**: Being open source, Kibana is free to use and offers a vibrant community for support and development.

Microservices architectures involve multiple, independent services working together. Kibana shines in this environment for several reasons:

- **Monitoring performance**: Visualize key metrics from your microservices on Kibana dashboards to monitor their health and performance. This helps identify bottlenecks and ensure smooth operation.

- **Log analysis**: Centralize and analyze logs from all your microservices within Kibana. This unified view simplifies troubleshooting issues and pinpointing errors across the system.

- **Application insights**: Gain insights into how users interact with your microservices by visualizing usage patterns and trends within Kibana. This data can guide development efforts and improve user experience.

Learning about the ELK stack, diving into details of Elasticsearch querying and Kibana-related topics, such as custom dashboards, and working with metrics are beyond the scope of this book and that is why we finish our chapter only with a simple introduction to them.

Summary

This chapter delved into the crucial aspects of monitoring and logging in microservices architecture, emphasizing the importance of observability in maintaining the health and performance of distributed systems. We began by explaining how observability provides deep insights into system behavior through key components such as logs, metrics, alerts, and traces.

We then shifted focus to the importance of logging in microservices, which is essential for capturing detailed records of system events, identifying performance bottlenecks, and diagnosing issues in real time. We explored different log levels—error, warning, info, debug, and trace—and discussed how they help categorize log messages based on severity, making troubleshooting more efficient. Additionally, the chapter covered popular logging libraries in Node.js such as `winston` and `morgan`.

Following the theoretical foundation, we demonstrated how to implement logging in a real-world scenario by integrating `winston` and `morgan` into the account microservice.

The chapter then moved on to centralized logging, introducing the powerful ELK stack. We explained how Logstash collects and processes log data, Elasticsearch stores and indexes the data for real-time search, and Kibana visualizes the information through interactive dashboards. By integrating these tools, we established a centralized logging system that simplifies log collection, analysis, and visualization.

In the next chapter, we will explore how to manage multiple microservices effectively using popular microservices architecture elements. You'll learn about using an API gateway, which acts as a single entry point to manage requests and direct them to the correct services, as well as organizing data and actions within your system through CQRS and Event Sourcing, two important methods that help handle complex data flows. By the end, you'll have a clear understanding of building and connecting services in a way that's efficient and easy to maintain.

Microservices Architecture

The world of software development is constantly evolving. As applications grow in complexity, traditional monolithic architectures struggle to keep pace. This chapter dives into some key design patterns that empower developers to build scalable and resilient systems – an API gateway, **Command Query Responsibility Segregation** (**CQRS**), event sourcing, and Service Registry and discovery.

These patterns, particularly when used together within a microservices architecture, offer numerous benefits. They promote loose coupling between services, making them easier to develop, maintain, and deploy independently. They also enhance scalability by allowing individual services to be scaled based on specific needs. Additionally, these patterns contribute to improved fault tolerance and resilience, ensuring that your application remains robust even if individual services encounter issues.

This chapter will provide a comprehensive introduction to each of these patterns, outlining their core concepts, benefits, and use cases. We will explore how to apply some of them to create a robust foundation for building modern, scalable applications. By understanding these patterns, you'll be equipped to design and develop applications that can thrive in the ever-changing landscape of software development.

This chapter covers the following topics:

- Getting started with an API gateway
- CQRS and event sourcing
- Service Registry and discovery in microservices

Let's get into the chapter!

Technical requirements

To follow us along the chapter, we need an IDE (we prefer Visual Studio Code), Postman, Docker, and a browser of your choice.

It is preferable to download the repository from `https://github.com/PacktPublishing/Hands-on-Microservices-with-JavaScript` and open the `Ch11` folder to easily follow our code snippets.

Getting started with an API gateway

An API Gateway integrates with a microservice architecture by acting as a central hub, managing communication between client applications and the distributed microservices. When we build our microservices, we want them independently developed, deployed, and scaled without affecting client applications. Clients only interact with the API gateway, which shields them from the complexities of the underlying microservice network.

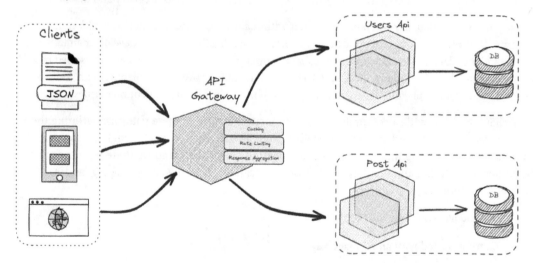

Figure 11.1: A simple API Gateway

The API Gateway receives requests from clients and intelligently routes them to the appropriate microservice(s), based on the request content or URL. It can handle simple routing or complex scenarios, involving multiple microservices working together to fulfill a request. Let's explore the importance of integrating an API Gateway into our microservice architecture:

- **Simplified client interaction**: Clients have a centralized entry point/single point of contact (the API gateway) to interact with an application, regardless of how many microservices are involved. This reduces development complexity on the client side.

- **Improved scalability**: An API Gateway can be independently scaled to handle increasing traffic volumes without impacting the individual microservices. Microservices can also be scaled independently based on their specific workloads, highlighting the importance of API gateways.

- **Enhanced security**: Centralized security management of an API Gateway strengthens overall application security. The API Gateway can implement authentication, authorization, and other security policies to protect microservices from unauthorized access.

- **Reduced development complexity**: Developers don't need to implement functionalities such as routing, security, and monitoring logic within each microservice. An API Gateway handles these cross-cutting concerns centrally.

Let's now see how an API Gateway might work.

How an API Gateway works

In a microservice architecture, an API Gateway acts as the central entry point for all client requests. It plays a crucial role in managing and optimizing the flow of communication between clients and backend services. By handling authentication, routing, load balancing, and other vital functions, the API Gateway ensures that the microservices remain loosely coupled and scalable.

Here's a step-by-step breakdown of how an API Gateway typically processes client requests:

1. **Client request**: A client (e.g., a web or mobile app) sends a request to an API Gateway. The request includes details such as the HTTP method, URL path, headers, and possibly a body.

2. **Request handling**: The API Gateway receives the request and examines its contents. Based on the URL path or other routing rules, the Gateway determines which backend service(s) should handle the request.

3. **Authentication and authorization**: The API Gateway checks the request for authentication tokens (e.g., JWT or OAuth tokens). It verifies the token's validity and checks whether the client has the necessary permissions to access the requested resource.

4. **Request transformation**: The API Gateway may modify the request to fit the requirements of the backend service. This might include changing the protocol, altering headers, or modifying the request body.

5. **Routing and aggregation**: The Gateway routes the request to the appropriate backend service(s). If the request involves multiple services, the Gateway will handle communication with each service and aggregate their responses into a single response for the client.

6. **Caching and load balancing**: The Gateway checks whether the response is cached to serve it quickly without hitting the backend service. It also distributes the request load among multiple instances of the backend service to balance traffic and improve performance.

7. **Rate limiting and throttling**: The API Gateway enforces rate limits to control the number of requests a client can make within a specified period. It may throttle requests if a client exceeds the allowed request rate.

8. **Response handling**: Once the backend service(s) respond, the Gateway may modify the response before sending it back to the client. This could include adding or removing headers, transforming data formats, or aggregating multiple responses.

9. **Logging and monitoring**: The API Gateway logs details of the request and response for monitoring and analysis. Metrics such as request counts, response times, and error rates are tracked to monitor the health and performance of the services.

Now that we know how an API Gateway works, let's see what the better choice in a given situation is – single or multiple API gateways.

Single versus multiple API gateways

You can implement multiple API gateways in a microservice architecture, but it's not always the most straightforward or recommended approach. There are situations where it might be beneficial, but generally, a single API Gateway is preferred for simplicity and maintainability.

A single API Gateway is ideal when you want centralized management, a consistent client experience, and simplified scalability – all of which streamline API operations and reduce complexity.

While a single Gateway is often preferred, there are some situations where multiple gateways might be considered:

- **Heterogeneous client types**: If you have clients using vastly different protocols or communication styles (e.g., mobile apps, web applications, and legacy systems), separate API gateways could be used to cater to these specific needs with custom protocols or functionalities. This approach can be complex to maintain in the long run.

- **Physical separation**: If your microservices are geographically distributed across different data centers or cloud regions, you might consider placing an API Gateway in each location for performance reasons. However, this introduces additional management overhead to maintain consistency across gateways.

- **Security segmentation**: In very specific security-sensitive scenarios, you might implement separate API gateways for different security zones within your application. This allows for stricter control over access to certain microservices. However, this requires careful design and expertise to avoid creating unnecessary complexity.

Generally, the benefits of a single API Gateway outweigh the potential advantages of using multiple gateways, as the former promotes simplicity, maintainability, and a consistent client experience.

If you want to reap the benefits of multiple API gateways without the complexity, here are some alternatives:

- **An API Gateway with routing by client type**: Consider using a single API Gateway with routing logic that can differentiate between different client types and tailor responses accordingly.

- **Microservice facades**: Implement a **facade** pattern (more on this shortly) within some microservices to handle specific client interactions, potentially reducing the need for multiple gateways.

You should carefully consider your specific needs before implementing multiple API gateways. In most cases, a well-designed single API Gateway will provide the optimal solution for your microservice architecture.

> **The facade pattern**
>
> A facade in this context refers to implementing a layer within some microservices that specifically handles interactions with clients. Instead of introducing multiple API gateways, which can add complexity, a microservice facade acts as a simplified interface or *front* that abstracts the internal workings of the microservice for the client.

It is time to implement and see the power of an API Gateway in practice. The next section will dive into the details of the practical implementation of an API gateway.

Implementing microservices using an API gateway

It is possible to implement the API Gateway pattern using different forms with different libraries. In this context, **forms** refers to the different ways or approaches available to implement the API Gateway pattern, depending on the specific technologies or libraries chosen. The API Gateway can be set up using various frameworks or methods, each offering unique features or capabilities. To make things clear and understandable, we will implement our API Gateway as simply as possible. Ultimately, you will understand how to implement an API Gateway with caching, rate limiting, and response aggregating. For more detailed implementation, check out the `Ch11/ApiGateway` folder in our repo.

To demonstrate the real value of the API Gateway pattern, we need to have at least two microservices. The reason for needing *at least two* microservices to show the true value of the API Gateway pattern is that the pattern is designed to handle multiple services and consolidate their functionality for clients. We will use the following two microservices in this chapter:

- The post-microservice
- The user microservice

Implementing post microservice

Our first microservice, the *post-microservice*, acts as a wrapper/abstraction over the jsonplaceholder service. jsonplaceholder is a free online service that provides a REST API with fake data. It's often used by developers to easily access and utilize realistic-looking sample data (users, posts, comments, etc.) without having to set up their databases. This allows them to quickly test API endpoints, frontend functionality, and user interactions.

1. Create a new folder (a post-microservice folder in our case).
2. Run npm install express axios to install the required packages.

Here is what your package.json should look like:

```
{
  "dependencies": {
    "axios": "^1.7.2",
    "express": "^4.19.2"
  }
}
```

For all chapters, you don't need to install the exact package versions listed. While our focus is on using the packages themselves rather than specific versions, if there are major changes or breaking differences in newer versions, refer to the official documentation for updates.

Now, let's create a new file called server.js in the folder we created (i.e., post-microservices) with the following code block:

```
const express = require('express');
const axios = require('axios'); // Requires the axios library for
making HTTP requests

const app = express();
const port = 3001; // Port on which the server will listen

app.get('/posts/:id', async (req, res) => {
  const postId = req.params.id; // Extract the ID from the URL
parameter

  try {
    const response = await axios.get(
      `https://jsonplaceholder.typicode.com/posts/${postId}`);
    const post = response.data;

    if (post) {
      res.json(post); // Send the retrieved post data as JSON response
```

```
      } else {
         res.status(404).send('Post not found'); // Respond with 404 if
  post not found
      }
    } catch (error) {
      console.error(error);
      res.status(500).send('Internal Server Error'); // Handle errors
  with 500 status
    }
  });

  app.listen(port, () => {
    console.log(`Server listening on port ${port}`);
  });
```

This code snippet uses the Express framework to create a simple web server that listens on port 3001. It imports the axios library to make HTTP requests. The server has a single route, /posts/:id, which responds to GET requests. When a request is made to this route, it extracts the id parameter from the URL. The server then makes an asynchronous request to https://jsonplaceholder.typicode.com/posts/${postId} to fetch a specific post. If the post is found, it sends the post data as a JSON response. If the post is not found, it responds with a 404 status code. If there are any errors during the request, it logs them and responds with a 500-status code, indicating an internal server error.

Let's run our microservice using the node server.js command and test whether everything is working. Open your favorite browser and navigate to localhost:3001/posts/1 (*Figure 11.2*).

Figure 11.2: A post-microservice response

Implementing user microsevice

Our second microservice is called a *user microservice*. It has approximately the same implementation as our post microservice, with a different port (3002) and different service abstraction (a GitHub service abstraction):

```
const express = require('express');
const axios = require('axios'); // Requires the axios library for
making HTTP requests

const app = express();
const port = 3002; // Port on which the server will listen

app.get('/users/:id', async (req, res) => {
    const userId = req.params.id; // Extract the ID from the URL
parameter

    try {
        const response = await
          axios.get(`https://api.github.com/users/${userId}`);
        const user = response.data;
        if (user) {
            res.json(user); // Send the retrieved employee data as
JSON response
        } else {
            res.status(404).send('User not found'); // Respond with
404 if employee not found
        }
    } catch (error) {
        console.error(error);
        res.status(500).send('Internal Server Error'); // Handle
errors with 500 status
    }
});

app.listen(port, () => {
    console.log(`Server listening on port ${port}`);
});
```

Let's run our microservice using the node server.js command and test whether everything is working. Open your favorite browser and navigate to localhost:3002/users/1 (*Figure 11.3*).

Figure 11.3: A user microservice response

Let's build our API Gateway as a third microservice and combine the post and user microservices.

Developing an API gateway

After implementing two microservices, we're ready to show the value and power of an API gateway. We plan to implement rate limit, cache, and response aggregation functionalities for the API gateway. You can add more features such as logging, appropriate exception handling, monitoring, and other interesting behaviors after understanding the essentials.

First things first – you need to understand that an API Gateway by itself acts as a separate microservice. So, create a new folder for it (it is called `api-gateway` in our GitHub repo). We have `package.json` with the following content:

```
{
  "dependencies": {
    "apicache": "^1.6.3",
    "axios": "1.7.2",
    "express": "4.19.2",
    "express-rate-limit": "7.3.1"
  }
}
```

We will use an `express-rate-limit` package to implement rate-limit functionality in our microservice. In a microservice architecture, where applications are broken down into smaller, independent services, **rate limiting** is a technique used to control the number of requests that a service can receive within a specific timeframe. It acts like a traffic controller, preventing a service from being overloaded by a surge of requests.

Conversely, `apicache` is used to implement cache behavior for an API gateway. **Caching** refers to a functionality that allows you to store responses from your backend services for a specific time. This cached data can then be served to subsequent requests, improving performance and reducing load on your backend.

Let's create a `server.js` file to implement an API gateway. Our imported packages look like this:

```
const express = require('express');
const apicache = require('apicache');
const axios = require('axios');
const rateLimit = require('express-rate-limit');
```

First, let's configure our rate limit:

```
const limiter = rateLimit({
    windowMs: 60000, // 1 minute window
    max: 100, // 100 requests per minute
    message: 'Too many requests, please slow down!'
});
```

We use `express-rate-limit` to control how many times users can access your API Gateway in a minute. It acts like a gatekeeper. If a user makes fewer than a hundred requests within a minute, they get through. If they go over a hundred, they'll be blocked with a `Too many requests, please slow down` message. This protects our API from overload and ensures a good user experience for everyone. We will use this `limiter` object later when we specify routing for our endpoint. Let's move on and implement data aggregation:

```
async function getAggregatedData(id) {
    const postResponse = await axios.get(
        `http://postmicroservice:3001/posts/${id}`);
    const userResponse = await axios.get(
        `http://usermicroservice:3002/users/${id}`);

    const aggregatedData = {
        data: {
            id: userResponse.data.login,
            followers_url: userResponse.data.followers_url,
            following_url: userResponse.data.following_url,
            subscriptions_url:
```

```
            userResponse.data.subscriptions_url,
        repos_url: userResponse.data.repos_url,
        post: postResponse.data
    },
    location: userResponse.data.location
  };


  return aggregatedData;
}
```

This function, `getAggregatedData`, retrieves data from two different microservices to build a combined response. It takes an ID as input:

1. First, it makes two separate asynchronous calls using `axios.get`. One fetches post data from the post microservice at port `3001`, and the other fetches user data from the user microservice at port `3002`.

2. Then, it combines the data into a single object, named `aggregatedData`. User data such as location, the followers' URLs, and the person followed by the URL are included. Additionally, the post data retrieved from the first call is added under the key post.

3. Finally, the function returns the `aggregatedData` object, containing all the relevant information about the user and their posts.

By aggregating data in an API gateway, we present a simplified API to client applications. They only need to call a single endpoint (within the gateway) to receive the combined user and post data, instead of making separate calls to each microservice.

For example, when requesting `localhost:3000/users/1`, we should get user information from both the post and user microservices. Here is how we get aggregated data from more than one microservice:

```
app.get('/users/:id', limiter, async (req, res) => {
    const id = req.params.id;
    try {
        const aggregatedData = await getAggregatedData(id);
        res.json(aggregatedData);
    }
    catch {
        res.status(400).json({ success: false, message:
          'Bad request' });
    }


});
```

This code defines a route handler for the API Gateway using Express.js. It handles GET requests to the /users/:id URL path, where :id is a dynamic parameter representing the user ID. The limiter middleware is applied before the route handler function, which ensures that only allowed requests (typically, a hundred per minute based on the previous code) can proceed. Inside the function, the API extracts the ID from the request parameters. It then calls the getAggregatedData function to asynchronously retrieve and combine user and post data. If successful, the function sends a JSON response with the retrieved aggregated data. If there are errors during data fetching, it sends a response with a status code of 400 (bad request) and a generic error message.

The last functionality in our API Gateway is caching. We need to add the following code snippet to the server.js file:

```
let cache = apicache.middleware;
app.use(cache('5 minutes'));
```

Using this code, we apply caching for five minutes for all types of endpoints.

We're done with our infrastructure (the post microservice, API Gateway, and user microservice); it is time to test all of them together.

Testing an API Gateway in Docker

To test an API Gateway, you can run every microservice separately, but as you know, we have different names for microservices in our getAggregatedData function – http://post-microservice:3001 and http://user-microservice:3002. To make these microservices work properly and not run every microservice every time, we will containerize them.

For every microservice, we have Dockerfile, as shown in the following figure:

Figure 11.4: An API Gateway project structure

A `Dockerfile` is a text file that contains instructions to build a Docker image. It acts like a recipe that tells Docker what steps to take to create a self-contained environment for your application.

All three Docker files are completely the same, with the following content:

```
FROM node:alpine
WORKDIR /app
COPY package*.json ./
RUN npm install
COPY . .
CMD [ "node", "server.js" ]
```

This `Dockerfile` creates an image for a Node.js application. It starts with a lightweight Node.js base image, installs dependencies, copies your entire project, and then runs your server code upon startup.

We have a `docker-compose.yml` file in our root folder that will combine all these three `Dockerfile` files and compose them:

```
services:
  post-microservice:
    build:
      context: ./post-microservice
      dockerfile: Dockerfile
    ports:
      - 3001:3001

  user-microservice:
    build:
      context: ./user-microservice # Correct the path if necessary
      dockerfile: Dockerfile
    ports:
      - 3002:3002

  api-Gateway:
    build:
      context: ./api-Gateway
      dockerfile: Dockerfile
    ports:
      - 3000:3000
    depends_on:
      - post-microservice
      - user-microservice
```

This `docker-compose.yml` file defines a multi-container application. It creates three services – `post-microservice`, `user-microservice`, and `api-gateway`. Each builds its own image from a separate directory (for example, `./post-microservice`) using a common `Dockerfile`.

Each service gets exposed on a specific port (`3001` for posts, `3002` for users, and `3000` for the Gateway).

The `api-Gateway` relies on both `post-microservice` and `user-microservice` to be active before starting itself, ensuring that the dependencies are available. To compose these microservices' Docker files, navigate to the folder where we have the `docker-compose.yml` file and run the `docker-compose up -d` command. It should build and run composed services together. Here is what running all required services together via Docker looks like:

		Name	Image	Status	Port(s)
☐	⌄ 🥞	**apigateway**		Running (3/3)	
☐	📦	**api-gateway-1** 7ebbbf96754f 📋	apigateway-api-gateway	Running	3000:3000 ⤢
☐	📦	**post-microservice-1** 8c2a790bd001 📋	apigateway-post-microservice	Running	3001:3001 ⤢
☐	📦	**user-microservice-1** f20e699eba72 📋	apigateway-user-microservice	Running	3002:3002 ⤢

Figure 11.5: An API Gateway in Docker

Navigate to `localhost:3000/users/1` from your browser, and you should get the following aggregated data:

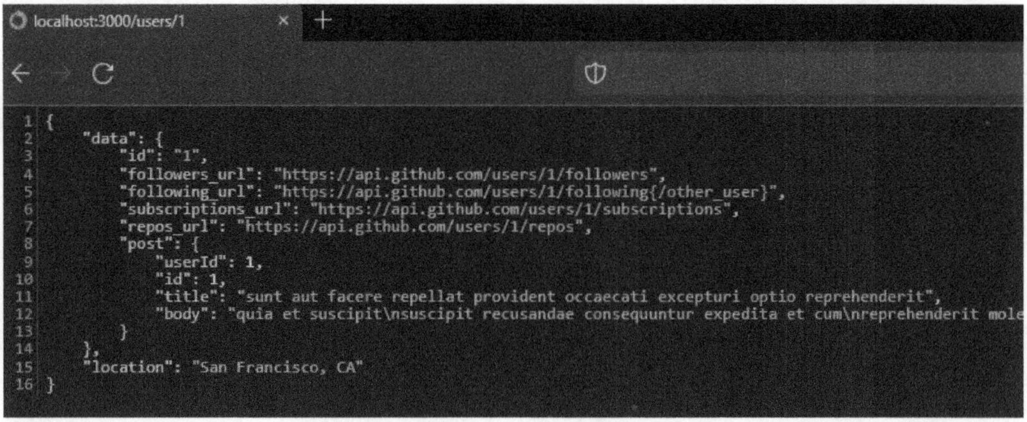

```
 1 {
 2     "data": {
 3         "id": "1",
 4         "followers_url": "https://api.github.com/users/1/followers",
 5         "following_url": "https://api.github.com/users/1/following{/other_user}",
 6         "subscriptions_url": "https://api.github.com/users/1/subscriptions",
 7         "repos_url": "https://api.github.com/users/1/repos",
 8         "post": {
 9             "userId": 1,
10             "id": 1,
11             "title": "sunt aut facere repellat provident occaecati excepturi optio reprehenderit",
12             "body": "quia et suscipit\nsuscipit recusandae consequuntur expedita et cum\nreprehenderit mole
13         }
14     },
15     "location": "San Francisco, CA"
16 }
```

Figure 11.6: An API Gateway in action

So far, we have explored the role of an API Gateway in a microservices architecture, emphasizing how it simplifies client interactions by acting as a central entry point for routing, security, and load balancing. We learned how the API Gateway aggregates data from multiple microservices, applies caching and rate limiting, and enhances scalability. By integrating it into our architecture, we improve both performance and security while maintaining the flexibility and independence of individual microservices. Finally, we containerized the microservices and API Gateway using Docker for efficient testing and deployment.

In our next section, we're going to explore other interesting patterns such as CQRS and event sourcing. First, we will learn what are they and why we use them.

CQRS and event sourcing

CQRS is a software design pattern used in distributed systems (often microservices) to separate read and write operations. This separation offers several advantages, particularly when dealing with applications with high read/write disparities or complex data models.

When you apply for jobs that use distributed architecture in their applications, you often hear about CQRS and, most probably, will be asked about its usage. First things first – we need to understand that CQRS is not an architecture style; it is neither an architecture nor architectural principle. It is just a design pattern that has no wide usage. So, what is CQRS? Before answering this question, let's understand the problem that CQRS seeks to resolve.

Traditional monolithic applications typically use a single database to both read and write data. This approach can lead to the following challenges as an application grows:

- **Scaling bottlenecks**: When read traffic spikes, it can impact write performance (and vice versa).
- **Data model mismatch**: Optimal read and write models may differ. Reads might benefit from denormalized data for faster retrieval, while writes might require a normalized structure for data integrity. This mismatch creates inefficiencies or duplication.
- **Transaction conflicts**: Updates and reads can compete for resources, potentially blocking each other or causing inconsistencies (violations of **ACID** (**Atomicity, Consistency, Isolation, Durability**) principles).
- **Optimization challenges**: Optimizing for reads might hinder write performance, and vice versa.

When we work with monolithic applications, we often use one single data store. This means we have multiple read and write instructions in the same database. We use the same data store model, and everything is simple when it comes to working with only one single storage in terms of development. But is that all? Well, not everything is okay when we have only one data store. Depending on our requirements, we may need to separate our database into read and write databases.

Understanding CQRS

CQRS helps us to separate data stores into read and write data stores. Why? One reason is that we need to optimize our read and write operations. Using CQRS, we can optimize our read data store to read data effectively. We can also configure our schema to optimize reading operations. The same is applicable for writing data stores.

When we have separate data storages, depending on loading, we can scale them independently. When we have separate data stores for reading and writing, we can scale them independently, based on the specific load requirements of each. This is particularly useful in applications that experience high demand for read operations. By decoupling the read and write operations, we can scale the read data store to handle the load without affecting the performance of the write data store, or vice versa. This approach allows more efficient resource allocation, ensuring that each data store is optimized for its specific role.

With CQRS, read and write are separated storages, and we have two different data models. We can now focus on optimizing and building them to support only one operation – either read or write.

In summary, here are the benefits of CQRS:

- **Improved performance**: Optimized read and write models can significantly enhance performance for both read and write operations.

- **Enhanced scalability**: You can scale read and write models independently based on their access patterns. This allows you to handle fluctuating read/write loads more effectively.

- **Flexibility in data modeling**: Each model can be designed for its specific purpose, improving overall data management and reducing complexity.

Is CQRS a silver bullet? Of course not. You should consider the following when you integrate CQRS into your projects:

- **Added complexity**: Implementing CQRS introduces additional complexity compared to a single store. Careful design and trade-off analysis are necessary for successful implementation.

- **Data consistency**: Maintaining consistency across read and write models requires careful consideration. Strategies such as eventual consistency or materialized views can be employed.

CQRS is a valuable pattern for applications with *high read/write disparities* (e.g., e-commerce with frequent product views and infrequent purchases), *complex data models* with different requirements for reads and writes, and scenarios that require *independent scaling* of read and write operations.

Before adopting CQRS, carefully analyze your application's needs. While it offers significant benefits in specific scenarios, the added complexity might not be necessary for simpler applications.

When discussing CQRS, it is also important to discuss event sourcing. They are complementary patterns that work well together, but they address different aspects of an application's architecture.

Event sourcing

Event sourcing is a design pattern to persist data as a sequence of events. Instead of storing the current state of an entity (such as a user account), you record each action that modifies that entity. This creates an immutable history of changes, allowing you to do the following:

- Replay events to rebuild state at any point in time.

- Gain deep insights into an application's history for auditing and debugging purposes.

- Simplify data evolution, as new events can be added without modifying existing ones.

These events represent what happened, not the current state of the data. By replaying an event stream, you can reconstruct the state at any point in time. Traditional databases in CQRS can be used to write models (i.e., store commands). Event sourcing shines on the read model side of CQRS. The event stream from event sourcing serves as the source of truth for read models. Read models are materialized projections built by replaying relevant events.

However, it is very important to note that CQRS can be implemented without event sourcing. Event sourcing often benefits from CQRS when managing read models, as the two patterns work well together in many scenarios:

- CQRS handles the high volume of reads efficiently by using optimized read models.

- Event sourcing provides a complete history to build these read models.

- Updates to an event stream automatically trigger updates in the read models, ensuring consistency (although eventual consistency might apply).

Event sourcing versus event streaming

Event streaming is not the same as event sourcing, although they are closely related and often used together. The key difference is that event streaming is a mechanism for transmitting a sequence of events between different parts of a system, or even between different systems. Event streaming focuses on the delivery of events, ensuring that they are received by interested parties. It can be used for various purposes, such as real-time notifications, data pipelines, or triggering actions in other microservices.

Conversely, event sourcing is a data persistence pattern where the entire history of changes to an entity is stored as a sequence of events. It focuses on the storage and utilization of events as a system's source of truth. These events are used to replay the history and rebuild the current state of data if needed.

Here's an analogy for better understanding. Imagine event streaming as a live stream – it continuously delivers updates (events) to anyone subscribed. Event sourcing is like a detailed log – it keeps a permanent record of all past updates (events) for future reference.

But how are these two connected? Event sourcing often leverages event streaming to efficiently store and transmit the sequence of events. The event stream from event sourcing can be used by other systems or services subscribed to it. Some event stores (to be discussed further shortly), which are specialized databases for event sourcing, might have built-in functionalities for event streaming. In essence, event streaming is a broader concept for data in motion. Event sourcing utilizes event streaming to preserve its event history.

Let's take a quick look at an event store next.

Event store

The other element we need to consider in our CQRS, and event-sourcing ecosystem is an **event store**. This is a specialized type of database designed specifically to store sequences of events. Unlike traditional relational databases that focus on the current state of data, event stores record every change made to an entity as a unique event. This creates an immutable history of all actions that have occurred, allowing several benefits:

- **Auditability and debugging**: You can easily track changes and identify issues by reviewing the sequence of events. This provides a detailed log of what happened, when, and why.

- **Data evolution**: As your application evolves, new events can be added to a store without modifying existing logic. This makes it easier to adapt to changing requirements without breaking existing functionality.

- **Replayability**: By replaying an event stream in a specific order, you can reconstruct the state of an entity at any point in time. This is useful for various purposes, such as rebuilding materialized views or disaster recovery.

- **Scalability**: Event stores are often optimized to handle high volumes of writes, making them well-suited for event-driven architectures with frequent data changes.

In essence, an event store not only captures a complete and immutable history of changes but also enhances flexibility and scalability. By preserving every event that modifies the state of an entity, the event store provides a foundation for reliable audit trails, effortless adaptation to new business requirements, and the ability to reconstruct the state as needed. These features make it a vital component in modern architectures, especially where high data throughput and accountability are important.

Here's how event stores typically work:

- **Events**: Each action or change to an entity is represented as an event. These events contain relevant data about the change, such as timestamps, user IDs, and the specific modifications made.

- **Append-only**: Events are stored in an append-only fashion, meaning they cannot be modified or deleted after being added. This ensures the immutability of the event history.

- **Event stream**: Each entity typically has its event stream, which is a sequence of all events related to that entity.

Event stores typically work by representing each action or change to an entity as an event. These events capture relevant information about the change, such as the time it occurred, the user responsible, and the specific details of the modification. Once an event is recorded, it is stored in an append-only fashion, meaning that it cannot be altered or deleted after being added. This ensures that the event history remains immutable, providing a reliable audit trail. Additionally, each entity is associated with its own event stream, which is a chronological sequence of all the events related to that specific entity. This stream allows you to trace the life cycle of the entity from its initial state to its current form, based entirely on the sequence of events recorded in a store.

Event stores offer the following significant benefits that make them highly suitable for modern architectures, especially those driven by events:

- One of the key advantages is the creation of an **immutable history**. Every change to a system is stored as an event, ensuring that past actions cannot be tampered with or altered. This creates a reliable, tamper-proof audit trail that allows you to track the complete life cycle of an entity, making it particularly useful for debugging, compliance, and historical analysis.

- In terms of **scalability**, event stores are designed to handle high volumes of writes efficiently. Since events are appended to a store rather than modifying existing records, they can support applications with frequent data changes and ensure that performance remains consistent, even as the volume of data grows. This makes them an excellent choice for systems that need to process large amounts of data or handle real-time event streams.

- Another important benefit is **data evolution**. As applications evolve and new business requirements emerge, event stores allow you to adapt without disrupting existing functionality. New events can be added to reflect changes in a system, while the old event data remains intact, preserving the full history. This flexibility simplifies the process of evolving your application over time while maintaining backward compatibility with previous versions of the data.

- **Replayability** is another important feature of event stores. By replaying the event stream, you can reconstruct the state of an entity at any point in time. This capability is invaluable for disaster recovery, rebuilding materialized views, or even simulating past system states for analysis or testing. It gives you the power to revisit the past and see exactly how an entity reached its current state, something that's not possible with traditional databases that only store the latest state of data.

These benefits make event stores a powerful tool for building scalable, flexible, and resilient systems, particularly in event-driven architectures where maintaining a detailed history of changes is critical.

Here are the challenges of using event stores:

- **Querying**: Traditional relational database querying techniques might not be directly applicable. Designing efficient queries on event streams can require different approaches.

- **Increased complexity**: Event stores require a different data management mindset compared to traditional databases.

Finally, let's look at some popular event store options, including the following:

- **EventStoreDB**: A leading dedicated event store solution.

- **Apache Kafka**: A distributed streaming platform that can be used for event storage.

- **Traditional databases (with modifications)**: Relational databases such as PostgreSQL can be configured for append-only functionality to act as basic event stores.

In conclusion, event stores are a valuable tool for building event-driven architectures and applications that require a detailed history of changes, data evolution capabilities, and resilience.

That's enough theory; it's time to put CQRS and event sourcing into practice.

Implementing CQRS and event sourcing

Let's create a simple application that uses CQRS and event-sourcing. Our application will allow us to attach multiple payment mechanisms to our account. It will be possible to register payment mechanisms to accounts, disable them, and enable them. We will use NestJS, but you can use any other framework. In Ch11, in the CQRS_EventSourcing folder, we have the cqrs_app folder in our Git repository. You can download it to properly follow throughout the chapter, but the other option is to implement everything from scratch, as we plan to do here:

1. Create any folder and open your favorite IDE. Load the empty folder to your IDE, and from the command line, type npx @nestjs/cli new cqrs_app or npm i -g @nestjs/cli with nest new cqrs_app.

2. This should install the NestJS template in the folder. Now, let's install the required packages:

```
npm i @nestjs/cqrs
npm i @eventstore/db-client
npm i uuid
npm i prettier
```

3. Before switching to development, we need to configure our EventStoreDB for Docker. You can easily run it using a simple Dockerfile; however, to operate it with all the necessary infrastructure components, you'll need to compose them together in the future. Create a docker-compose.yml file with the following content:

```yaml
services:
  eventstore.db:
    image: eventstore/eventstore:24.2.0-jammy
    environment:
      - EVENTSTORE_CLUSTER_SIZE=1
      - EVENTSTORE_RUN_PROJECTIONS=All
      - EVENTSTORE_START_STANDARD_PROJECTIONS=true
      - EVENTSTORE_HTTP_PORT=2113
      - EVENTSTORE_INSECURE=true
      - EVENTSTORE_ENABLE_ATOM_PUB_OVER_HTTP=true
    ports:
      - '2113:2113'
    volumes:
      - type: volume
        source: eventstore-volume-data
        target: /var/lib/eventstore
      - type: volume
        source: eventstore-volume-logs
        target: /var/log/eventstore
  volumes:
```

```
eventstore-volume-data:
eventstore-volume-logs:
```

4.   This Docker Compose file defines a service named `eventstore.db`. It uses the `eventstore/eventstore:24.2.0-jammy` image, which is a specific version of `EventStoreDB`. You can use any other versions with a bit different configuration. The service runs with several environment variables to configure `EventStore`, including starting all projections and enabling insecure connections (which is not recommended for production). The service maps port `2113` on the host machine to port `2113` within the container, allowing access to the `EventStoreDB` instance. Finally, it defines persistent volumes for data and logs to ensure that information is preserved even if the container restarts.

5.   Run `docker-compose up -d` command to run it. After a successful run, you can navigate to `localhost:2213` for the `EventStoreDB` dashboard.

Dashboard

Queue Name	Length		Rate (items/s)
	Current	Peak	
Index Committer	0	2	0
MainQueue	1	9	29
MonitoringQueue	0	0	1

Figure 11.7: The event store dashboard

6.   Now, in our `src` folder, create an `eventstore.ts` file with the following content:

```
import {EventStoreDBClient, FORWARDS, START} from
  '@eventstore/db-client'
const client = EventStoreDBClient.connectionString(
  'esdb://localhost:2113?tls=false',
)
const connect = () => {
  try {
    client.readAll({
      direction: FORWARDS,
      fromPosition: START,
      maxCount: 1,
```

```
    })
  } catch (error) {
    console.error('Failed to connect to
      EventStoreDB:', error) }
  }
  export {client, connect}
```

This code snippet utilizes the `@eventstore/db-client` library to interact with `EventStoreDB`. It establishes a connection (stored in the client), using a connection string that points to a local `EventStoreDB` instance (`localhost:2113`) with **Transport Layer Security** (**TLS**) encryption disabled (which is not recommended for production). The reason that it's not recommended to disable TLS in your connection to `EventStoreDB` for production is that it provides encryption for data transmitted over a network. Without TLS, data transmitted between the client and `EventStoreDB`, such as commands, events, and sensitive information, is sent in plain text. This means anyone with access to the network could potentially intercept and read the data, leading to security vulnerabilities, including data theft or man-in-the-middle attacks.

The provided `connect` function attempts to read a single event (`maxCount: 1`) from the beginning (`direction: FORWARDS, fromPosition: START`) of the event stream. Any errors encountered during this read operation are caught and logged to the console. Finally, both the client connection and the connect function are exported for potential use in other parts of the code.

7. We will store account-based elements such as events, commands, and aggregates together. Storing account-based elements such as events, commands, and aggregates together helps maintain consistency and clarity within the domain model. These elements are tightly interconnected commands that initiate actions that change the state of an aggregate, and these changes are captured as events. Keeping them together simplifies the logical flow of operations, ensuring that all related components are easily accessible and organized. That is why we need to create a folder called `account` under `src`. After creating a folder, create a new file called `account.commands.ts` under `src/account` with the following content:

```
import {ICommand} from '@nestjs/cqrs'
export class RegisterAccountUnitCommand implements
  ICommand {
  constructor(
    public readonly aggregateId: string,
    public readonly paymentmechanismCount: string,
  ) {}
}
export class DisableAccountUnitCommand implements
  ICommand {
  constructor(public readonly aggregateId: string) {}
}
```

```
export class EnableAccountUnitCommand implements
  ICommand {
  constructor(public readonly aggregateId: string) {}
}
```

This code defines three commands for an account unit system in a NestJS application, using CQRS:

- `RegisterAccountUnitCommand`: This command takes an `aggregateId` (a unique identifier for the account unit) and a `paymentmechanismCount` (the number of payment methods associated). It's used to create a new account unit.

- `DisableAccountUnitCommand`: This command simply takes `aggregateId` and presumably disables the account unit.

- `EnableAccountUnitCommand`: Similar to the disabling command, this takes `aggregateId` and typically reenables a previously disabled account unit.

These commands represent different actions that users might take on account units, and they follow the CQRS pattern by focusing on modifying the system state (i.e., creating, disabling, or enabling).

8. Instead of calling the required functionalities directly, we will encapsulate them using commands. Our commands work based on a command design pattern. Using a command pattern, it is possible to encapsulate every action/request as an object. This encapsulation brings a lot of additional features, depending on the context; you can implement late execution, redo, undo, transactional operations, and so on. The `ICommand` interface helps us to achieve this.

The other contracts we need to implement to cover CQRS with event sourcing are events. In the `src/account` folder, create a new file called `account.events.ts` with the following content:

```
import {UUID} from 'uuid'
import {IEvent} from "@nestjs/cqrs";
export class AccountEvent implements IEvent {
  constructor(
      public readonly aggregateId: UUID,
      public readonly paymentmechanismCount: string
  ) {}
}
export class AccountRegisteredEvent extends
  AccountEvent {}
export class AccountDisabledEvent extends AccountEvent {}
export class AccountEnabledEvent extends AccountEvent {}
```

In CQRS, events are used to communicate changes that occur in a system. By inheriting from `IEvent` (provided by the `@nestjs/cqrs` package), we ensure that `AccountEvent` and its subclasses conform to the expected event structure within the CQRS framework. This allows the framework to handle these events appropriately, such as publishing them to an event bus or persisting them for eventual consistency:

- `AccountEvent` (the base class): Acts as a base for all account events. It inherits from `IEvent` (from `@nestjs/cqrs`) and holds common properties such as `aggregateId` and `paymentmechanismCount`.

- **Concrete events**: Classes such as `AccountRegisteredEvent` inherit from `AccountEvent`, customizing it for specific actions (i.e., registration, disabling, and enabling) with potentially additional properties if needed.

This approach promotes code reuse and keeps event data consistent across different account unit events.

We have specified our commands and events, but we haven't used them. The purpose of the `account.aggregate.ts` file under `src | account` is exactly for that. We need first to specify our command handler. If you have a command, there should be a handler to handle it.

Commands and handlers

Commands represent the actions that users or external systems want to perform on the domain model. They encapsulate the data needed to execute the action. In our example, `RegisterAccountUnitCommand`, `DisableAccountUnitCommand`, and `EnableAccountUnitCommand` are all commands that represent actions on account units.

Commands are typically defined as interfaces or classes. They often include properties that specify an action and any necessary data (e.g., `aggregateId` in our commands). Conversely, **command handlers** (also referred to as handlers in this chapter) are responsible for receiving commands, executing the necessary logic to modify the system state, and potentially producing events that reflect the changes. They act as the bridge between commands and the domain model.

Each command typically has a corresponding command handler. The handler receives the command, interacts with the domain logic (i.e., aggregate root, entities and services), and updates the system state accordingly. It might also trigger the creation of events to communicate the changes.

Our `account.aggregate.ts` contains `AggregateRoot`, `CommandHandler`, and `EventHandler` implementations. First, we will look at the command handler:

```
@CommandHandler(RegisterAccountUnitCommand)
export class RegisterAccountUnitHandler
  implements ICommandHandler<RegisterAccountUnitCommand>
{
  constructor(private readonly publisher: EventPublisher) {}
```

```
  async execute(command: RegisterAccountUnitCommand): Promise<void> {

    const aggregate = this.publisher.mergeObjectContext
      (new AccountAggregate())
    aggregate.registerAccount(command.aggregateId,
      command.paymentmechanismCount)
    aggregate.commit()
  }
}
```

This NestJS code defines a command handler to register account units using CQRS. The @
CommandHandler decorator associates it with the RegisterAccountUnitCommand. It injects
EventPublisher (for event sourcing). In the execute method, it creates an AccountAggregate
instance, calls its registerAccount method with command data, and potentially commits
the changes. This demonstrates processing a command by interacting with the domain model and
potentially publishing events. We will discuss AggregateRoot a bit later. For now, we will just
focus on the base idea behind the commands.

We have two more commands that have approximately the same implementation, with different
method calls:

```
@CommandHandler(DisableAccountUnitCommand)
export class DisableAccountUnitHandler implements
  ICommandHandler<DisableAccountUnitCommand> {
  constructor(private readonly publisher: EventPublisher){}

  async execute(command: DisableAccountUnitCommand):
    Promise<void> {
    const aggregate = this.publisher.mergeObjectContext(
        await AccountAggregate.loadAggregate
          (command.aggregateId)
    );
    if (!aggregate.disabled) {
      aggregate.disableAccount();
      aggregate.commit();
    }
  }
}
```

DisableAccountUnitHandler retrieves the AccountAggregate instance associated with
the command.aggregateId, using AccountAggregate.loadAggregate.

It verifies whether the account is already disabled, using `!aggregate.disabled`. If not disabled, it calls `aggregate.disableAccount` to perform the disabling logic and then `aggregate.commit` to potentially persist the change as an event.

This handler ensures that an account unit is only disabled once and triggers event publication (if applicable) upon successful disabling. The last handler is `EnableAccountHandler`, which is a counterpart of `DisableAccountUnitHandler`:

```
@CommandHandler(EnableAccountUnitCommand)
export class EnableAccountUnitHandler implements
  ICommandHandler<EnableAccountUnitCommand> {
  constructor(private readonly publisher: EventPublisher){}

  async execute(command: EnableAccountUnitCommand):
    Promise<void> {
    const aggregate = this.publisher.mergeObjectContext(
        await AccountAggregate.loadAggregate
          (command.aggregateId)
    );
    if (aggregate.disabled) {
      aggregate.enableAccount();
      aggregate.commit();
    }
  }
}
```

We're done with handlers. It is time to explore **event handlers**. In this context, event handlers are classes that implement the `IEventHandler<T>` interface from the `@nestjs/cqrs` package. These handlers respond to specific domain events that are emitted by the aggregate.

An event handler in the context of CQRS is responsible for handling the domain events that occur within a system. The events represent significant state changes within your aggregates, and the event handlers respond to these changes by performing side effects or additional logic outside the aggregate itself.

In the same file (`account.aggregate.ts`), we have three event handlers (`AccountRegisteredEventHandler`, `AccountDisabledEventHandler`, and `AccountEnabledEventHandler`):

```
interface AccountEvent {
  aggregateId: string;
  paymentmechanismCount: string;
}
async function handleAccountEvent(eventType: string, event:
  AccountEvent): Promise<void> {
  const eventData = jsonEvent({
```

```
    type: eventType,
    data: {
      id: event.aggregateId,
      paymentmechanismCount: event.paymentmechanismCount,
    },
  });
  await eventStore.appendToStream(
    'Account-unit-stream-' + event.aggregateId,
    [eventData],
  );
}
```

All event handlers have the same contract, and that is why we use the `AccountEvent` interface. It then implements a function, `handleAccountEvent`, that takes an event type and an event object as arguments. The function prepares data in a JSON-compatible format and uses an event store service to persist the event information, under a stream specific to the involved account aggregate.

Now, let's take a look at concrete event handler implementations:

```
@EventsHandler(AccountRegisteredEvent)
export class AccountRegisteredEventHandler
  implements IEventHandler<AccountRegisteredEvent> {
  async handle(event: AccountRegisteredEvent):
    Promise<void> {
    await handleAccountEvent('AccountUnitCreated', event);
  }
}

@EventsHandler(AccountDisabledEvent)
export class AccountDisabledEventHandler implements
  IEventHandler<AccountDisabledEvent> {
  async handle(event: AccountDisabledEvent): Promise<void> {
    await handleAccountEvent('AccountUnitDisabled', event);
  }
}

@EventsHandler(AccountEnabledEvent)
export class AccountEnabledEventHandler implements
  IEventHandler<AccountEnabledEvent> {
  async handle(event: AccountEnabledEvent): Promise<void> {
    await handleAccountEvent('AccountUnitEnabled', event);
  }
}
```

In this code, we define event handlers for account registration, disabling, and enabling. When an account is registered, the `AccountRegisteredEventHandler` triggers logic related to account creation. Similarly, `AccountDisabledEventHandler` and `AccountEnabledEventHandler` handle account disabling and enabling events, respectively. These handlers leverage the `handleAccountEvent` function for centralized event processing.

That is great, but how do these commands interact with events? To demonstrate this, we need to discuss one more concept, called an aggregate root, a popular pattern in **Domain-Driven Design (DDD)**.

Implementing an aggregate root

In DDD, an **aggregate root** is a fundamental concept for modeling complex domains. It acts as the central entity within a cluster of related objects, also known as an **aggregate**.

An aggregate root encapsulates the core data and logic associated with a particular domain concept. In our example, `AccountAggregate` will hold all the essential information about an account (i.e., ID, payment mechanism count, and disabled status). This centralizes the account's state and promotes data integrity.

An aggregate root plays a crucial role in event sourcing, a technique for persisting domain object changes as a sequence of events. In our code, `AccountAggregate` methods such as `registerAccount` apply events to the aggregate, reflecting state changes. By reconstructing the state from the event stream, the aggregate root becomes the central source of truth for the account's history.

An aggregate root defines the transactional boundaries within our domain. Within an aggregate, changes to the state of all related entities (including the root itself) must happen atomically. This ensures data consistency within the aggregate.

An aggregate root also serves as the sole entry point for external interactions with the aggregate. This means other parts of your application (or other aggregates) should interact with the domain through the aggregate root's methods. This promotes loose coupling and simplifies reasoning about domain logic.

Aggregate roots promote data consistency and integrity by centralizing state management and defining transactional boundaries. They simplify domain logic by providing a clear entry point for interactions. They also improve code maintainability by encapsulating related entities and their behavior.

By effectively utilizing aggregate roots in DDD, we can build robust and maintainable domain models that accurately reflect your business processes. Now, let's see how it is possible to rebuild the state of `AccountAggregate` by reading its event stream from the event store:

```
export class AccountAggregate extends AggregateRoot {
.........
static async loadAggregate(aggregateId: string):
  Promise<AccountAggregate> {
    const events = eventStore.readStream(
      'Account-unit-stream-' + aggregateId);
```

```
    let count = 0;
    const aggregate = new AccountAggregate();
    for await (const event of events) {
      const eventData: any = event.event.data;
      try {
        switch (event.event.type) {
          case 'AccountUnitCreated':
            aggregate.applyAccountRegisteredEventToAggregate({
              aggregateId: eventData.id,
              paymentmechanismCount:
                eventData.paymentmechanismCount,
            });
            break;
          case 'AccountUnitDisabled':
            aggregate.accountDisabled();
            break;
          case 'AccountUnitEnabled':
            aggregate.accountEnabled();
            break;
          default:
            break
        }
      } catch(e) {
        console.error("Could not process event")
      }
      count++;
    }
    return aggregate;
}}
```

This NestJS code defines an asynchronous function named `loadAggregate` that takes an aggregate ID as input. It retrieves a `stream` of events related to that ID from the event store. The function then iterates through each event and applies the changes it describes to an `AccountAggregate` object. There are cases for handling different event types, such as `AccountUnitCreated`, `AccountUnitDisabled`, and `AccountUnitEnabled`. If an event type isn't recognized, it's skipped. If there are errors processing an event, it logs an error message but keeps iterating. Finally, the function returns the populated `AccountAggregate` object.

Download our Git repository for a more complete example of implementing an aggregate root. Here is a snippet from an aggregate root that handles the operations:

```
export class AccountAggregate extends AggregateRoot {
……
  registerAccount(aggregateId: string,
```

```
    paymentmechanismCount: string) {
    this.apply(new AccountRegisteredEvent(aggregateId,
      paymentmechanismCount));
  }
  enableAccount(): void {
    if(this.disabled) {
      this.apply(new AccountEnabledEvent(this.id,
        this.paymentmechanismCount))
    }
  }
  disableAccount() {
    if (!this.disabled) {
      this.apply(new AccountDisabledEvent(this.id,
        this.paymentmechanismCount));
    }
  }
  ...
}
```

As you might guess, commands interact with events using an aggregate root, and the latter encapsulates the logic that triggers events.

Implementing projection

In CQRS and event sourcing architectures, **projections** play a crucial role in efficiently retrieving data for reads. Event sourcing acts like a film reel, storing a sequence of events that represent all the changes that happened in a system. Each event captures a specific action (such as `Account Created` or `Account Disabled`).

Projections are like the projection booth in a movie theater. They take the event stream (the film reel) and *project* it into a specific format, suitable for reading. This format, called a **read model**, is optimized to query data efficiently.

With that, let's understand why projections are important:

- **Read efficiency**: Projections help rebuild the entire system state from the event stream, as doing so for every read query would be slow. Projections pre-process the event stream, creating a separate, optimized data structure for frequently accessed information.

- **Flexibility**: We can create multiple projections tailored to different reading needs with projections. One projection might focus on account details, while another might analyze purchase history.

Next, let's see how projections work:

1. **Event listeners**: Projections act as event listeners, subscribing to the event stream.

2. **Processing events**: As new events arrive, a projection processes them one by one, updating its internal read model accordingly.

3. **Read model access**: When a read query arrives, a system retrieves the relevant data from a projection's read model instead of the entire event stream.

Projections are not a replacement for an event store. The event store remains the single source of truth for all historical events. Projections simply offer a way to efficiently access specific data from that history. Having said that, let's look at some of the benefits of projections:

*   **Faster reads**: Queries run against read models are significantly faster than replaying an entire event stream.

*   **Scalability**: Projections can be scaled independently to handle increasing read traffic.

*   **Flexibility**: Different projections cater to diverse read needs without impacting write performance.

We plan to implement a simple projection that demonstrates the usage of projection in CQRS and event sourcing architectures.

Under the `src`/`paymentmechanism` folder, create a `paymentmechanism-total.projection.ts` file with the following functionalities:

```
@EventsHandler(AccountRegisteredEvent,
  AccountDisabledEvent, AccountEnabledEvent)
export class PaymentMechanismProjection implements
  IEventHandler<AccountRegisteredEvent |
  AccountDisabledEvent | AccountEnabledEvent> {
  private currentPaymentMechanismTotal: number = 0;
  constructor() {
    console.log('Account info Projection instance created:', this);
  }

  handle(event: AccountRegisteredEvent |
    AccountDisabledEvent | AccountEnabledEvent): void {
    if (event instanceof AccountRegisteredEvent) {
      this.handleAccountRegistered(event);
    } else if (event instanceof AccountDisabledEvent) {
      this.handleAccountDisabled(event);
    } else if (event instanceof AccountEnabledEvent) {
      this.handleAccountEnabled(event);
    }
  }
```

```
. . . . . . . .
. . . . . . .
```

This code defines an event handler class named `PaymentMechanismProjection` in a CQRS architecture with event sourcing. It listens for three specific events related to account management:

- `AccountRegisteredEvent`: Triggers when a new account is created.
- `AccountDisabledEvent`: Triggers when an account is deactivated.
- `AccountEnabledEvent`: Triggers when a deactivated account is reactivated.

The class keeps track of the total number of payment mechanisms (`currentPayment MechanismTotal`), but its initial value is zero.

The `handle` method is the core functionality. It checks the type of the incoming event and calls a specific handler function, based on the event type:

- `handleAccountRegistered`: Handles `AccountRegisteredEvent` by incrementing `currentPaymentMechanismTotal`, based on information in the event data.
- `handleAccountDisabled`: Handles `AccountDisabledEvent` and decrements `currentPaymentMechanismTotal`.
- `handleAccountEnabled`: Handles the `AccountEnabledEvent` and applies the opposite operation of `handleAccountDisabled`.

This is a simplified example, but it demonstrates how an event handler projection can listen for specific events and update its internal state accordingly, maintaining a view of the data optimized for a particular purpose (e.g., tracking total payment mechanisms). Here are our detailed handler methods in this class:

```
handleAccountRegistered(event: AccountRegisteredEvent) {
    const pmCount = parseInt(event.paymentmechanismCount,
      10);
    this.currentPaymentMechanismTotal += pmCount;
    console.log("currentPaymentMechanismTotal",
      this.currentPaymentMechanismTotal)
  }

  handleAccountDisabled(event: AccountDisabledEvent) {
    const pmCount = parseInt(event.paymentmechanismCount,
      10);
    this.currentPaymentMechanismTotal -= pmCount;
    console.log("currentPaymentMechanismTotal",
      this.currentPaymentMechanismTotal)
  }
```

```
handleAccountEnabled(event: AccountEnabledEvent) {
  const pmCount = parseInt(event.paymentmechanismCount,
    10);
  this.currentPaymentMechanismTotal += pmCount;
  console.log("currentPaymentMechanismTotal",
    this.currentPaymentMechanismTotal)
}
```

Our handlers simply interact with `currentPaymentMechanismTotal` and build logic around it. The idea is simple, but you can implement more complex logic based on this knowledge.

Implementing API functionalities

We use controllers as an entry point to our request flow. In a classical flow, controllers accept requests and forward them to the related services. When we apply CQRS and event sourcing, we usually use the same controllers, but instead of specifying direct services, we apply a command pattern to provide commands and their handlers. Controllers serve as the intermediary between a client and the backend logic, determining how an application should respond to various requests. Controllers map specific routes to corresponding methods that contain business logic. By organizing request handling within controllers, the application maintains a clear separation of concerns, making it more structured, scalable, and easier to manage.

Create a new folder called `api` under the `src` folder. Then, create a new file called `account.controller.ts` under `src / api`, with the following content:

```
@Controller('Account')
export class AccountUnitController {
  constructor(private readonly commandBus: CommandBus) {}

  @Post('/register')
  async registerAccount(@Query('paymentmechanismCount')
    paymentmechanismCount: string): Promise<any> {
    const aggregateId = uuid()
    await this.commandBus.execute(new
      RegisterAccountUnitCommand(aggregateId,
        paymentmechanismCount))
    return { message: 'Request received as a command',
      aggregateId };
  }
  @Post('/:id/disable')
  async disableAccount(@Param('id') id: string):
    Promise<any> {
    await this.commandBus.execute(new
```

```
      DisableAccountUnitCommand(id))
    return { message: 'Request received as a command' };
  }
  @Post('/:id/enable')
  async enableAccount(@Param('id') id: string):
    Promise<any> {
    await this.commandBus.execute(new
      EnableAccountUnitCommand(id))
    return { message: 'Request received as a command' };
  } }
```

This NestJS controller handles account management. It's named `AccountUnitController` and is mapped to the `/Account` route. The controller uses a command bus to send commands. There are three functionalities exposed through `POST` requests:

- `registerAccount` allows you to create a new account with a payment mechanism count, by sending `RegisterAccountUnitCommand`.

- `disableAccount` deactivates an account by ID using `DisableAccountUnitCommand`.

- `enableAccount` reactivates an account using an `EnableAccountUnitCommand`, based on its ID.

All successful requests return a message indicating the command was received and the aggregate ID (for registration).

In order to enable a controller's functionality, we need to import several essential elements. `Controller`, `Param`, `Post`, and `Query` from `@nestjs/common` are necessary to define the controller, handle route parameters, and process HTTP `POST` requests with query parameters. `CommandBus` from `@nestjs/cqrs` allows us to dispatch commands, following the CQRS pattern. We import the specific commands (`DisableAccountUnitCommand`, `EnableAccountUnitCommand`, and `RegisterAccountUnitCommand`) from the `account.commands` file to perform specific operations on the account unit. Finally, we import the `uuid` package to generate unique IDs for these operations:

```
import {Controller, Param, Post, Query} from
  '@nestjs/common'
import {CommandBus} from '@nestjs/cqrs'
import {
  DisableAccountUnitCommand,
  EnableAccountUnitCommand,
  RegisterAccountUnitCommand
} from '../account/account.commands'
import {v4 as uuid} from 'uuid'
```

Our controller doesn't know about events. It only interacts with commands. The request will flow to command handlers, and they will trigger our events.

Besides the controller, we have the `account.module.ts` file, which contains `AccountModule`:

```
export class AccountModule implements OnModuleInit {
  async onModuleInit() {
    this.startSubscription();
  }

  private startSubscription() {
    (async (): Promise<void> => {
      await this.subscribeToAll();
    })();
  }

  private async subscribeToAll() {
    const subscriptionList = eventStore.subscribeToAll({
      filter: streamNameFilter({ prefixes: ["Account-unit-stream-"]
        }),
    });

    for await (const subscriptionItem of subscriptionList){
      console.log(
          `Handled event ${subscriptionItem.event?.
revision}@${subscriptionItem.event?.streamId}`
      );
      const subscriptionData: any =
        subscriptionItem.event.data;
      console.log("subscription data:", subscriptionData);
    }
  }
}
```

For a complete example with imported functionalities, check out our repository.

This code defines `AccountModule` used in a CQRS architecture with event sourcing. It implements the `OnModuleInit` life cycle hook, which gets called after the module is initialized.

Here's a breakdown of the functionality:

- `onModuleInit`: This method is called when the module is ready.

- `startSubscription (private)`: This private method initiates a subscription to an event stream. It uses an **Immediately Invoked Function Expression (IIFE)** to encapsulate the asynchronous logic.

Finally, we will take a look at `subscribeToAll` `(private, async)`; this private asynchronous method does the actual subscription work. It uses `eventStore.subscribeToAll` to subscribe to all event streams that start with the `Account-unit-stream-` prefix. This method typically captures all events related to account management. It iterates through the subscription using `for await...` of the loop. For each event received, it logs the event revision number and stream ID, extracts the event data, and logs it as well. The `AccountModule` subscribes to a specific category of events in the event store (events related to accounts). Whenever a new event related to accounts arrives, it logs details about the event and its data for potential processing or monitoring.

Testing an application

Before running our application, you should run the provided `docker-compose` file via the `docker-compose up -d` command. It ensures that we already have `EventStoreDB` as a data store. To make sure if data store is running, just navigate to `localhost:2113`, and you should see the `EventStoreDB`'s dashboard.

To run our application, execute the `nest start` command from the command line. Open your Postman application, and create a new tab. Select the **POST** command for the `http://localhost:8080/account/register?paymentmechanismCount=67` URL. Here, we register a new account, with the value of `paymentmechanismcount` set to `67`. Then, click the **Send** button.

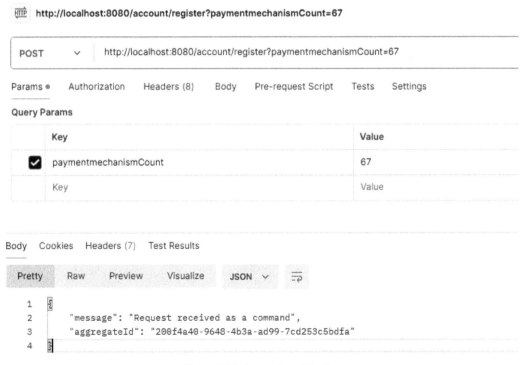

Figure 11.8: Account registration

After successful operation, you should get the following message to your VS Code console.

```
PROBLEMS  19    OUTPUT    TERMINAL    PORTS    GITLENS    SQL CONSOLE    ...          no

currentPaymentMechanismTotal 67
Handled event 0@Account-unit-stream-27a47b90-c328-4037-8cf7-05b32998de0f
subscription data: {
  id: '27a47b90-c328-4037-8cf7-05b32998de0f',
  paymentmechanismCount: '67'
}
```

Figure 11.9: Account registration logs

The ID will be different in your case because it is automatically generated by the system. After running the same command with a different payment mechanism count (it is twenty-three in our case), you should get the following message with `currentPaymentMechanismCount=90`. The ID is different again, but if you use the same payment mechanism count, the values should be totaled based on the `currentPaymentMechanismTotal = currentPaymentMechanismTotal + paymentMechanismCount` formula:

```
currentPaymentMechanismTotal 90
Handled event 0@Account-unit-stream-90f80d89-4620-4526-ae3e-02a8156df9a1
subscription data: {
  id: '90f80d89-4620-4526-ae3e-02a8156df9a1',
  paymentmechanismCount: '23'
}
```

Figure 11.10: Account registration calculation

Now, we have two different IDs (aggregate IDs), and we can use any of them to enable and disable requests.

Open a new tab on Postman and send a POST request to `http://localhost:8080/account/YOUR_AGGREGATE_ID/disable`. The last aggregate ID stores the value of `paymentmechanismCount`, which is twenty-three. So, disabling the endpoint should end up making a value of `currentPaymentMechanismTotal = 67`. The logic is ninety minus twenty-three equals to sixty-seven.

Let's run the **POST** command for `http://localhost:8080/account/90f80d89-4620-4526-ae3e-02a8156df9a1/disable` and click **Send**:

```
currentPaymentMechanismTotal 67
Handled event 1@Account-unit-stream-90f80d89-4620-4526-ae3e-02a8156df9a1
subscription data: {
  id: '90f80d89-4620-4526-ae3e-02a8156df9a1',
  paymentmechanismCount: '23'
}
```

Figure 11.11: The disabled account response

To enable the account, just replace `disable` with `enable` and run the command again. It should restore `currentPaymentMechanismTotal` to `90`.

Besides CQRS and event sourcing, we have a Service Registry and discovery for microservices. The next section will help us to understand them in more detail.

Service Registry and discovery in microservices

Microservices development by itself consists of huge amounts of patterns and best practices. It is indeed not possible to cover all of them in one book. In this section, we will provide popular patterns and techniques used in microservices development.

In a microservice architecture, applications are built as a collection of small, independent services. These services need to communicate with each other to cover user requests. Service Registry and discovery is a mechanism that simplifies this communication by enabling services to find each other dynamically.

Understanding Service Registry and discovery

Imagine a central database. This database, called the **Service Registry**, acts as a directory of all the microservices in your system. Each service instance (i.e., an individual running a copy of a microservice) registers itself with the registry. During registration, the service provides details such as the following:

- **Network location**: The address (IP address and port) where the service can be found.

- **Capabilities**: What the service can do (e.g., processes payments or provides user data).

- **Health Information**: Status details such as whether the service is currently healthy and available to handle requests.

You can use tools such as Consul, ZooKeeper, and Eureka Server (as used by Netflix) for real-world service registries.

Service Registry often integrates with API gateways, which are a single-entry point for external clients to access microservices. An API Gateway might leverage the Service Registry to discover the latest locations of the microservices it needs to route requests to.

Conversely, **Service discovery** is the process where microservices find the location of other services they need to interact with. There are two main approaches:

- **Client-side discovery**: The service that needs another service (the client) directly queries the registry to find the address of the target service.

- **Server-side discovery**: A separate component, such as a load balancer, sits in front of the services. This component retrieves service locations from the registry and routes requests to the appropriate service instance.

Let's look at some benefits of Service Registry and discovery:

- **Dynamic service location**: Services don't need to be hardcoded with the addresses of other services. They can discover them on-demand from the registry, making the system more adaptable to changes.

- **Scalability and elasticity**: As you add or remove service instances, the registry automatically reflects the changes. This ensures that clients always interact with available services.

- **Loose coupling**: Services become loosely coupled, as they rely on the registry for communication. This promotes independent development and deployment of microservices.

By using a central registry and enabling dynamic discovery, Service Registry and discovery simplify communication and promote flexibility in a microservice architecture.

Approaches for implementing Service Registry and Discovery

There are two main approaches to implementing Service Registry and discovery in Node.js microservices:

- The first option is using a dedicated Service Registry tool. This approach leverages a separate service specifically designed for Service Registry and discovery functionalities. We can use popular options such as Consul, ZooKeeper, and Eureka Server (Netflix). These tools offer robust features for registration, discovery, health checks, and so on.

- The second option is Node.js client libraries. Each registry tool typically provides a Node.js client library that simplifies interaction with the registry. The library allows your microservices to register themselves, discover other services, and monitor their health.

Finally, let us look at how we can implement a Service Registry before wrapping up this chapter.

Implementing Service Registry

Now, let's take a brief look at implementing a Service Registry:

1. Choose a Service Registry tool, and install its Node.js client library:

   - During startup, each microservice registers itself with a registry using the library. It provides its network location, capabilities, and health information.

   - In client-side discovery, the service needing another service uses the library to query the registry for the target service's address.

   - In server-side discovery, a separate component, such as a load balancer, retrieves service locations from the registry and routes requests accordingly.

2. Now, let's move on to building a simple registry with Node.js: For smaller deployments or learning purposes, you can implement a basic Service Registry using Node.js itself. Here's a simplified example:

   - **For data storage**: Use a lightweight in-memory data store, such as Redis, or a simple Node.js object to store service information

   - **Registration**: During startup, each microservice registers itself with the registry by sending a message containing its details

   - **Discovery**: Services can query the registry to retrieve a list of available services and their addresses

Before we end this section, let's look at some important considerations of Service Registry and discovery, the first being **security**. When implementing your own registry, ensure proper authentication and authorization mechanisms to control access to registration and discovery functionalities. Next is **scalability**. A homegrown registry might not scale well for large deployments. Consider a dedicated tool for production environments. Finally, **health checks** are very important. Regularly check the health of registered services to ensure that they are available.

We've covered everything about microservice architecture in this chapter. It's now time to wrap up.

Summary

This chapter dived into the building blocks of a strong microservice architecture. It covered API gateways, explaining their purpose, use cases, and how to implement them for optimal performance, with caching, rate limiting, and response aggregation. The chapter then explored CQRS and event sourcing patterns, along with event streaming, a technology that makes them work. Finally, it discussed Service Registry and discovery, essential for microservices to communicate with each other. This chapter provided the knowledge and practical examples to build a well-designed and scalable microservice infrastructure.

In the next chapter, we will explore testing strategies in depth and cover how to write effective unit and integration tests for your microservices.

12

Testing Microservices

Testing is a critical phase within the **software development life cycle** (**SDLC**) that's integral to ensuring the software meets the required standards and functions as expected. Testing detects bugs introduced during development. It verifies that the software performs its intended functions correctly and efficiently and ensures the software meets user requirements and specifications. By applying tests, we can reduce the risks associated with software failure or malfunction.

In this chapter, we'll talk about different strategies for software testing within microservices. By the end, you'll know how to write unit and integration tests for your microservices both in isolation and integrated with other microservices.

We're going to cover the following topics:

- Understanding testing in a microservice architecture
- Understanding and implementing unit tests
- Implementing unit tests for the account microservice
- Writing unit tests for the transaction microservice
- Comparing mocks, stubs, and spies in unit tests
- Understanding and implementing integration tests

Technical requirements

To implement our tests, we'll need the following:

- An IDE of your choice (we prefer Visual Studio Code).
- This book's GitHub repository, which can be downloaded from `https://github.com/PacktPublishing/Hands-on-Microservices-with-JavaScript`. Open the `Ch12` folder so that you can follow along with ease.

Understanding testing in a microservice architecture

Microservice architecture divides an application into smaller, loosely coupled services, each responsible for a specific business function. This approach offers numerous benefits, such as improved scalability and flexibility. However, it also introduces complexity, particularly in terms of testing. Comprehensive testing is crucial to ensure that these independent services function correctly and cohesively. Let's try to understand the importance of testing in a microservice architecture:

- The first reason for using tests in a microservice architecture is to ensure **functionality**. Each service performs a distinct function in a microservice architecture and is developed independently. Testing ensures that each service performs its intended function correctly. We mostly use unit and functional testing to achieve this goal:

  - **Unit testing** focuses on individual components within a service, verifying that each function works as expected. This helps us catch bugs early in the development process.

  - On the other hand, **functional testing** ensures that the service as a whole meets its functional requirements. This involves testing the service's endpoints and ensuring that they return the expected results.

- The second reason for using tests in microservices is to maintain **interoperability**. Microservices must communicate with each other to function as a cohesive application. Ensuring seamless interoperability between services is critical. To achieve this, we mostly focus on integration and contract testing:

  - **Integration testing** focuses on interactions between services, verifying that data exchange and communication protocols are implemented correctly.

  - **Contract testing** ensures that services adhere to defined APIs or contracts. This is particularly important when different teams develop services independently as it helps maintain consistent communication standards.

- The third reason is **performance** assurance. Performance testing ensures that services operate efficiently under various load conditions, which is vital for maintaining a good user experience. We can achieve this goal using load testing and stress testing:

  - **Load testing** evaluates how services handle expected load levels. This helps identify performance bottlenecks and ensures services can handle real-world usage.

  - **Stress testing** examines how services perform under extreme conditions, such as high traffic or resource shortages. This helps in understanding the service's breaking point and resilience.

- Testing is also important for **security** validation. Security is a critical concern in microservice architecture as each service may handle sensitive data and must be protected against vulnerabilities. We can use security testing and penetration testing to achieve our goal:

  - **Security testing** identifies vulnerabilities and ensures that services can protect sensitive data. This includes testing for common security issues such as SQL injection, **cross-site scripting (XSS)**, and authentication flaws.

  - **Penetration testing** simulates attacks to identify potential security gaps. This helps in proactively securing services against real-world threats.

- Microservices need to be reliable and stable, especially during updates or changes. Testing ensures that services remain **dependable** over time. We have regression and chaos testing to make sure we have reliable and stable microservices:

  - **Regression testing** ensures that new changes or updates don't introduce new bugs or break existing functionality. This is crucial for maintaining service reliability after each deployment.

  - **Chaos engineering** involves intentionally introducing failures into the system to test its resilience. This helps us understand how services respond to unexpected issues and improves overall stability.

Having understood testing as a whole, let's move on to unit tests.

Understanding unit tests

Unit testing is a software testing technique that matters most when you want to ensure that individual units or components of the software are tested in isolation. The goal of unit testing is to validate that each unit of the software performs as expected.

It's an important aspect of software development, especially in microservices architectures. Node.js, with its asynchronous and event-driven nature, poses unique challenges and opportunities for unit testing. In this context, unit testing involves testing individual functions, methods, or classes within your Node.js application. Let's cover the importance of unit testing for microservices:

- **It ensures code quality**: Unit testing helps identify bugs early in the development cycle, ensuring that individual units of code function as intended. This is particularly important in microservices, where services are designed to be small, independent, and modular.

- **It facilitates refactoring**: With a comprehensive suite of unit tests, developers can confidently refactor code, knowing that any changes will be verified by the tests. This is crucial for maintaining and improving the code base over time.

- **It supports continuous integration/continuous deployment (CI/CD)**: Unit tests are an integral part of CI/CD pipelines. They provide immediate feedback on code changes, enabling quick iterations and stable deployments.

- **Better documentation**: Well-written unit tests serve as documentation for the code. They demonstrate how individual units are expected to behave, making it easier for new developers to understand the code base.

Let's look at some of the benefits of performing unit testing in Node.js microservices:

- **Improved reliability**: Unit tests ensure that each microservice behaves as expected, reducing the likelihood of runtime errors and improving overall system reliability.

- **Faster development cycles**: Automated unit tests speed up the development process by allowing developers to quickly identify and fix issues. This is particularly beneficial in microservices, where services are developed and deployed independently.

- **Reduced debugging time**: With unit tests in place, bugs can be detected and isolated quickly, reducing the time spent on debugging.

- **Increased confidence in code changes**: Unit tests provide a safety net for developers, giving them the confidence to make changes and add new features without breaking existing functionality.

Unit testing in Node.js microservices enhances reliability, accelerates development by catching issues early, reduces debugging time, and boosts developer confidence in making code changes without breaking functionality. Now, let's focus on unit testing packages we need to use to write unit tests.

Introducing unit testing packages

Before writing a line of code, we need to prepare our environment. To be precise, we need to install the required packages to write unit tests.

Chai, Mocha, and Sinon are popular libraries that are used for testing in Node.js applications, including microservices. Each of these libraries has a specific role and they often work together to provide a comprehensive testing framework.

Introducing Mocha

First, let's talk about **Mocha**. Mocha is a feature-rich JavaScript test framework that runs on Node.js, making asynchronous testing simple and fun. It provides a testing environment where you can define your tests and run them.

It has the following features:

- **Descriptive**: It allows for descriptive and structured test suites using `describe` and `it` blocks.

- **Allows asynchronous testing**: It supports both synchronous and asynchronous tests.

- **Variety of hooks**: It provides life cycle hooks (`before`, `after`, `beforeEach`, and `afterEach`) for setting up and tearing down conditions for tests.

- **Extensible**: It can be extended with various plugins and reporters to customize the testing setup.

You can install it using the `npm install --save-dev mocha` command.

Introducing Chai

Chai is a popular assertion library that's used with Node.js, often in combination with testing frameworks such as Mocha. It provides a variety of interfaces and styles for writing tests, making it flexible and easy to use.

It supports different assertion styles, two of which we'll look at here:

- The first and maybe the most used style is known as **behavior-driven development** (BDD). In this style, we have `expect` and `should` interfaces. They're used for writing expressive and readable assertions. This style allows for natural language assertions, making tests easier to understand.

- The second style is known as **test-driven development** (TDD). The `assert` interface is used for writing classical unit test assertions. This style is more traditional and straightforward, which makes it suitable for developers familiar with xUnit frameworks.

We can install it using the `npm install --save-dev chai` command.

While Chai has many features, let's understand three of the most relevant ones. The first feature we'll look at is its **plugins**. Chai has a rich ecosystem of plugins that extend its functionality. Popular plugins include `chai-as-promised` for promise assertions and `chai-http` for HTTP assertions. The second key feature is **extensibility**. Chai can be extended to create custom assertions using its plugin API. This allows developers to add domain-specific language to their tests On the other hand, Chai has a cool feature known as readable and expressive syntax. Chai's BDD-style assertions are designed to be readable and expressive, making tests easier to write and understand. Finally, Chai also **integrates** seamlessly with Mocha, providing a powerful combination for writing and running tests.

Introducing Sinon

Sinon is another powerful library for testing in JavaScript that's particularly useful for creating spies, stubs, and mocks to control and monitor the behavior of functions. It's especially valuable in unit testing to isolate the code under test from its dependencies, ensuring that the tests focus on the specific functionality being tested.

Before we learn how to implement unit tests, let's take a look at some of the key features of Sinon:

- **Spies**: Track and monitor the behavior of functions.
- **Stubs**: Replace functions with predefined behaviors.
- **Mocks**: Create fake objects with expectations for their behavior.

- **Fakes**: Combine the behavior of spies and stubs for simpler use cases.

- **Timers**: Control and simulate the passage of time in tests.

- **XHR and Fetch**: Simulate `XMLHttpRequest` and the Fetch API to test AJAX requests.

We can install it using the `npm install --save-dev sinon` command. Sinon can mock functions, HTTP requests, and more, making it ideal for unit testing.

Other packages in Node.js

Along with `Chai`, we have other popular assertion libraries such as Jest. **Jest** has its own assertion library, which is fully integrated and optimized for use with Jest.

When implementing unit tests, we also need mocking and stubbing libraries. In unit testing, mocks and stubs are used to isolate the unit of code being tested by simulating the behavior of dependencies. This allows you to test the functionality of a specific unit without having to rely on external components, such as databases, network services, or other modules.

Along with `Sinon`, we use the **Testdouble** library. `Testdouble` is a minimal, standalone test double library for JavaScript. You can use the `npm install --save-dev testdouble` command to install it. Testdouble provides tools for creating, using, and verifying test doubles in JavaScript.

What should we test in unit testing?

Before implementing unit tests in our project, we need to answer one simple question: what should we unit test? Let's take a look:

- **Business logic**: This is the most critical part to test. Business logic includes the rules and operations that dictate how data is transformed, manipulated, and controlled. It ensures the application behaves correctly under various conditions.

- **Edge cases**: Test the boundaries and limits of your application. This includes checking how the application handles unexpected, extreme, or invalid inputs.

- **Error handling**: Ensure that the application responds correctly to error conditions, such as invalid input or failed operations.

- **State transitions**: If the application involves state changes (such as a status update), make sure these transitions occur as expected.

- **Return values**: Verify that functions return the correct values for given inputs.

- **Dependencies and interactions**: While unit tests should ideally test a unit in isolation, it's important to mock dependencies and verify interactions between components to ensure they collaborate correctly.

Now that we know what we should test, it's time to implement unit testing so that we can see it in practice.

Implementing unit tests for the account microservice

A copy of the source code for *Chapter 7* can be found in the Ch12 folder of this book's GitHub repository. This chapter will demonstrate how to test different microservices. We'll start with the account microservice.

Create a new folder at the same level as the src folder and name it tests. Our main focus here is to test the src/services/account.js file. It contains the main logic and the required business rules that are implemented in our application.

Next, create a file called accountservice.test.mjs under the tests folder. Why the .mjs extension? This extension is used in Node.js projects to indicate that a JavaScript file should be treated as an **ECMAScript (ES)** module. This distinction is important because JavaScript supports two module systems: *CommonJS* and *ES modules*. Each has different syntax and behaviors. ES modules use import and export syntax. By using .mjs, Node.js can unambiguously determine that the file should be treated as an ES module, even if it exists alongside CommonJS files with a .js extension. This avoids confusion and potential conflicts, especially in projects that use both module systems. Using .mjs makes it explicit to developers and tools that the file is an ES module, helping them avoid making mistakes and misconfigurations.

Simply put, using the .mjs extension in Node.js projects helps separate ES modules from CommonJS modules. This ensures Node.js handles them correctly and keeps your code compatible with modern JavaScript standards. By using .mjs, you can simplify your module setup and make your code more future proof as JavaScript continues to evolve.

We plan to implement unit tests for the account.js file, which can be found in the src / services folder.

We have multiple functions inside this service. First, let's consider some unit tests for the getAccountById function. Here's the original function:

```
function getAccountById(id) {
    return Account.findById(id);
}
```

From an implementation perspective, we haven't implemented valid exception handling. We *throw* the same exception from the database layer to the API layer directly. It's generally better to handle exceptions either at the lowest level (database layer) or at the highest level (API layer). *Lower layers* should primarily focus on detecting and throwing exceptions when unexpected conditions arise. This maintains a clean separation of concerns and prevents lower layers from exposing implementation details. Some exceptions, such as database connection failures or file read/write errors, might require immediate handling at the lowest level to prevent data corruption or resource leaks. For instance, if a file write operation fails due to a full disk, handling the exception at this level can prevent further issues.

If the exception is expected and can be handled within the lower layer without exposing internal details, it's reasonable to do so. A centralized error-handling mechanism at the highest layer can provide consistent error management across the application.

First, let's install the required packages. To do so, run the `npm install --save-dev mocha chai sinon` command. After installation, we'll have the following `devDependencies` section in the `package.json` file:

```
"devDependencies": {
    "chai": "^5.1.1",
    "mocha": "^10.7.0",
    «sinon": "^18.0.0"
  }
```

Now, it's time to import the necessary packages and functionalities:

```
import * as chai from 'chai';
import sinon from 'sinon';
const expect = chai.expect;
import * as accountService from '../src/services/account.js';
import account from '../src/models/account.js'
const { errorCodes } = accountService.default;
```

What should we test in our account service? The first function that needs to be tested is `getAccountById`. We should check whether the function will return the exact account information if the given account exists in our database. Here's our first test case:

```
describe('getAccountById service', () => {
    let findByIdStub;
    beforeEach(() => {
        findByIdStub = sinon.stub(account, 'findById');
    });

    afterEach(async () => {
        await findByIdStub.restore();
    });

    it('should return the account if found by id', async () => {
        const expectedAccountId = '12345';
        const expectedAccount = { name: 'Test Account',
          number: '123-456-7890' };
        findByIdStub.withArgs(expectedAccountId)
          .resolves(expectedAccount);
        const account = await accountService
          .getAccountById(expectedAccountId);
```

```
            expect(account).to.deep.equal(expectedAccount);
            expect(findByIdStub.calledOnceWith(expectedAccountId))
                .to.be.true;
        });
    });
```

Well, this code may seem a little bit complicated at first glance, but the detailed explanation provided in this section will help you understand it with ease.

In Mocha, the `describe` and `it` blocks are fundamental structures that are used to write and organize tests.

The `describe` block is used to group related test cases. It helps organize tests into logical sections, making them easier to read and understand. It's typically used to group tests related to a particular feature or function. The `describe` block has two parameters:

- `description`: A string that describes the group of tests. This description will appear in the test's output.

- `function`: A callback function that contains the test cases (using it blocks) and any setup/teardown logic.

The `it` block is used to define individual test cases. Each `it` block represents a single test that performs a specific assertion or set of assertions.

You can nest `describe` blocks to create a hierarchical structure for your tests, making it easier to organize and understand complex test suites. Here's an example of this:

```
describe('Math operations', function() {
  describe('Addition', function() {
    it('should add two numbers correctly', function() {
      expect(1 + 1).to.equal(2);
    });
  });
  describe('Subtraction', function() {
    it('should subtract two numbers correctly', function()
    {
      expect(2 - 1).to.equal(1);
    });
  });
});
```

In practice, you typically use `describe` to group tests by the feature or unit of code being tested and `it` to define the specific behaviors you expect from that code.

Let's get back to our example. Our code snippet describes a unit test for a service function called getAccountById. The test uses a mocking library called Sinon to simulate the behavior of a function named findById within the account module.

In simpler terms, this test checks whether the getAccountById service function correctly retrieves an account by its ID using the findById function. It ensures that the service returns the expected account data when the ID is found.

Here's a line-by-line explanation of our first unit test:

- *Line 1* declares a test suite named getAccountById service. The function that's passed to describe will contain the test cases related to getAccountById service.

- *Line 2* declares the findByIdStub variable, which will be used later to hold the stub created by Sinon.

- *Line 3* sets up a function to run before each test case within this describe block.

- Inside the beforeEach function in *Line 4*, Sinon creates a stub for the findById method of the account model. This stub will replace the original findById method, allowing us to control its behavior during tests.

- *Line 7* sets up a function to run after each test case within this describe block.

- Inside the afterEach function in *Line 8*, the restore method is called on findByIdStub. This restores the original findById method of the account model, ensuring that stubs don't affect other tests.

- *Line 11* declares a test case with a description of should return the account if found by id. The function that's passed to it contains the test logic.

- *Line 12* declares a constant, expectedAccountId, and assigns it a value of '12345'. This is the ID that will be used to search for the account.

- *Line 13* declares a constant, expectedAccount, and assigns it a mock account object. This is the account that the stubbed findById method will return.

- *Line 14* sets up findByIdStub to resolve (return a promise that resolves to) expectedAccount when it's called with expectedAccountId. This simulates the behavior of finding an account in the database.

- *Line 15* calls the getAccountById service function with expectedAccountId and awaits its result. The result is assigned to the account variable.

- *Line 16* asserts that the account that's returned by the service function is deeply equal to expectedAccount. Deep equality checks that all properties of the objects are equal.

- *Line 17* asserts that findByIdStub was called exactly once with expectedAccountId. This verifies that the service function attempted to find the account by the correct ID.

Here are the next few unit tests inside the same `describe` block:

```
describe('getAccountById service', () => {
    .........
    .........
    it('should return null if account not found', async () => {
        const expectedAccountId = '54321';
        findByIdStub.withArgs(expectedAccountId).resolves(null);
        const account = await accountService
          .getAccountById(expectedAccountId);
        expect(account).to.be.null;
        expect(findByIdStub.calledOnceWith(expectedAccountId))
          .to.be.true;
    });

    it('should rethrow errors from findById', async () => {
        const expectedAccountId = '98765';
        const expectedError = new Error('Database error');
        findByIdStub.withArgs(expectedAccountId)
          .rejects(expectedError);

        try {
            await accountService.getAccountById(expectedAccountId);
        } catch (error) {
            expect(error).to.equal(expectedError);
            expect(findByIdStub.calledOnceWith(expectedAccountId))
              .to.be.true;
    } }); });
```

In this unit test suite, two test cases have been defined for the `getAccountById` service:

- The first test case, named `should return null if account not found`, sets up a scenario where the account with an ID of `'54321'` doesn't exist. Here, `findByIdStub` is configured to return `null` when called with this ID. The test then calls `getAccountById` with `'54321'` and expects the result to be `null`. It also verifies that `findByIdStub` was called exactly once with `'54321'`.

- The second test case, named `should rethrow errors from findById`, tests the behavior when the `findById` method throws an error. Here, `findByIdStub` is set up to throw `Database error` when called with ID `'98765'`. The test calls `getAccountById` and expects the call to throw the same error. This is verified using a try-catch block, where it's checked that the caught error is equal to the expected error. Additionally, it verifies that `findByIdStub` was called exactly once with `'98765'`. These tests ensure that the `getAccountById` service correctly handles cases where the account isn't found and when errors occur during database access. Please keep in mind that rethrowing errors should include meaningful handling, such as logging or adding additional context to the error.

Other tests except `updateAccountById` follow approximately the same testing style. In a given service, the most complex implementation exists inside the `updateAccountById` function. Please refer to *Chapter 5* to learn more about the `Account` microservice and its business cases.

We should cover every business rule that's implemented in our original functionality. Here's the first condition that we need to cover when updating the account:

```
async function updateAccountById(id, { name, number, type, status }) {
    if (!name && !number && !type && !status) {
        return { error: 'provide at least one valid data to be
updated', code: NO_VALID_DATA_TO_UPDATE };
    }
    ........
}
```

This function ensures that an account update is meaningful by requiring at least one valid piece of information (name, number, type, or status) to be provided. If none are given, it returns an error, to enforce the business rule of avoiding invalid updates.

Here's the unit test fragment:

```
describe('updateAccountById service', () => {
    let findByIdStub, saveStub;
    beforeEach(() => {
        findByIdStub = sinon.stub(account, 'findById');
        saveStub = sinon.stub(account.prototype, 'save');
    });
    afterEach(async () => {
        await findByIdStub.restore();
        await saveStub.restore();
    });
    it('should return error for no data to update', async () => {
        const id = '12345';
        const updateData = {};
        const result = await accountService.updateAccountById(id,
          updateData);
        expect(result).to.deep.equal({
            error: 'provide at least one valid data to be updated',
            code: errorCodes.NO_VALID_DATA_TO_UPDATE,
        });
          expect(findByIdStub.calledOnceWith(id)).to.be.false;
        expect(saveStub.calledOnce).to.be.false;
    });
```

```
    . . . . . .
    . . . . . . .  });
```

The preceding code snippet describes a unit test for a service function called `updateAccountById`. This function is responsible for updating an account based on a given ID and update data. The test employs `Sinon` to substitute the behavior of the `findById` and `save` methods within the account module.

Before each test case, `Sinon` stubs are established for both the `findById` and `save` methods to enable controlled test scenarios. After each test, these stubs are restored to their original state.

The specific test case focuses on validating the error handling process when no update data is provided. It constructs an account ID and an empty update object. Subsequently, it invokes the `updateAccountById` service with these parameters and captures the result that's returned.

The test then asserts that the returned result is an error object containing a specific error message and code, indicating the absence of valid update data. To ensure the correct behavior, it further verifies that neither the `findById` nor the `save` method was called as no account retrieval or update was necessary in this scenario.

Long story short, this unit test guarantees that the `updateAccountById` service correctly handles cases where no update data is supplied, returning an appropriate error response without performing unnecessary operations.

The next piece of logic in the `updateAccountById` function is defined like this:

```
async function updateAccountById(id, { name, number, type, status }) {
    . . . . . .
  if (status && !(status in availableAccountStatusesForUpdate)) {
        return { error: 'invalid status for account', code: INVALID_
STATUS_CODE };    }
    . . . . . .
}
```

The preceding code snippet indicates that if the status isn't part of the allowed statuses defined by the business rules, it returns an error message, preventing the update with an invalid or unsupported status. This ensures that only acceptable status changes are made, maintaining business consistency and data integrity.

The following unit test validates error handling for invalid status updates:

```
it('should return error for invalid status update', async () => {
        const id = '12345';
        const updateData = { status: 'invalid_status' };
        const result = await accountService.updateAccountById(id,
          updateData);
        expect(result).to.deep.equal({
```

```
        error: 'invalid status for account',
        code: errorCodes.INVALID_STATUS_CODE,
    });
    expect(findByIdStub.calledOnceWith(id)).to.be.false;
    expect(saveStub.calledOnce).to.be.false;
});
```

The preceding unit test verifies error handling for invalid status updates in the updateAccountById service. It simulates an update with an invalid status. The test expects an error object with specific details when the service encounters this invalid input. To isolate the test, stubs prevent database interactions. By asserting the correct error, the test ensures the service behaves as expected when faced with incorrect data.

Using the same approach we implemented for the preceding unit tests, we can test all the possible cases for our services. For more complete implementation, check out this book's GitHub repository and the respective folder for this chapter.

To run unit tests, navigate to the root folder from the command line (for us, this is the Ch12/accountservice folder) and run the following command:

```
npx mocha .\tests\accountservice.tests.mjs
```

Here's the result:

```
getAccountById service
  ✓ should return the account if found by id
  ✓ should return null if account not found
  ✓ should rethrow errors from findById

getAllAccounts  service
  ✓ should return all accounts
  ✓ should return null if accounts is empty

createAccount service
  ✓ should create a new account with correct data
  ✓ should handle errors from create

updateAccountById service
  ✓ should return error for no data to update
  ✓ should return error for invalid status update
  ✓ should return error for invalid type update
  ✓ should return error for account not found
  ✓ should return error for invalid status transition
  ✓ should allow valid status transition

updateAccountById - Type Transition Check
  ✓ should return error for invalid type transition
  ✓ should allow valid type transition


15 passing (87ms)
```

Figure 12.1: Results of the test run

With that, we've demonstrated how to write tests for the Express.js project. The same unit testing logic is the same for Nest.js applications. You can easily apply the aforementioned ideas to your Nest.js applications.

Writing unit tests for the transaction microservice

Now, it's time to demonstrate how easily you can write unit tests for your Nest.js applications. In this book's GitHub repository, in the Ch12 folder, we have the same transaction service we implemented in *Chapter 7*.

Open the `transaction.service.spec.ts` file, which can be found in the `src/test` folder. It contains all the essential tests to help us understand how to write unit tests. If you want to follow along and implement everything from scratch, just create a folder named `test` inside the `src` folder.

First things first, we need to install the required packages to implement unit testing for our project. To write unit tests for `transaction.service.js`, we need to install the `@nestjs/testing` package. Here's how you can do it:

```
npm install --save-dev jest @nestjs/testing
```

Once it's been installed, create a file called `transaction.service.spec.ts`. First, we need to import the required references:

```
import { Test, TestingModule } from '@nest.js/testing';
import { TransactionService } from '../transaction/transaction.
service';
import { PrismaService } from '../prisma/prisma.service';
import { HttpService } from '@nest.js/axios';
import { KafkaService } from '../kafka/kafka.service';
import { CreateTransactionDto } from '../transaction/dto/create-
transaction.dto';
```

The preceding code imports the necessary services for testing: `TransactionService` handles transaction logic, `PrismaService` interacts with the database, `HttpService` handles external HTTP requests, `KafkaService` performs message handling, and `CreateTransactionDto` defines the structure of transaction data. The `Test` and `TestingModule` imports are from the Nest.js testing module and are used to create a testing environment for `TransactionService`.

Here's what a simple unit test looks like:

```
describe('TransactionService', () => {
   let service: TransactionService;
   let prismaService: PrismaService;
   let httpService: HttpService;
   let kafkaService: KafkaService;
```

```
beforeEach(async () => {
  const module: TestingModule = await Test.createTestingModule({
    providers: [
      TransactionService,
      {
        provide: PrismaService,
        useValue: {
          transaction: {
            create: jest.fn(),
            findMany: jest.fn(),
            findUnique: jest.fn(),
            update: jest.fn(),
          },
        },
      },
      {
        provide: HttpService,
        useValue: {
          axiosRef: {
            get: jest.fn(),
          },
        },
      },
      {
        provide: KafkaService,
        useValue: {
          send: jest.fn(),
        },
      },
    ],
  }).compile();
```

We already know about the describe block and its role in unit testing. The preceding code snippet establishes a testing environment for TransactionService. It begins by importing the necessary modules and services: TransactionService, PrismaService for database interactions, HttpService for external requests, KafkaService for message handling, and CreateTransactionDto for data transfer.

A `describe` block encapsulates the tests for `TransactionService`. Inside, variables are declared to hold instances of the services. The `beforeEach` block sets up the testing module using `Test.createTestingModule`. It provides mock implementations for `PrismaService`, `HttpService`, and `KafkaService` to isolate `TransactionService` during testing. The `PrismaService` mock includes methods such as `create`, `findMany`, `findUnique`, and `update` to simulate database operations. If you open `transaction.service.ts`, you'll realize that we use these methods to implement the functionalities of the transaction service. Similarly, the `HttpService` and `KafkaService` mocks mimic their respective functionalities using Jest's `jest.fn()`. This setup allows for controlled testing of `TransactionService` without the need to rely on actual external dependencies.

Here, `jest.fn()` is a function provided by Jest, a popular JavaScript testing framework, to create mock functions. A mock function is essentially a dummy function that can be used to replace real functions during testing. There are a lot of benefits and values to using such types of functionalities in unit testing. Here are the benefits of using `jest.fn()`:

- **Isolation**: It allows us to isolate the component or function you're testing by replacing dependencies with mock functions. This helps us focus on the specific behavior of the code under test without being affected by external factors.

- **Verifiability**: We can assert how many times the mock function was called, with what arguments, and what it returned. This helps in verifying the correct behavior of the code.

- **Custom implementation**: We can define the behavior of the mock function using mock implementation to control its return value or actions.

By using `jest.fn()`, we can effectively test different scenarios and edge cases without relying on the actual implementation of the mocked function:

```
service = module.get<TransactionService>(TransactionService);
prismaService = module.get<PrismaService>(PrismaService);
httpService = module.get<HttpService>(HttpService);
kafkaService = module.get<KafkaService>(KafkaService);
```

The `module.get` method is used to access the providers that were defined in the `TestingModule` setup. It takes the service class as an argument and returns an instance of that service. By calling `module.get` for each service (`TransactionService`, `PrismaService`, `HttpService`, and `KafkaService`), the code obtains references to these services, which can then be used for testing purposes.

These service instances are typically used within the test cases to interact with the system under test and verify its behavior.

First, let's start with a simple test case:

```
it(<should be defined', () => {
   expect(service).toBeDefined();
 });
```

This code snippet defines a basic test case to ensure the service instance is injected correctly.

The `it('should be defined', () => { ... })` block creates a test case with a description of `should be defined` Inside this block, the `expect(service).toBeDefined();` assertion checks whether the `service` variable has a defined value. This is a fundamental test to verify that the dependency injection process has successfully provided an instance of `TransactionService`. If the service is `null` or `undefined`, the test will fail.

Essentially, this test case acts as a sanity check to ensure the testing environment has been set up correctly before we proceed with more complex test scenarios. Now, let's switch to testing the transaction creation process:

```
describe('create', () => {
    it('should create a transaction with status CREATED if account
status is new or active', async () => {
      const createTransactionDto: CreateTransactionDto = {
        accountId: '1',
        description: 'Test transaction',
      };
      const accountApiResponse = {
        data: {
          account: {
            id: '1',
            status: 'active',
          },
        },
      };

      jest.spyOn(httpService.axiosRef, 'get').
mockResolvedValue(accountApiResponse);
      jest.spyOn(prismaService.transaction, 'create').
mockResolvedValue({
        id: 1,
        accountId: '1',
        description: 'Test transaction',
        status: 'CREATED',
        createdAt: new Date(),
        updatedAt: new Date(),
      });
```

```
        const result = await service.create(createTransactionDto);
        expect(result).toEqual(expect.objectContaining({
          id: 1,
          accountId: '1',
          description: 'Test transaction',
          status: 'CREATED',
        }));
        expect(httpService.axiosRef.get).toHaveBeenCalledWith('http://
localhost:3001/v1/accounts/1');
        expect(prismaService.transaction.create).toHaveBeenCalledWith({
          data: {
            accountId: '1',
            description: 'Test transaction',
            status: 'CREATED',
          }, }); });
```

This test case aims to verify the `create` method of `TransactionService` under specific conditions.

It starts by defining a test scenario where the account status is either `new` or `active`. A `CreateTransactionDto` object is created with the necessary data. To simulate external dependencies, `httpService` and `prismaService` are mocked using `jest.spyOn`.

Here, `jest.spyOn` is a function in Jest that's used to create a spy on an existing function. Unlike `jest.fn()`, which creates a new mock function, `jest.spyOn` wraps an existing function to track calls and potentially modify its behavior.

We can use `jest.spyOn` to observe how a particular function is used within your code without altering its original implementation. It also records information about function calls, such as arguments, return values, and the number of times it was called. This is useful for verifying the interaction between different parts of our code.

While optional, we can change the behavior of the spied function. This is helpful when we want to control the output of the function for specific test cases. After testing, we can restore the original function's behavior.

The `httpService.axiosRef.get` method is mocked to return a successful account response with an `active` status. The `prismaService.transaction.create` method is also mocked to return a created transaction with the CREATE status.

The `service.create` method is then called with the prepared `createTransactionDto` object. The test asserts that the returned result matches the expected transaction data, indicating successful creation. Additionally, it verifies that `httpService.axiosRef.get` was called with the correct URL to fetch account information, and `prismaService.transaction.create` was called with the correct data to persist the transaction.

Essentially, this test case ensures that the `create` method interacts with `httpService` correctly to fetch account details, determines the transaction status based on account status, and persists the transaction to the database through `prismaService` with the expected data. By mocking dependencies, the test isolates the `create` method's logic and verifies its behavior without relying on external systems.

It should now be easy for you to understand the rest of the unit tests that have been implemented inside our `transaction.service.spec.ts` file.

When implementing unit tests, you may hear a lot about mocks, stubs, and spies. As our last topic regarding unit tests, let's explore and understand their responsibilities.

To run all your tests, you simply need to run the `npm test` command (*Figure 12.2*).

There may be cases where tests fail to run properly. To resolve this, please refer to this book's GitHub repository and ensure that the `package-lock.json` file matches the package versions specified in the repository:

```
PASS  src/test/transaction.service.spec.ts (14.941 s)
  TransactionService
    √ should be defined (26 ms)
    create
      √ should create a transaction with status CREATED if account status is new or active (6358 ms)
      √ should create a transaction with status FAILED if account status is not new or active (25 ms)
      √ should throw an error if account is not found (39 ms)

Test Suites: 1 passed, 1 total
Tests:       4 passed, 4 total
Snapshots:   0 total
Time:        15.352 s, estimated 16 s
```

Figure 12.2: Running transaction tests

As mentioned previously, we can use various building blocks for testing, such as mocks, stubs, and spies. Let's try to understand and differentiate them.

Comparing mocks, stubs, and spies in unit tests

We'll spend this section comparing mocks, stubs, and spies in unit tests because they're essential tools for isolating and simulating components' behaviors during testing. Understanding their differences will help us choose the right approach to test various interactions and functionalities in the system effectively.

Mocks

A **mock** is a simulated object that replaces a real dependency in a unit test. It's designed to mimic the behavior of the original object but with complete control over its actions. Why? This isolation allows for focused testing of the code under scrutiny without the need to rely on external factors.

We can define exact return values, exceptions, or sequences of actions for mock objects. This enables us to test various scenarios and edge cases. Mocks can record interactions, allowing us to verify that methods were called with correct arguments, in the right order, and with the expected frequency. By replacing real dependencies with mocks, we can create a controlled environment, preventing unexpected side effects and ensuring test reliability.

Let's go over the benefits of using mocks:

- **Improved test focus**: Mocks help you concentrate on the logic of the code being tested, without being distracted by the intricacies of external components.
- **Faster test execution**: Since mocks don't involve real interactions (such as database calls or network requests), tests run significantly faster
- **Increased test coverage**: Mocks allow you to test different scenarios and edge cases that might be difficult or impossible to reproduce in a real environment.
- **Enhanced code reliability**: By thoroughly testing code in isolation, you can identify and fix potential issues early in the development process.

Next, we'll look at stubs.

Stubs

On the other hand, a **stub** is a simplified implementation of a component that's used to replace a real component in a test. It provides canned answers to calls that are made during the test, focusing on the specific behavior needed for the test case.

A stub only contains the essential logic required for the test and returns predetermined values or exceptions. It typically doesn't verify interactions or expectations. That is great, but when can you use them?

- When you need to isolate the unit under test by providing controlled responses.
- When the behavior of the dependency isn't critical to the test case.
- When you want to speed up test execution by avoiding complex logic.

While both stubs and mocks are used to replace real components in tests, there's a key difference. Stubs focus on providing predefined responses and don't verify interactions, whereas mocks allow for more complex behavior, including expectations and verifying interactions.

In many cases, stubs can be sufficient for basic testing, but as test requirements become more complex, mocks offer greater flexibility and control.

Spies

A **spy** is a wrapper around an existing object or function that records information about how it's used. Unlike stubs and mocks, which replace the original object, spies observe the behavior of the real object.

Here are some of the key characteristics of spies:

- **Wrap real object**: Spies can be created around existing objects or functions.
- **Record interactions**: They track method calls, arguments, and return values.
- **Verify behavior**: Spies are used to ensure that methods are called correctly and with the expected parameters.

You can use spies in the following instances:

- When you want to verify that a specific method is called with certain arguments.
- When you need to check the sequence of method calls.
- When you want to observe the side effects of a function without controlling its behavior.

While both spies and mocks can verify interactions, there's a key difference – spies observe the behavior of the real object, whereas mocks replace the real object with a simulated one.

Additionally, stubs provide canned responses without verifying interactions. Mocks replace objects and allow for complex behavior and verification. On the other hand, spies observe the behavior of real objects without modifying them.

Understanding and implementing integration tests

Integration tests are an important component of a robust testing strategy and focus on the interactions between different parts of your application. Unlike unit tests, which isolate individual components, integration tests evaluate how these components work together as a cohesive system.

In the context of Express.js, integration tests ensure that routes, controllers, models, and databases interact seamlessly. They verify that data flows correctly between these components and that the application produces the expected outcomes.

Why are integration tests essential? They help prevent integration issues, which can often be complex and time-consuming to debug. By testing the interactions between components, you can catch potential problems early in the development cycle, reducing the risk of unexpected behavior in production.

Integration tests aren't a replacement for unit tests. Unit tests focus on the correctness of individual functions and modules, while integration tests verify how these components work together. A comprehensive testing strategy should include both unit and integration tests.

By investing time in writing effective integration tests, you can significantly improve the quality and reliability of your Express.js applications. They help prevent integration issues, increase confidence in your code base, and ultimately deliver a better user experience.

Integration testing in Node.js microservices focuses on verifying the interactions between different components or services. It ensures that these components work together seamlessly to deliver the expected outcomes.

Integration tests catch issues early in development, reducing production failures. By writing comprehensive integration tests, you encourage better code design and maintainability. Successful integration tests build confidence in the system's overall reliability.

Before we move on, let's understand the key aspects of integration testing in microservices:

- **Testing boundaries**: Integration tests primarily focus on the interfaces between microservices. They verify data exchange, contract adherence, and error handling.
- **Dependency management**: Effectively managing dependencies is essential. You might use mocking, stubbing, or test doubles to isolate components for testing.
- **Data consistency**: Integration tests should validate data integrity across different services. This includes testing data transformations, consistency checks, and error handling.
- **Performance considerations**: Integration tests can help identify performance bottlenecks and scalability issues.

Having said this, it's also important to understand exactly when you'd use integration testing. Let's look at the instances when you would use this here:

- **API interactions**: Test how different microservices communicate through APIs, verifying request/response formats, error handling, and authentication.
- **Database interactions**: Ensure data is stored, retrieved, and updated correctly across multiple services.
- **Message queues**: Verify message delivery, processing, and error handling in asynchronous communication patterns.
- **External systems**: Test interactions with external systems such as payment gateways, email services, or third-party APIs.

Long story short, integration tests in Node.js microservices verify that different components or services interact correctly, ensuring seamless functionality and preventing complex issues in production. Now, let's implement integration tests for the transaction microservice.

The purpose of this subsection is to show you how you can implement integration tests for your Node.js services, particularly for Nest.js. The general idea of integration testing applies to all types of applications, regardless of whether you use Express.js or other frameworks.

As always, we need to install the required package to write integration tests for our project. Go to `Ch12/transactionservice` and run the following command to install the `jest` and `supertest` packages:

```
npm install --save-dev jest @types/jest supertest @nestjs/testing
```

We've already talked about the `jest` package. The `supertest` package is a high-level abstraction for testing HTTP servers. It makes it easy to send HTTP requests to your Nest.js application and inspect the responses, simulating real-world client behavior.

Nest.js provides excellent integration with both Jest and Supertest, making it straightforward to set up and run integration tests. You can test various aspects of your Nest.js application, including controllers, services, and database interactions. Integration tests can be included in your CI/CD pipeline so that you can catch issues early in the development process.

Go to the root folder (`Ch12/transactionservice`) and create the `jest.config.js` file with the following content:

```js
// jest.config.js
module.exports = {
    moduleFileExtensions: [
        'js',
        'json',
        'ts',
    ],
    rootDir: 'src',
    testRegex: '.*\\.spec\\.ts$',
    transform: {
        '^.+\\.(t|j)s$': 'ts-jest',
    },
    collectCoverageFrom: [
        '**/*.(t|j)s',
    ],
    coverageDirectory: '../coverage',
    testEnvironment: 'node',
    globalSetup: './test/global-setup.js',
    globalTeardown: './test/global-teardown.js',
};
```

Let's break down the code here:

- The `jest.config.js` file is a configuration file that customizes Jest's behavior. This particular configuration specifies that Jest should look for TypeScript, JavaScript, and JSON files (`moduleFileExtensions`). It sets the project root directory to `src`, defines test files as those ending with `.spec.ts`, and uses `ts-jest` to process TypeScript files. The configuration also enables code coverage reporting to `../coverage`, sets the test environment to Node. js, and executes `global-setup.js` before all tests and `global-teardown.js` after.

- Next, we have `globalSetup` and `globalTeardown` in our Jest configuration to execute code before and after the entire test suite runs, respectively.

- Then, `globalSetup` runs once before all tests. It's ideal for setting up resources such as databases, servers, or other external dependencies that are required for the tests.

- Finally, `globalTeardown` runs once after all tests have been completed. It's used to clean up resources that are created in `globalSetup`, such as closing database connections or stopping servers.

In the provided configuration, the scripts for these operations are located in the `./test/global-setup.js` and `./test/global-teardown.js` files. However, we don't have these files yet. So, let's create them. Go to the `test` folder and create both files.

Here's our `global-setup` file:

```
const { execSync } = require('child_process');
module.exports = async () => {
    console.log('Starting Docker Compose...');
    execSync('docker-compose -f docker-compose.tests.yml up
      --build -d', { stdio: 'inherit' });
    // You might need to add a delay here to give services time to
initialize
    await new Promise(resolve => setTimeout(resolve, 15000)); };
```

This global setup script initiates a Docker Compose environment for testing. It starts by logging a message, and then executes the `docker-compose up --build -d` command using the specified `docker-compose.tests.yml` file. Finally, it introduces a fifteen second delay to allow services sufficient time to start before test execution begins.

Here's the `global-teardown` file:

```
const { execSync } = require('child_process');
module.exports = async () => {
    console.log(<Stopping Docker Compose...>);
    execSync('docker-compose -f docker-compose.tests.yml down',
      { stdio: 'inherit' });
};
```

This `global-teardown` script terminates the Docker Compose environment. It logs a message indicating the process and then executes the `docker-compose down` command using the specified `docker-compose.tests.yml` file to stop all running containers and remove networks.

We run all dependent services from the Docker file, hence why we have a special file called `docker-compose.tests.yml` under `Ch12/transactionservice`. Check out this book's GitHub repository for the source code for the `docker-compose.tests.yml` file.

This Docker Compose file defines a multi-container environment for a microservices application. It includes services for a PostgreSQL database, `PgAdmin` for database management, MongoDB, Zookeeper, Kafka, and a Kafka UI. The file also defines an account service built from a local `Dockerfile` file, configuring its dependencies on MongoDB and Kafka. Environment variables, ports, volumes, and network configurations are specified for each service. Here, `app-network` is used for internal communication between containers.

When writing integration tests for Nest.js applications, we often create a test configuration file. This configuration file specifies configuration values that are necessary for the test environment, such as database connections, API keys, or other sensitive information. You can set up in-memory or temporary databases for testing purposes to isolate test data and prevent conflicts with production data. It also helps us to configure mocking libraries or frameworks so that we can replace real external services with test doubles, improving test isolation and performance. We mostly define configuration options for testing frameworks or libraries, such as Jest or Supertest, to customize their behavior for integration tests. By centralizing test-specific configurations in a separate file, you enhance code organization, maintainability, and reusability. It also helps to prevent sensitive information from being accidentally committed to the main code base. Check out the `Ch12/transactionservice/test-configuration.ts` file for more content.

Our test configuration file sets up a Nest.js testing module for integration tests. It imports the necessary modules for database connection (`TypeOrm`), microservices (`ClientsModule`), and the target module (`TransactionModule`). It also configures a PostgreSQL database using environment variables or default values and establishes a Kafka client. Finally, the `testConfiguration` function compiles the testing module and returns it for use in integration tests.

If you haven't installed it yet, don't forget to run the following command to make sure your test configuration will run properly:

```
npm install --save @nestjs/microservices @nestjs/testing @nestjs/
typeorm
```

Here, `@nestjs/typeorm` is a package that seamlessly integrates `TypeORM`, a popular **object-relational mapper (ORM)**, with the Nest.js framework. It provides a convenient way to interact with relational databases such as PostgreSQL, MySQL, SQLite, and others within your Nest.js application.

You must define your database tables as TypeScript classes (*entities*). Here, `TypeORM` handles the mapping between your code and the database schema. It supports features such as repositories, migrations, transactions, and more, making database operations efficient and reliable.

Now, it's time to write our simple integration test for the transaction microservice. The `transaction. controller.spec.ts` file can be found under `Ch12/transactionservice/src/test` and contains the following content:

```
import { INestApplication } from '@nest.js/common';
import { testConfiguration } from '../test/test-configuration';
import * as request from 'supertest';

describe('AppController (e2e)', () => {
  let app: INestApplication;
  beforeAll(async () => {
    const moduleFixture = await testConfiguration();
    app = moduleFixture.createNestApplication();
    await app.init();
  });

  afterAll(async () => {
    await app.close();
  });
  it('/transactions (POST) should create a transaction', async () => {
    const createTransactionDto = {
      accountId: '6658ae5284432e40604018d5', // UUID
      description: 'Test transaction',
    };
    return request(app.getHttpServer())
      .post('/transaction')
      .send(createTransactionDto)
      .expect(400);
  }, 10000); });
```

This test imports the necessary modules for testing and HTTP requests. The `beforeAll` hook sets up the test environment by creating a Nest.js application using the `testConfiguration` function, while the `afterAll` hook cleans up by closing the application. The test case focuses on creating a transaction. It constructs a transaction DTO with sample data and sends a POST request to the `/transaction` endpoint. The expected response status is `400` (*Bad Request*), indicating an error in the request. A timeout of `10000` milliseconds (`10` seconds) is set for the test. This test case verifies the basic functionality of the transaction creation endpoint and provides a foundation for further testing scenarios.

To run your tests, simply execute the `npm run test` command. Make sure Docker is running before executing any integration tests:

```
[+] Running 8/8
✓ Network transactionservice_app-network        Created      0.1s
✓ Container transactionservice-postgres-1        Started      0.2s
✓ Container mongodb                              Started      0.2s
✓ Container transactionservice-zookeeper-1       Started      0.2s
✓ Container transactionservice-pgadmin-1         Started      0.2s
✓ Container transactionservice-kafka1-1          Started      0.2s
✓ Container transactionservice-account-service-1 Started      0.1s
✓ Container transactionservice-kafka-ui-1        Started      0.1s
```

Figure 12.3: Docker services

When running integration tests with a Dockerized account microservice, the primary challenge is ensuring a consistent data state for each test. This involves doing the following:

- **Data preparation**: Creating necessary accounts or records before each test.

- **Data cleanup**: Removing test data after each test to prevent data pollution.

- **Database isolation**: Ensuring test data doesn't interfere with other tests or environments.

To handle these challenges, we can use multiple solutions:

- **Database migration scripts**: Use tools such as `typeorm` and `sequelize` to create migration scripts for your account database:

  - **Run migrations before tests**: Execute these scripts in your `globalSetup` or `beforeEach` hooks to populate the database with test data.

  - **Rollb ack migrations after tests**: Execute the reverse migrations in your `globalTeardown` or `afterEach` hooks to clean up the database.

- **Docker volumes**: Define a Docker volume for your account microservice's database:

  - **Mount the volume**: Mount the volume to the container to persist data between test runs.

  - **Truncate or delete data**: Before each test, truncate or delete the database's content to ensure a clean state.

- **Test containers**: For complex scenarios, use a dedicated container for test data preparation and cleanup:

  - **Orchestrate with Docker Compose**: Use Docker Compose to manage the relationship between the test container and the account microservice.

- **In-memory databases**: For simpler scenarios, use in-memory databases such as SQLite for testing:

    - **Benefits**: Faster startup, isolation, and no need for data migration.

With that, we've come to the end of this chapter! Let's recap what we learned.

Summary

In this chapter, we delved into the critical role of testing in microservice architecture. Building upon our previous exploration of microservice creation, we emphasized the importance of rigorous testing for ensuring code quality and reliability. We introduced the concepts of unit and integration testing, explaining their distinct purposes and benefits.

To solidify our understanding, we implemented unit tests for both the account and transaction microservices. These tests verified the correct behavior of individual code units in isolation. Additionally, we explored the nuances of mocks, stubs, and spies, demonstrating their utility in isolating components during testing.

To assess the interactions between different microservices, we introduced integration testing. By combining unit tests with integration tests, we established a robust testing strategy for our microservices.

In the next chapter, we will dive into the practical implementation of CI/CD pipelines. We will explore how to utilize GitHub Actions to automate workflows and streamline the deployment of our microservices, particularly focusing on deploying to Azure Cloud. You'll learn how to build a fully automated pipeline that ensures your applications are consistently ready for deployment with minimal manual intervention.

13

A CI/CD Pipeline for Your Microservices

Continuous integration (CI) and **continuous delivery/deployment (CD)** are fundamental practices in modern software development, forming the backbone of efficient DevOps workflows. Together, they automate and streamline the processes of integrating code changes, testing, and deploying applications, ensuring that software is always in a deployable state.

One of the modern software development requirements for developers is to at least understand and have essential skills for building pipelines and working with different automation systems.

This chapter is about understanding and applying CI/CD to your microservices. Developing these fundamental DevOps skills will help you stay aligned with modern development practices.

We'll cover the following topics:

- The essentials of CI/CD processes
- Working with Azure Cloud
- Working with GitHub actions
- Building a pipeline

You don't need any previous experience of CI/CD to cover and understand the current chapter.

The essentials of CI/CD processes

CI and CD are essential practices in Node.js microservice development to streamline both the development and release processes. CI automates the integration of code changes into the main branch, ensuring each update is tested and validated through automated testing. This reduces the risk of integration issues and helps maintain code quality.

In the CD pipeline, every successful build from CI is automatically deployed to production or staging environments. This automation significantly reduces the time between development and release, allowing teams to quickly iterate on features and address issues.

Understanding CI

CI is the practice of frequently integrating code changes into a shared repository. This process is typically automated, with code being merged and tested multiple times a day. The main goals of CI are to detect integration issues early, reduce the chances of bugs reaching production, and ensure that new code is always compatible with the existing code base.

As developers, we commit our code changes frequently (often several times a day) to a shared repository. This reduces the chances of conflicts and integration issues. When we have automated systems such as CI, after every commit, an automated build process is triggered. The code is compiled, and necessary dependencies are resolved. This ensures that the code base remains in a buildable state at all times. A successful build is an indication that the code base is in a healthy state and can proceed to the next steps, such as testing.

Automated tests are executed after the build process. These tests can include unit tests, integration tests, and sometimes even end-to-end tests. The goal is to catch any bugs or issues early in the development cycle. If the build or tests fail, developers receive immediate feedback. This allows them to address issues quickly before they become bigger problems.

Every time a new code change is committed, an automated build process is triggered. This process compiles the code, resolves dependencies, and packages the application if necessary.

CI encourages the use of a single shared repository, which acts as the *single source of truth* for the project. This repository contains the most up-to-date and stable version of the code base, ensuring that all team members are working from the same foundation. This practice especially helps in maintaining consistency across the team.

Now, let's try to cover the benefits of CI:

- **Early bug detection**: By integrating code changes frequently and running automated tests with each integration, CI allows teams to detect bugs and issues early in the development process. This early detection reduces the cost and complexity of fixing bugs.

- **Reduced integration conflicts**: Frequent integration of code changes means that conflicts are detected and resolved quickly.

- **Faster development cycles**: Automated builds and tests free up developer time by eliminating the need for manual testing and build processes. This leads to faster development cycles and quicker delivery of new features and bug fixes.

- **Improved code quality**: Automated testing as part of CI ensures that only code that passes a predefined set of tests is integrated into the mainline. This improves the overall quality and stability of the code base.

- **Enhanced collaboration**: CI encourages collaboration among team members by making it easier to integrate and share code. This fosters a culture of transparency and collective ownership of the code base.

- **Continuous feedback**: Continuous feedback loops provide developers with immediate information about the impact of their changes. This helps in maintaining high code quality and reduces the time spent on debugging and troubleshooting.

A CI workflow helps the team to catch bugs early, reduce integration challenges, and improve collaboration among team members. By automating the process of testing and building, CI ensures that the code base remains stable and ready for further development or deployment, promoting a faster and more reliable release cycle. Here is how it works:

1. **Developer makes changes**: Step one is about making changes. A developer writes new code or modifies existing code on their local machine. Once the changes are complete, they commit the changes to the **version control system (VCS)**, such as Git.

2. **Code is pushed to the repository**: The developer pushes the committed changes to the shared repository. This triggers the CI process.

3. **CI server detects changes**: A CI server (e.g., Jenkins, Travis CI, CircleCI, or GitHub Actions) monitors the repository for new changes. When a change is detected, the CI server automatically triggers a build process.

4. **Build is automated**: The CI server pulls the latest code and initiates the build process. This involves compiling the code, resolving dependencies, and creating build artifacts if necessary. Tools such as Maven, Gradle, and Ant are used to automate the build process, manage dependencies, and compile the code.

5. **Testing is automated**: After a successful build, the CI server runs automated tests. These tests can include unit tests, integration tests, and other types of tests specific to the project. If the tests pass, the CI process continues. If any test fails, the process is halted, and the developer is notified of the failure. JUnit, NUnit, Mocha, Jest, and Selenium are examples of testing frameworks used to write and execute automated tests.

6. **Feedback is given to developers**: The CI server provides feedback to the developer, typically through notifications or a web interface. If the build or tests fail, the feedback includes details about the failure, helping the developer to quickly identify and fix the issue.

7. **Changes are merged to mainline**: Once the build and tests pass, the changes are merged into the mainline or master branch of the repository. This branch always represents the latest stable version of the code.

8. **Builds are deployed**: In some cases, successful builds might be automatically deployed to a staging environment for further testing. This can be part of a CD pipeline.

The CI workflow is designed to automate the integration of code changes, ensuring that new updates are quickly tested and validated before being merged into the mainline. By following this structured process, teams can catch issues early, reduce integration headaches, and deliver high-quality code more efficiently.

Several tools and platforms play an important role in implementing CI in software development projects. These tools ensure that code integration, building, and testing processes are automated and efficient. VCSs such as Git and Subversion, manage and track changes in the code base, while CI servers such as Jenkins and GitHub Actions automate the build and test process. Build tools such as Maven and Gradle handle dependencies and compilation, and testing frameworks such as Mocha and Jest enable automated testing, ensuring code quality at every stage of development.

Understanding CD

CD is a software engineering practice that enables teams to develop and release software in shorter, more frequent cycles, ensuring it can be deployed at any moment with confidence. As an evolution of CI, CD emphasizes not just building and testing code but also automating the deployment process to production environments, allowing for faster and more reliable releases.

Here are the core principles of CD:

- **Automated testing**: Every change goes through an automated testing process to ensure that it is production-ready.

- **Automated deployment**: The deployment process is automated, reducing the risks and errors associated with manual deployments.

- **Incremental updates**: Software is released in small, manageable chunks rather than large, monolithic updates.

- **Environment parity**: The testing, staging, and production environments are kept as similar as possible to avoid unexpected issues during deployment.

- **Continuous feedback**: Constant monitoring and feedback from the production environment allow for quick detection and resolution of issues.

That is great, but how do we apply it to our Node.js microservices? Applying CD to a Node.js microservice architecture involves several steps.

Integrating CI/CD into microservices

Integrating CI/CD into microservices ensures seamless, automated deployment and testing of independent services, enabling faster development cycles and consistent, reliable updates. This approach enhances scalability and agility by streamlining the release process across distributed microservice architectures. Here is how we can integrate it in terms of Node.js microservices:

1. First, you need to set up CI. You can use a CI tool such as **GitHub Actions**, **Jenkins**, or another tool to automate the process of building, testing, and packaging your Node.js microservices. Make sure that your CI pipeline runs unit tests, integration tests, and static code analysis on every commit.

2. Use Docker to containerize each Node.js microservice. This ensures that the service runs consistently across different environments. Define a Docker file for each microservice to specify the dependencies, environment variables, and startup commands.

3. The next step is writing automated tests for each microservice, covering unit tests, integration tests, and end-to-end tests. Use a test framework such as **Mocha**, **Jest**, or **Supertest** to write and run your tests.

4. In the end, ensure your CI pipeline runs these tests on every code change.

5. The second huge step is to set up a CD pipeline. Extend your CI pipeline to deploy your microservices to a staging environment automatically. This can be done using the previously mentioned tools such as GitHub Actions, Jenkins, or other tools. Use a deployment tool such as **Kubernetes**, **Docker Swarm**, or **AWS ECS** (**Elastic Container Service**) to manage your containers in the staging and production environments.

6. Automate the deployment process by defining scripts that push the Docker images to a container registry (such as Docker Hub or AWS ECR) and update the services in the staging environment.

7. Ensure that your local, testing, staging, and production environments are as similar as possible. This reduces the chances of environment-specific bugs.

8. To manage different configurations for each environment, don't forget to use environment variables.

9. Implement monitoring and logging for your microservices using tools such as Prometheus, Grafana, ELK Stack, or Datadog. Set up alerts to notify your team of any issues in the production environment.

10. Use deployment strategies such as canary releases or blue-green deployments to minimize the risk when deploying new versions of your microservices. This allows you to test new versions with a small percentage of users before rolling them out to the entire user base.

11. Monitor the performance and logs of your services in production. Gather feedback from users and automatically roll back if a deployment causes issues.

12. Continuously iterate on your processes and tools to improve your CD pipeline. By following these steps, you can effectively implement CD in your Node.js microservice development process, allowing for faster, safer, and more reliable deployments.

CI and CD are closely related concepts in modern software development, but they focus on different stages of the software development life cycle. Here's how they differ.

The main focus of CI is integrating code changes from multiple developers into a shared repository, multiple times a day. It also ensures that the code is always in a deployable state by catching integration issues early. Hence, a CI pipeline focuses on integrating and testing code. It includes stages such as code linting, unit tests, integration tests, and sometimes code coverage reports.

On the other hand, CD builds on CI by automating the delivery of code changes to various environments, such as staging and production, after they pass the CI pipeline. The primary goal of CD is to then ensure that code is always ready to be released to production, and releases can happen frequently and reliably. A CD pipeline extends the CI pipeline to include steps for deploying the code to various environments. This can include deployment scripts, environment configuration, and automated rollback mechanisms.

In essence, CI is the foundation, and CD extends it to cover the deployment aspect, allowing for continuous delivery of new features and updates to end users.

Working with Azure Cloud

The **cloud** refers to a network of remote servers hosted on the internet, which are used to store, manage, and process data, rather than relying on a local server or personal computer. It allows businesses and individuals to access computing resources on-demand, such as storage, computing power, databases, and more, from anywhere in the world.

Azure is Microsoft's cloud computing platform, providing a wide range of services such as virtual machines, databases, AI tools, and more. It enables developers and businesses to build, deploy, and manage applications through a global network of Microsoft-managed data centers. Azure offers flexibility, scalability, and cost-effectiveness, making it suitable for everything from small startups to large enterprises.

Using **Azure cloud** provides several advantages, including seamless integration with Microsoft's ecosystem, high availability, and robust security features. It also supports hybrid cloud environments, allowing businesses to connect their on-premises infrastructure with the cloud. Azure's global presence ensures low latency and compliance with regional regulations. Additionally, it offers advanced analytics, AI, and machine learning services, empowering businesses to innovate and stay competitive in the digital age.

To make our example as simple as possible, we will work on the Account microservice from *Chapter 5*. We will begin by obtaining all the resources necessary for our example.

Our Account service stores data in the Postgres database. We will deploy our application to Azure, but you can use any cloud infrastructure you want.

First, we need to create an **Azure Resource Group** to deploy our application. We can do that with the following steps:

1. First, let's create a Postgres resource to store data on Azure. Go to `http://portal.azure.com` and register to get a free account if you haven't registered yet. Using a free subscription, you can get $200 of free credit toward Azure products and services, plus twelve months of popular free services.

2. The next step is to set up Azure resources using the Azure portal and create a resource group:

    I.   Log in to the Azure portal.

    II.   In the left sidebar, select **Resource Groups**.

    III. Click **Create**.

    IV.   Fill in the necessary details, such as the subscription, resource group name, and region, then click **Review + create** (*Figure 13.1*):

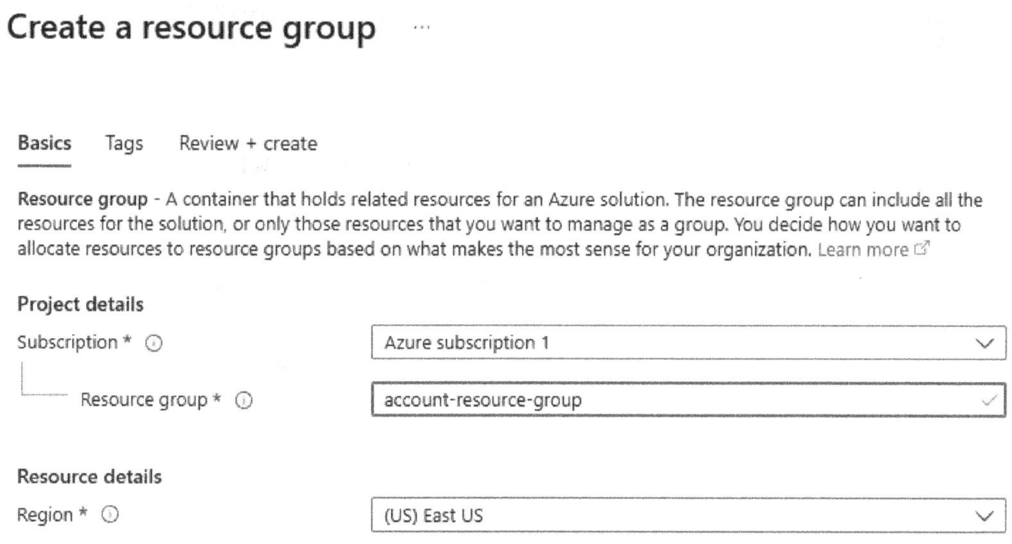

Create a resource group   ...

Basics   Tags   Review + create

Resource group - A container that holds related resources for an Azure solution. The resource group can include all the resources for the solution, or only those resources that you want to manage as a group. You decide how you want to allocate resources to resource groups based on what makes the most sense for your organization. Learn more

Project details

Subscription * ⓘ | Azure subscription 1   ⌄ |

    Resource group * ⓘ | account-resource-group   ✓ |

Resource details

Region * ⓘ | (US) East US   ⌄ |

Figure 13.1: Creating a resource group in Azure

3. The next step is to create an App Service plan:

I.   In the Azure portal, search for `App Service plans` in the search bar and select the top result.

II. Click **Create**.

III. Choose your subscription, select the resource group you just created, and enter a name for your App Service plan.

IV. Under **Operating System**, select **Linux**.

V.   Choose a pricing tier (e.g., **B1** for a basic plan).

VI. Click **Review + create**.

Creating an App Service plan in Azure is an essential step when deploying web apps, APIs, and other workloads using Azure App Services. The App Service plan defines the underlying infrastructure that powers your web app, API, or function app. It determines how your application is hosted, including the amount of CPU (processing power), memory (RAM), storage (disk space), and networking capacity it uses.

By creating an App Service plan, you specify the resources and capacity needed to run your application, ensuring it has the necessary performance to handle the expected load. It directly influences the cost of running your application in Azure by giving the following two options:

- **Pricing tier**: The plan you choose determines the pricing tier, which affects the cost based on the resources allocated. Azure offers various pricing tiers, from free and shared tiers for small apps to premium tiers for high-performance, production-grade apps.

- **Scaling options**: An App Service plan also defines the scaling options for your application. You can scale up (increase the size of the instance) or scale out (increase the number of instances) based on your application's needs. Different pricing tiers offer different scaling capabilities.

Figure 13.2 shows how to create an App Service plan in Azure:

Create App Service Plan   ...

Azure resource utilization. This way, if you want to save money on your testing environment you can share a plan across multiple apps. Learn more ⬈

Project Details

Select a subscription to manage deployed resources and costs. Use resource groups like folders to organize and manage all your resources.

Subscription * ⓘ	Azure subscription 1 ⌄
Resource Group * ⓘ	(New) account-resource-group ⌄
	Create new

App Service Plan details

Name *	account-api-service-plan
Operating System *	◉ Linux ◯ Windows
Region *	East US ⌄

Pricing Tier

App Service plan pricing tier determines the location, features, cost and compute resources associated with your app. Learn more ⬈

Pricing plan	Premium V3 P1V3 (195 minimum ACU/vCPU, 8 GB memory, 2 vCPU) ⌄
	Explore pricing plans

Zone redundancy

An App Service plan can be deployed as a zone redundant service in the regions that support it. This is a deployment time only decision. You can't make an App Service plan zone redundant after it has been deployed Learn more ⬈

Zone redundancy

◯ **Enabled:** Your App Service plan and the apps in it will be zone redundant. The minimum App Service plan instance count will be three.

◉ **Disabled:** Your App Service Plan and the apps in it will not be zone redundant. The minimum App Service plan instance count will be one.

[Review + create]   [< Previous]   [Next : Tags >]

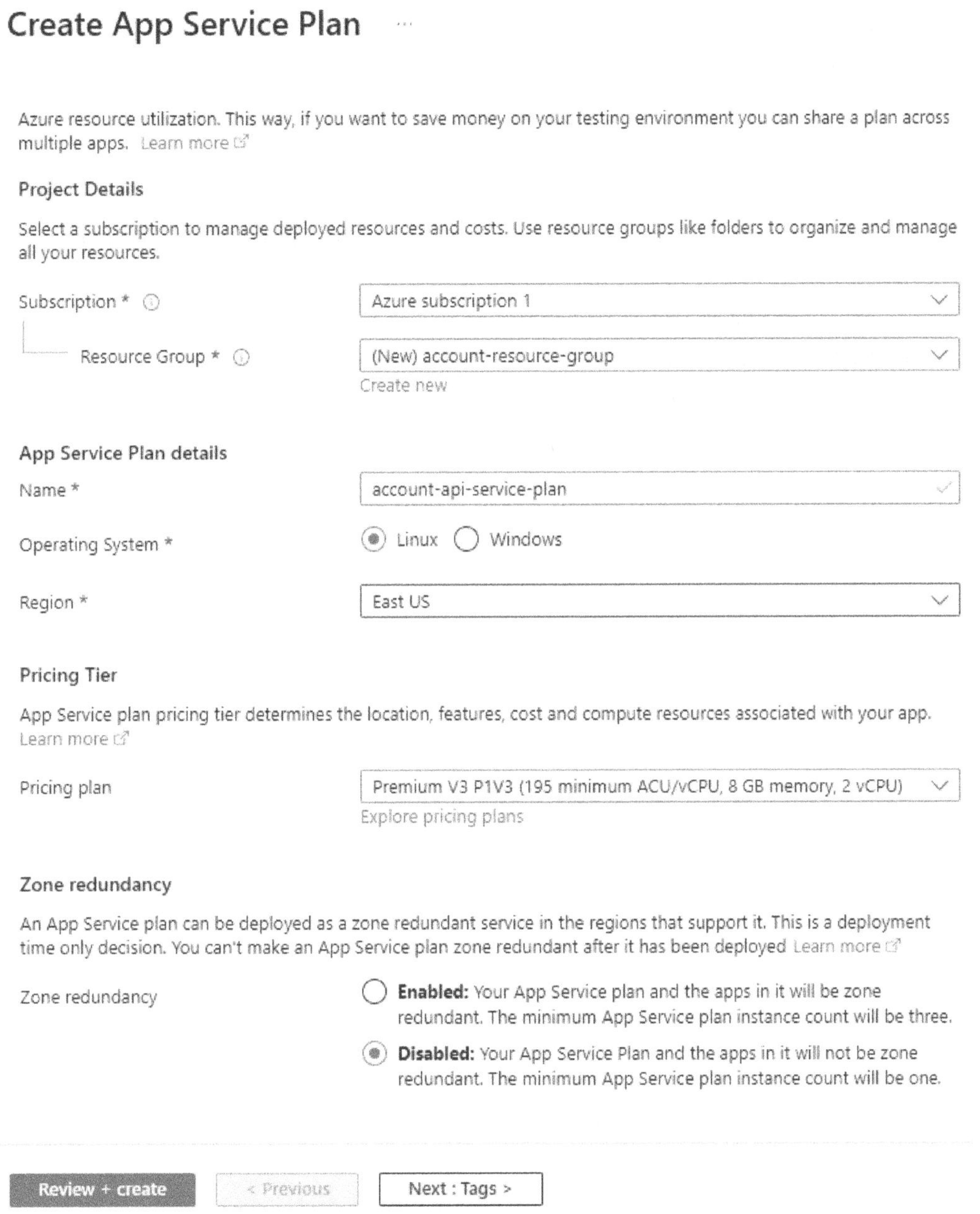

Figure 13.2: Creating an App Service Plan in Azure

4.   The next step is creating a web app:

I.   In the Azure portal, search for `App Services` and select the top result.

II.   Click **Create** and select **Web App**.

III. Choose your subscription, select your resource group, and enter a name for your web app. Make sure you have selected a unique name for your web app.

IV.   For **Publish**, select **Code**.

V.   For the **Runtime stack**, select **Node 20 LTS**. (Select the node version you think is better for your needs).

VI.   For **Operating System**, choose **Linux**.

VII. Under **Region**, select the region closest to you or your users.

VIII. Under **App Service Plan**, select the plan you created earlier.

IX.   Click **Review + create** and then **Create**. See *Figure 13.3*:

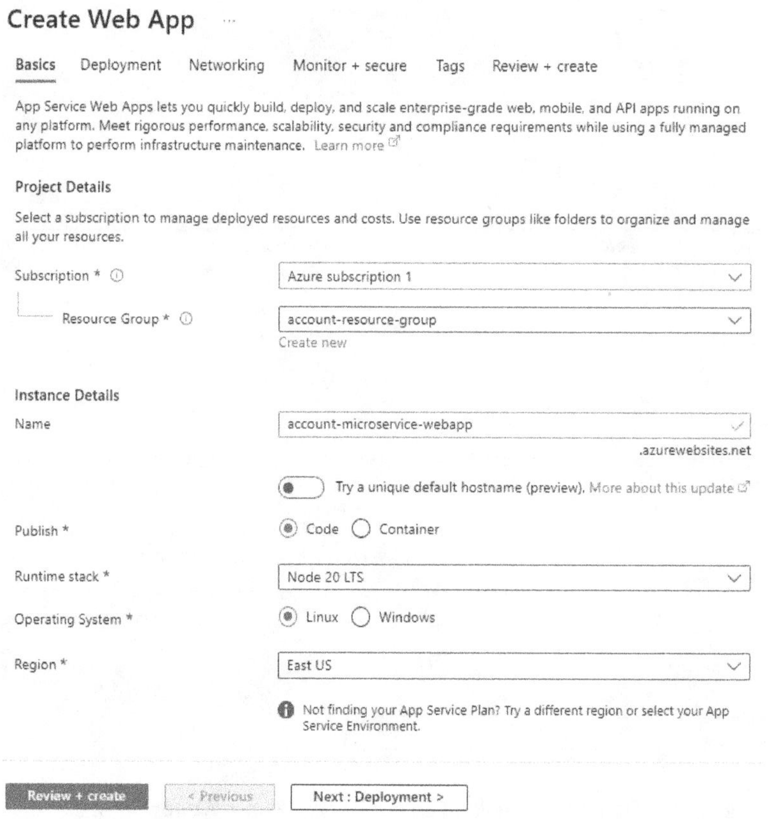

Figure 13.3: Creating a web app in Azure

5.   Next, create an Azure Cosmos DB for the MongoDB API:

    I.   In the Azure portal, search for `Azure Cosmos DB` and select **Create**.

    II.   Azure will ask you to select the type of resource, which will either be a requesting **unit database account** or **vCore cluster**. vCore Cluster is a recommended resource by Microsoft.

    III. Under **API**, choose **Azure Cosmos DB for MongoDB**.

    IV. Enter your **Subscription**, **Resource Group**, **Account Name**, and other necessary details.

    V.   Click **Review + create** and then **Create**:

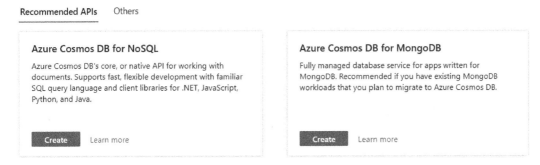

Figure 13.4: Selecting Azure Cosmos DB for MongoDB

You can see the Azure Cosmos DB account creation page in the following figure:

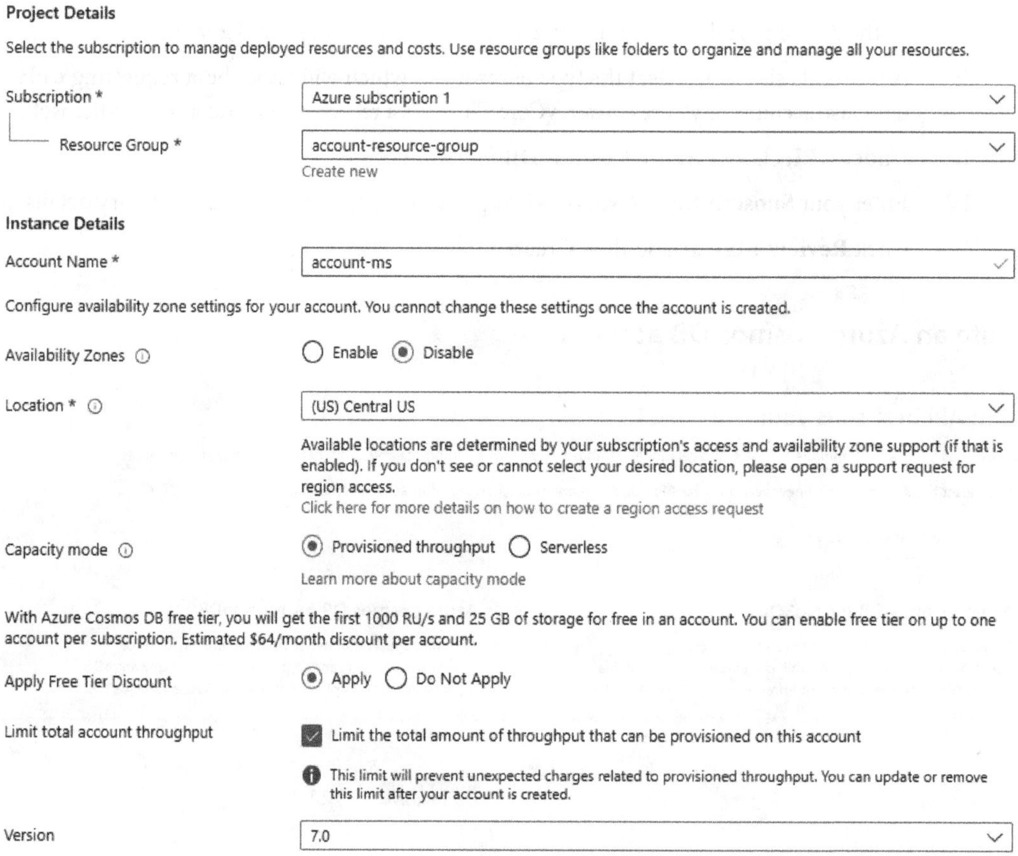

Project Details

Select the subscription to manage deployed resources and costs. Use resource groups like folders to organize and manage all your resources.

Subscription * | Azure subscription 1 ⌄

└─── Resource Group * | account-resource-group ⌄
                         Create new

Instance Details

Account Name * | account-ms ✓

Configure availability zone settings for your account. You cannot change these settings once the account is created.

Availability Zones ⓘ   ◯ Enable ⦿ Disable

Location * ⓘ | (US) Central US ⌄

Available locations are determined by your subscription's access and availability zone support (if that is enabled). If you don't see or cannot select your desired location, please open a support request for region access.
Click here for more details on how to create a region access request

Capacity mode ⓘ   ⦿ Provisioned throughput ◯ Serverless
                        Learn more about capacity mode

With Azure Cosmos DB free tier, you will get the first 1000 RU/s and 25 GB of storage for free in an account. You can enable free tier on up to one account per subscription. Estimated $64/month discount per account.

Apply Free Tier Discount ⦿ Apply ◯ Do Not Apply

Limit total account throughput   ☑ Limit the total amount of throughput that can be provisioned on this account

                        ⓘ This limit will prevent unexpected charges related to provisioned throughput. You can update or remove this limit after your account is created.

Version | 7.0 ⌄

Figure 13.5: The Azure Cosmos DB account creation page

6. Finally, let us obtain a MongoDB connection string:

   I. Once the Cosmos DB account is created, go to the **Overview** page.

   II. Click on **Connection String** under the **Settings** section.

   III. Click the eye icon.

IV.   Copy **Primary Connection String**:

HOST

account-ms.mongo.cosmos.azure.com

PORT

10255

USERNAME

account-ms

SSL

true

Azure Cosmos DB has strict security requirements and standards. Azure Cosmos DB

Read-write Keys   Read-only Keys

PRIMARY PASSWORD ⟳

****

ⓘ Last regenerated: 22/08/2024 (4 days ago). Learn more

SECONDARY PASSWORD ⟳

****

ⓘ Last regenerated: 22/08/2024 (4 days ago). Learn more

PRIMARY CONNECTION STRING

****

SECONDARY CONNECTION STRING

****

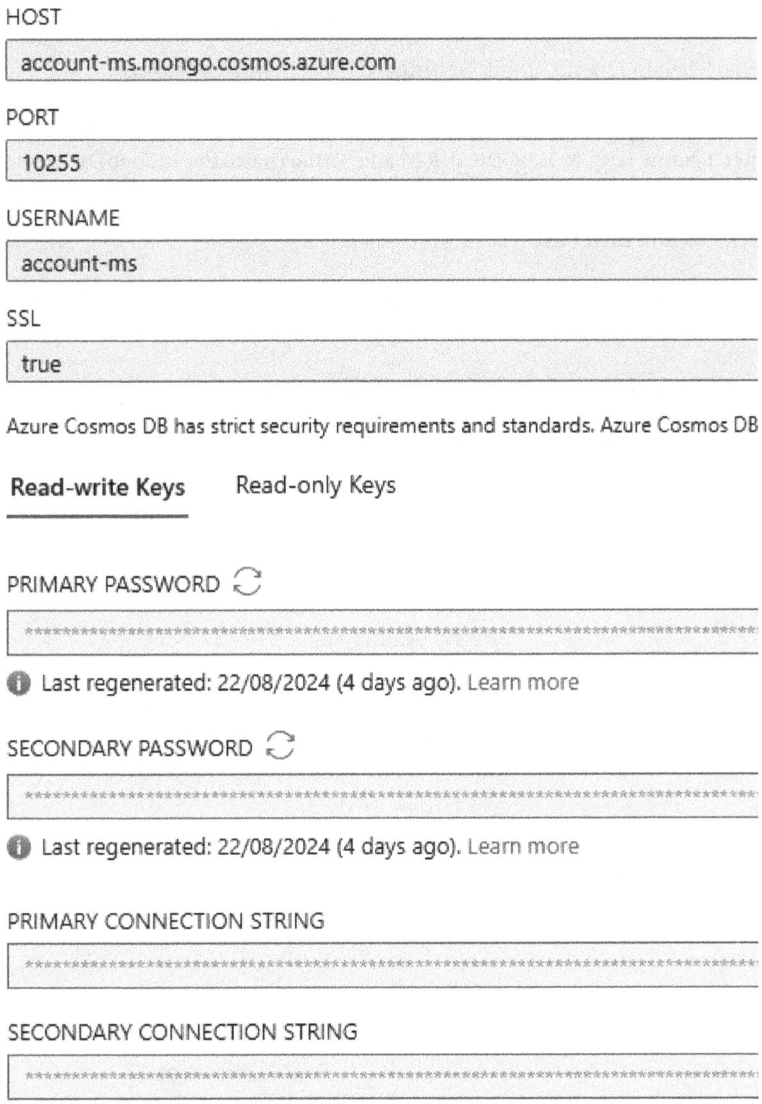

Figure 13.6: Connection string page in Azure

We're done with resource obtaining. It is time for configuration.

7. Now, let's configure the Azure web app to use MongoDB. For that, navigate to your web app:

    I.   In the Azure portal, go to **App Services** and select your web app.

    II.   In the left-hand menu, under **Settings**, click on **Configuration**.

    III.   Under **Environment Variables | Application settings**, click on + **Add**.

    IV.   Enter a **Name** (e.g., MONGODB_URL) and **Value** (paste the MongoDB connection string you copied earlier).

    V.   Click **OK** and then **Save**.

Finally, it's time to prepare your Node.js application. Ensure your Node.js application is set up to read the MongoDB connection string from environment variables. Here are the steps to achieve it:

1. Go to the `src/config/config.js` file and change the `createConfig` function like so:

```
function createConfig(configPath) {
        dotenv.config({ path: configPath });
        const { value: envVars, error } = envVarsSchema
            .prefs({ errors: { label: 'key' } })
            .validate({
                PORT: process.env.PORT || dotenv
                        .config({ path: configPath })
                        .parsed.PORT,
                MONGODB_URL: process.env.MONGODB_URL
                        || dotenv.config({
                        path: configPath }).parsed
                        .MONGODB_URL
            });
        if (error) {
            throw new Error(`Config validation error:
              ${error.message}`);
        }
        return {
            port: envVars.PORT,
            mongo: {
                url: envVars.MONGODB_URL,
            } }; }
```

2. When we run our Node.js application, it automatically connects to a port number equal to 3001 (depending on what you encoded in the .env file). We updated the .env file by default to use PORT=443. Here is what it looks like:

```
PORT=443
MONGODB_URL=mongodb://localhost:27017/account-microservice
```

3. We also applied minor changes to the src/index.js file to support the winston library and to use the port from the process:

```
async function execute() {
    logger.info('preparing account service ...');
    const configPath = path.join(__dirname,
      '../configs/.env');
    const appConfig = createConfig(configPath);
    logger.info({configPath:configPath});
    await db.connect(appConfig);
    const port = process.env.PORT || appConfig.port;
    const server = app.listen(port, () => {
        logger.info('account service started',
        { port: port });
    });

    const closeServer = () => {
        if (server) {
            server.close(() => {
                logger.error('server closed');
                process.exit(1);
            });
        } else {
            process.exit(1);
        } };
```

As you might guess, for both previous examples, we used process.env. Using process.env.PORT and process.env.MONGODB_URL in Node.js applications is a best practice for managing environment-specific configurations.

Node.js applications often need to run in different environments (development, testing, staging, production), each with its own set of configurations. Using environment variables allows you to customize behavior based on the environment without changing the code. Now, let's take a closer look at the environment variables used in our code:

- `process.env.PORT` is used to define the port number on which the Node.js application will listen for incoming requests. By using an environment variable for the port, you can easily run the application on different ports depending on the environment. For example, in a development environment, you might want to run it on port 3000, while in production, the application might need to run on a port assigned by a hosting provider (e.g., Azure, Heroku). Cloud providers often assign dynamic ports to applications. By using `process.env.PORT`, your application can adapt to whatever port is assigned at runtime.

- `process.env.MONGODB_URL`, on the other hand, is used to define the connection string for your MongoDB database. Storing sensitive information such as database connection strings in environment variables keeps them out of your source code, which is a security best practice. This prevents accidental exposure in VCSs (e.g., Git). Different environments may use different databases or database servers. For example, a development environment might use a local MongoDB instance, while production uses a managed MongoDB service such as MongoDB Atlas. By using `process.env.MONGODB_URL`, you can easily switch between these without changing your code.

4. After successful deployment, Azure should run your application. That is why you need to update the `package.json` file to have the `start` script, like the following:

```
"scripts": {
    "start": "node src/index.js",
    ...other commands }
```

But how about the package installation process? As you know, we don't publish `node_modules`, but it should be on the server to run your application properly. To handle node module installation and execute the start command from `package.json`, you can follow the following steps:

1. Go to **App Services** from the Azure portal.

2. Select your web app.

3. Navigate to **Settings**.

4. Select **Configuration**.

5. Go to **General Settings**.

6. Go to **Startup Command** and type `npm install && npm start`:

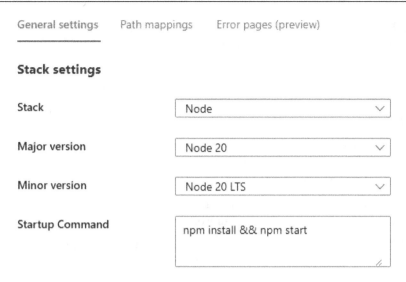

Figure 13.7: Startup command for an Azure web app

Of course, this is not the only option for running Node.js applications properly but for this example, it is more than enough.

Now, everything is ready. We can implement our pipeline using GitHub Actions.

Working with GitHub Actions

GitHub Actions is a powerful feature of GitHub that allows you to automate, customize, and execute software development workflows directly in your GitHub repository. It's designed to help you build, test, and deploy your code right from GitHub. GitHub Actions is a tool that helps you automate tasks within your software development life cycle. For our case, we'll create a workflow that automatically deploys your Node.js microservice to Azure whenever you push changes to the main branch.

First, create an account if you haven't yet. After account creation, create a repository that will store your source code. Next, let's look at some key features of GitHub Actions:

- **Automation of workflows**: GitHub Actions enables you to automate tasks such as running tests, building applications, deploying to cloud services, and more whenever specific events occur in your repository (e.g., a push to a branch, a pull request, or the creation of an issue). You can also use GitHub Actions to run linting tools or static analysis on your code, ensuring that code quality standards are maintained.

- **YAML-based configuration**: Workflows in GitHub Actions are defined in YAML files, typically located in the `.github/workflows/` directory of your repository. These files describe the automated processes you want to run.

- **Event-driven**: Actions can be triggered by various GitHub events, such as pushes, pull requests, issue creation, or on a scheduled basis. This flexibility allows you to create workflows that are finely tuned to your development process.

- **Built-in CI/CD**: GitHub Actions provides built-in support for CI and CD. You can use it to automatically test your code and deploy it to production or a cloud service such as AWS, Azure, or Heroku after every commit.

- **Reusable actions**: You can reuse actions created by the community or share your own actions across projects. GitHub has a marketplace where you can find actions for various tasks such as setting up languages, deploying to cloud services, and more.

- **Secrets management**: You can securely manage and use sensitive information such as API keys, tokens, and other credentials in your workflows without exposing them in your code.

- **Scheduling tasks**: You can use GitHub Actions to run scripts or maintenance tasks, such as nightly builds or database backups, on a schedule.

GitHub Actions integrates seamlessly with other GitHub features, such as *Issues*, *Pull Requests*, and *Packages*, making it easy to create workflows that encompass the full development life cycle.

Now let's look at Secrets in GitHub Actions.

Understanding Secrets

Secrets in GitHub Actions are encrypted environment variables that you use in your workflows. They are stored securely and can be accessed within your workflows without exposing sensitive information.

To securely pass your Azure credentials (such as the publish profile) to GitHub Actions, you need to add them as **Secrets**. Here is how you can do it:

1. Go to the Azure portal and navigate to your web app.

2. On the web app's **Overview** page, look for the **Get Publish Profile** button and download the publish profile file. It's an XML file that contains the credentials your GitHub Actions workflow will use to deploy the app. Don't forget to change **Platform settings** from your Azure web app's **Settings-Configuration** tab.

3. Once you do it, you will be able to download the publish profile (*Figure 13.8*).

4. Now go to the **Overview** page of your Azure web app and click **Download Publish Profile**. It should download a file that matches `<web_app_name>.PublishSettings` (it is `account-microservice-webapp.PublishSettings` in our case).

Providing an Azure publish profile to GitHub Actions is essential for automating the deployment of your application to Azure. The publish profile contains credentials that GitHub Actions uses to authenticate and authorize the deployment to your Azure resources. This ensures that only authorized processes can deploy your application.

It also includes all the necessary settings for deploying your application to a specific Azure App Service or other resources. It simplifies the configuration, avoiding manually defining all the deployment details in your workflow.

Using a publish profile in GitHub Actions allows you to securely store and manage the credentials as secrets within your GitHub repository. This prevents exposing sensitive information in your workflow files. Here is what platform settings should look like to download the publish profile:

⟳ Refresh   💾 Save   ✕ Discard   ♡ Leave Feedback

Platform settings

SCM Basic Auth Publishi...   ◉ On ◯ Off

FTP Basic Auth Publishi...   ◉ On ◯ Off

ⓘ Disable basic authentication for FTP and SCM access. Learn more

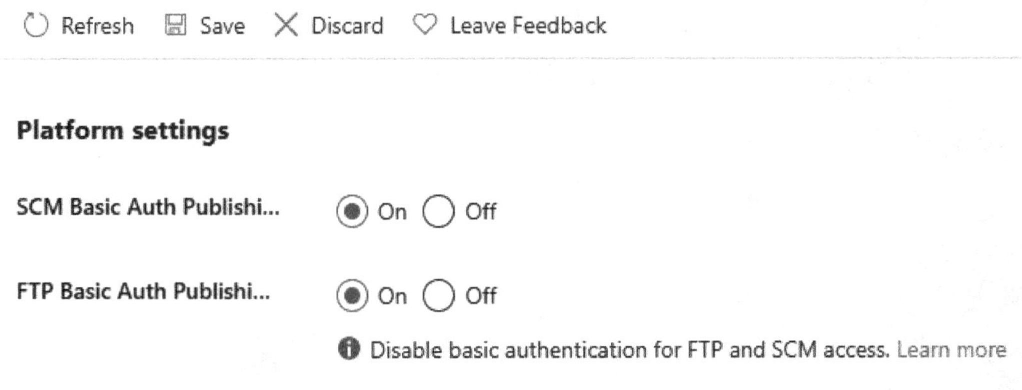

Figure 13.8: Platform settings to download the publish profile

Let's create Secrets in GitHub:

1. Go to your GitHub repository.

2. Navigate to **Settings** | **Secrets** | **Actions**.

3. Add the following secrets:

   - `AZURE_WEBAPP_PUBLISH_PROFILE`: The entire contents of the publish profile from Azure (*Figure 13.9*).

- MONGODB_URL: At this point, you should paste the MongoDB connection string that you copied earlier. If you have not yet retrieved it, please do so now before continuing. Here is how we can do it:

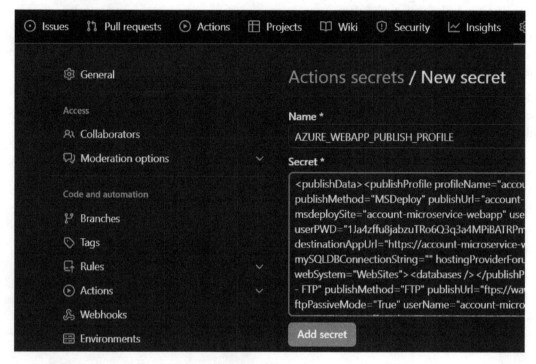

Figure 13.9: Adding the Azure web app's publish profile

Using Secrets is crucial because it prevents sensitive data from being exposed in your repository's code or logs. Only authorized workflows can access these secrets.

We have now provided all the secret information to GitHub, so let's focus on building a simple pipeline using GitHub Actions.

Building a pipeline

While GitHub Actions doesn't explicitly use the term **pipeline** in its documentation, a pipeline is a broader concept that represents the sequence of processes that code goes through from development to production. In many CI/CD tools, a pipeline typically consists of multiple stages (such as build, test, and deploy) that are executed in a specific order.

A **workflow** in GitHub Actions is a configurable automated process made up of one or more jobs. It is defined in a YAML file within the `.github/workflows/` directory of a repository. Workflows are triggered by events, such as pushes to the repository, pull requests, or scheduled events. Each workflow can have multiple jobs that run in parallel or sequentially, and each job can have multiple steps that execute commands or actions.

A workflow is defined in a `.yml` file. Here is how we define it:

1. To create this file, you should open your web browser and go to your GitHub repository. Inside your repository, click on the **Add file** button, then choose **Create new file**.

2. Name the file `.github/workflows/azure-deploy.yml`. This will create the necessary directory structure and file. Commit the `azure-deploy.yml` file and push it to your GitHub repository.

3. The `azure-deploy.yml` file consists of multiple steps. For a more complete example, check our GitHub repository (`Ch13/.github/workflows/azure-deploy.yml`). Here is our first step:

```
name: CI/CD Pipeline
on:
  push:
    branches:
      - main  # The workflow will trigger on pushes to the main
branch
```

The GitHub Actions workflow file, named `CI/CD Pipeline`, is set up to automatically trigger whenever there is a push to the `main` branch of the repository. This means that any changes committed and pushed to the `main` branch will activate the defined workflow. The `on: push:` section specifies the event that starts the workflow – in this case, a push event to the `main` branch. This setup is commonly used for CI/CD, ensuring that updates to the `main` branch automatically go through the build, test, and deployment processes defined in the workflow.

4. Let's continue by discussing the next lines in our workflow file:

```
jobs:
  security-scan:
    name: Run Security Scan
    runs-on: ubuntu-latest
    steps:
    - name: Checkout code
      uses: actions/checkout@v3
    - name: Set up Node.js
      uses: actions/setup-node@v3
      with:
        node-version: '20'
```

```
    - name: Install dependencies
      run: npm install
    - name: Run npm audit
      run: npm audit --audit-level=high
```

This part of the GitHub Actions workflow defines a job named `security-scan`, which is responsible for running a security scan on your code base. The job will execute on the latest version of Ubuntu, as specified by `runs-on: ubuntu-latest`.

Within this job, several steps are outlined. The first step, `Checkout code`, uses the `actions/checkout@v3` action to clone the repository's code into the workflow's environment. Next, the `Set up Node.js` step sets up Node.js version 20 in the environment using the `actions/setup-node@v3` action. After the environment is ready, the `Install dependencies` step runs `npm install` to install all required Node.js packages. Finally, the `Run npm audit` step executes the `npm audit --audit-level=high` command, which checks for security vulnerabilities in the installed packages, focusing on those with a high severity level. This job ensures that your application is scanned for critical security issues as part of the CI/CD pipeline.

5. The following code of the GitHub Actions workflow defines a job called `check-dependencies`, which is designed to check whether any dependencies in your project are outdated. The job will run on the latest version of Ubuntu, as indicated by `runs-on: ubuntu-latest`:

```
check-dependencies:
    name: Check Dependencies
    runs-on: ubuntu-latest
    needs: security-scan
    steps:
    - name: Checkout code
      uses: actions/checkout@v3
    - name: Install dependencies
      run: npm install
    - name: Check for outdated dependencies
      run: npm outdated
```

The `needs: security-scan` line specifies that this job will only run after the `security-scan` job has successfully completed. This creates a dependency between the two jobs, ensuring that the security scan must pass before checking for outdated dependencies.

The job contains several steps. First, the `Checkout code` step uses the `actions/checkout@v3` action to clone the repository's code into the environment. Then, the `Install dependencies` step runs `npm install` to install all the necessary Node.js packages for the project. Finally, the `Check for outdated dependencies` step runs `npm outdated`, which lists any dependencies that have newer versions available. This job helps maintain the health of your project by ensuring that you are aware of any outdated packages that might need updating.

6. The following part of the GitHub Actions workflow defines a job named `test`, which is responsible for running tests on your code base. The job runs on the latest version of Ubuntu, as specified by `runs-on: ubuntu-latest`:

```
test:
    name: Run Tests
    runs-on: ubuntu-latest
    needs: check-dependencies
    steps:
    - name: Checkout code
      uses: actions/checkout@v3
    - name: Set up Node.js
      uses: actions/setup-node@v3
      with:
        node-version: '20'

    - name: Install dependencies
      run: npm install
    - name: Run tests
      run: npm test
```

The `needs: check-dependencies` line indicates that this job will only start after the `check-dependencies` job has successfully completed. This ensures that all dependencies are up-to-date before tests are run, which is important for ensuring consistency and reliability in your testing process.

The job consists of several steps. First, the `Checkout code` step uses the `actions/checkout@v3` action to clone the repository's code into the workflow environment. Then, the `Set up Node.js` step configures Node.js version 20 in the environment using the `actions/setup-node@v3` action. Following this, the `Install dependencies` step runs `npm install` to install the necessary packages for the project. Finally, the `Run tests` step executes the `npm test` command, which runs the test suite defined in your project. This job ensures that your code is tested in a controlled environment, catching any issues before changes are merged or deployed.

7. The following part of the workflow is responsible for deploying your application to the Azure web app after the tests have been completed. The job runs on an Ubuntu-based virtual machine provided by GitHub Actions. Before deployment, the workflow checks out the latest version of your code to ensure that the most recent changes are included:

```
deploy:
    name: Deploy to Azure Web App
    runs-on: ubuntu-latest
    needs: test  # Run this job after testing succeeds
    steps:
```

```
    - name: Checkout code
      uses: actions/checkout@v3

    - name: Clean up unnecessary files
      run: |
        rm -rf .git
        rm -rf .github
        rm -rf _actions
        rm -rf _PipelineMapping
        rm -rf _temp

    - name: Deploy to Azure Web App
      uses: azure/webapps-deploy@v3
      with:
        app-name: 'account-microservice-webapp'  # Matches the
"msdeploySite" in your publish profile
        publish-profile: ${{ secrets.AZURE_WEBAPP_PUBLISH_PROFILE
}}  # Ensure this secret contains the publish profile XML
content
        package: ${{ github.workspace }}
```

8. In preparation for deployment, the workflow cleans up unnecessary files and directories, such as the .git folder (which contains the repository's Git history), the .github folder (used for GitHub-specific configurations), and other temporary or internal folders that aren't needed in the deployed application. This cleanup helps reduce the deployment package size and eliminates any files that aren't required for the application to run.

9. Finally, the workflow uses the azure/webapps-deploy@v3 action to deploy the application to the specified Azure web app. The app-name configuration is set to match the site name in your Azure publish profile, and the publish-profile secret contains the necessary credentials. The package to be deployed is set to the entire workspace, ensuring that the cleaned-up code is what gets deployed.

Once you push your changes, GitHub Actions will automatically trigger the workflow. Monitor the deployment process in the **Actions** tab of your GitHub repository:

Figure 13.10: GitHub Actions workflow

Here is what success deployment logs look like:

```
{
  id: '77ef5e3e-161d-4b4c-afb2-e44d537ec921',
  *******
  is_temp: false,
  is_readonly: true,
  url: 'https://account-microservice-webapp.scm.azurewebsites.net/api/
deployments/77ef5e3e-161d-4b4c-afb2-e44d537ec921',
  log_url: 'https://account-microservice-webapp.scm.azurewebsites.net/
api/deployments/77ef5e3e-161d-4b4c-afb2-e44d537ec921/log',
  site_name: 'account-microservice-webapp',
  build_summary: { errors: [], warnings: [] }}
Deploy logs can be viewed at https://account-microservice-webapp.
scm.azurewebsites.net/api/deployments/77ef5e3e-161d-4b4c-afb2-
e44d537ec921/log
Successfully deployed web package to App Service.
App Service Application URL: https://account-microservice-webapp.
azurewebsites.net
```

Once deployment succeeds, you can check the deployed files using a simple FTPS connection. To connect to your server using an FTP client, you can use any FTP client tools you want. We use FileZilla, which is free and easy to use. You can download it from `https://filezilla-project.org/`.

To find FTP credentials for your server, follow these steps:

1. Go to the Azure portal.
2. Select **App Services**.
3. Find your web app.
4. Got to **Deployment** | **Deployment Center**

5. Select the **FTPS credentials** tab. See *Figure 13.11*:

Settings   Logs   FTPS credentials

App Service supports multiple technologies to access, publish and modify the content of your app. FTPS credentials can be scoped to the application or the user.

FTPS endpoint

ftps://waws-prod-blu-147.ftp.azurewebsites.windows.net/site/wwwroot

Application scope

Application scope credentials are auto-generated and provide access only to this specific app or deployment slot. These credentials can be used with FTPS, Local Git and WebDeploy. They cannot be configured manually, but can be reset anytime. Learn more

FTPS Username

account-microservice-webapp\$account-microservice-webapp

Password

••

Figure 13.11: FTPS credentials tab for an Azure web app

Now you can use these credentials to connect to the server. Here is what it looks like after connecting and navigating to the wwwroot folder:

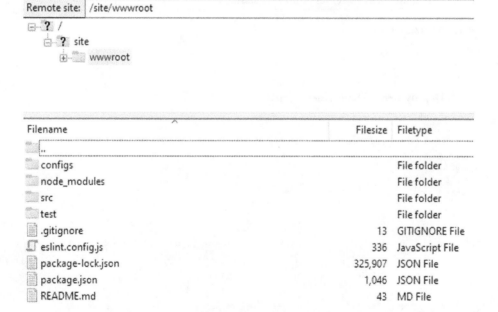

Figure 13.12: FTP view of the deployed repository

Now we're ready to test whether things are working or not. As you might guess, after investigating the Account microservice's source code, we added a simple middleware to `app.js`:

```
. . . . . . . . . . . . . .
// Define a route for the welcome page
app.get('/welcome', (req, res) => {
    res.send('<h1>Welcome to Express.js Application!</h1>');
});
. . . . . . . . . . . . . .
```

Just go to the Azure portal, select your web app, and in the **Overview** section, you will find the default domain:

 Domains

Default domain	account-microservice-webapp.azurewebsites.net
Custom domain	Add custom domain

Figure 13.13: Domains section for an Azure web app

Open any browser and type `<Default_domain>/welcome` as the URL:

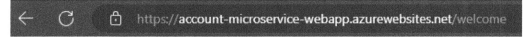

Welcome to Express.js Application!

Figure 13.14: Welcome page for the deployed Node.js application

To test whether it is possible to connect to MongoDB and create account information, follow these steps:

1. Open Postman.
2. Click on the + button to create a new tab.
3. Select **POST** and **HTTP verb** and paste your API URL that follows the `<default_domain>/v1/accounts` template (it is `https://account-microservice-webapp.azurewebsites.net/v1/accounts` for us).
4. Go to the **Body** section and select **raw | Json**.
5. Paste your payload to create an account and click **Send**.

Here is what it looks like for us:

Figure 13.15: Creating an account using Postman

To test whether it is possible to retrieve account information, follow these steps:

1. Open Postman.
2. Click on the + button to create a new tab.
3. Select **GET** and **HTTP verb** and paste your API URL that follows the `<default_domain>/v1/accounts` template (it is `https://account-microservice-webapp.azurewebsites.net/v1/accounts` for us).
4. Click **Send**.

Here is what it looks like for us:

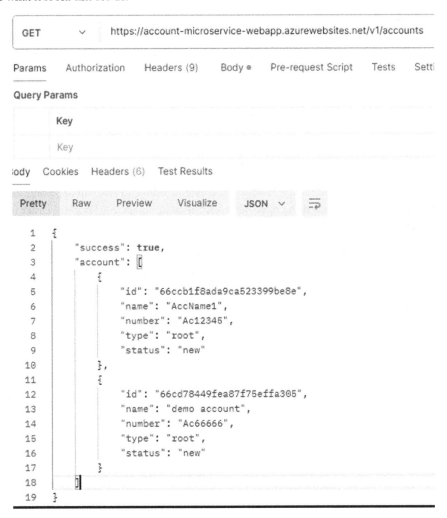

Figure 13.16: Retrieving account information

In this section, we explored the process of deploying an application to Azure and testing its functionalities. We walked through how to verify that everything is working as expected using Postman, ensuring your application is ready for production environments. Now you have a solid understanding of how to deploy and validate your microservice in the cloud.

Summary

In this chapter, we embarked on a comprehensive exploration of CI/CD processes, emphasizing their critical role in modern software development. We began by understanding the fundamentals of CI and CD and how they streamline the process of integrating and deploying code changes.

Our journey continued with an in-depth look at working with Azure Cloud, where we discussed how to leverage its robust infrastructure for deploying and managing applications. We then delved into GitHub Actions, a powerful tool for automating workflows, enabling us to build, test, and deploy our code efficiently.

Most of the chapter was dedicated to building a CI/CD pipeline. We walked through the steps necessary to create a seamless and automated pipeline, ensuring that our applications are always in a state ready for deployment.

In this book, we have covered everything you need to start building microservices with JavaScript. From designing the basic structure to deploying and monitoring your services, each chapter has given you practical steps and knowledge to help you create flexible and efficient applications. Now, you're ready to take on real projects using microservices, which can make your systems easier to scale, update, and manage.

However, remember that microservices are not a silver bullet. The best design depends on many factors, including the size of your project, team structure, and business needs. As you continue learning and practicing, stay curious and keep in mind that technology is always changing. Enjoy your journey in the world of microservices!

Keep going and may you code for a lifetime. Until we meet again.

Index

`packtpub.com`

Subscribe to our online digital library for full access to over 7,000 books and videos, as well as industry leading tools to help you plan your personal development and advance your career. For more information, please visit our website.

Why subscribe?

- Spend less time learning and more time coding with practical eBooks and Videos from over 4,000 industry professionals

- Improve your learning with Skill Plans built especially for you

- Get a free eBook or video every month

- Fully searchable for easy access to vital information

- Copy and paste, print, and bookmark content

Did you know that Packt offers eBook versions of every book published, with PDF and ePub files available? You can upgrade to the eBook version at `packtpub.com` and as a print book customer, you are entitled to a discount on the eBook copy. Get in touch with us at `customercare@packtpub.com` for more details.

At `www.packtpub.com`, you can also read a collection of free technical articles, sign up for a range of free newsletters, and receive exclusive discounts and offers on Packt books and eBooks.

Other Books You May Enjoy

If you enjoyed this book, you may be interested in these other books by Packt:

Mastering JavaScript Functional Programming - Third Edition

Federico Kereki

ISBN: 978-1-80461-013-8

- Understand when to use functional programming versus classic object-oriented programming
- Use declarative coding instead of imperative coding for clearer, more understandable code
- Know how to avoid side effects and create more reliable code with closures and immutable data
- Use recursion to help design and implement more understandable solutions to complex problems
- Define functional programing data types with or without TypeScript, add type checking, and implement immutability
- Apply advanced containers to get better structures to tackle errors and implement async programming

JavaScript Design Patterns

Hugo Di Francesco

ISBN: 978-1-80461-227-9

- Find out how patterns are classified into creational, structural, and behavioral
- Implement the right set of patterns for different business scenarios
- Explore diverse frontend architectures and different rendering approaches
- Identify and address common asynchronous programming performance pitfalls
- Leverage event-driven programming in the browser to deliver fast and secure applications
- Boost application performance using asset loading strategies and offloading JavaScript execution

Packt is searching for authors like you

If you're interested in becoming an author for Packt, please visit `authors.packtpub.com` and apply today. We have worked with thousands of developers and tech professionals, just like you, to help them share their insight with the global tech community. You can make a general application, apply for a specific hot topic that we are recruiting an author for, or submit your own idea.

Share Your Thoughts

Now you've finished *Hands-On Microservices with JavaScript*, we'd love to hear your thoughts! Scan the QR code below to go straight to the Amazon review page for this book and share your feedback or leave a review on the site that you purchased it from.

https://packt.link/r/1-788-62540-4

Your review is important to us and the tech community and will help us make sure we're delivering excellent quality content.

Download a free PDF copy of this book

Thanks for purchasing this book!

Do you like to read on the go but are unable to carry your print books everywhere?

Is your eBook purchase not compatible with the device of your choice?

Don't worry, now with every Packt book you get a DRM-free PDF version of that book at no cost.

Read anywhere, any place, on any device. Search, copy, and paste code from your favorite technical books directly into your application.

The perks don't stop there, you can get exclusive access to discounts, newsletters, and great free content in your inbox daily

Follow these simple steps to get the benefits:

1. Scan the QR code or visit the link below

https://packt.link/free-ebook/978-1-78862-540-1

2. Submit your proof of purchase
3. That's it! We'll send your free PDF and other benefits to your email directly

www.ingramcontent.com/pod-product-compliance
Lightning Source LLC
Chambersburg PA
CBHW060651060326
40690CB00020B/4601